W9-BZV-385

FREEWHEELIN'

FREE-WHEELIN'

A Solo Journey Across America

Richard A. Lovett

  Ragged Mountain Press

CAMDEN, MAINE

Published by Ragged Mountain Press, a division of
McGraw-Hill, Inc.

10 9 8 7 6 5 4 3 2

Library of Congress Cataloging-in-Publication Data

Lovett, Richard A.
    Freewheelin' : a solo journey across America / Richard A. Lovett.
      p.   cm.
    ISBN 0-87742-352-0
    1. Bicycle touring—United States. 2. —United States—
Description and travel—1981- I. Title.
    GV1045.L68 1992
    796.6'4'0973—dc20   92-24112
                                           CIP

For every book sold, Ragged Mountain Press will make a
contribution to an environmental cause.

Freewheelin' is printed on 60-pound Renew Opaque
Vellum, which contains 50 percent recycled waste paper
(preconsumer) and 10 percent postconsumer waste paper.

Typeset by A&B Type, Bow, NH.
Printed by Fairfield Graphics, Fairfield, PA.
Edited by Jim Babb and Pamela Benner.
Text design by James Brisson.
Production by Molly Mulhern.

To Vera

for always believing

CONTENTS

ACKNOWLEDGMENTS

This book owes its genesis to my grandfather's retirement more than two decades before this trip had even become an idea. For the next ten years, he and my grandmother traveled the world to locales that to my grade-school perception were only distantly imagined points on the globe. From the beginning, my grandmother assumed the role of family historiographer, recording amusing anecdotes, her impressions of foreign travel, and details of the cultures they visited.

When my grandparents were overseas, these stories would trickle into our house on a series of aerograms bearing stamps from such exotic origins as Spain, Yugoslavia, Japan, or Peru. My mother, a retired English teacher who may have missed a profession as an editor, painstakingly transcribed these epistles, typing out as many carbon copies as were necessary to bring the news to a family scattered across half of the country.

Reading my grandmother's letters became a family tradition, one that in my childhood I took for granted, and that I often anticipated almost as eagerly as I did the arrival of the packages of souvenirs they always brought with them on their first visit after a trip.

When I was old enough to begin my own travels, the mystique of journal writing was firmly planted in my soul. For some reason, I kept no record of my first bicycle excursion—a gloriously mismatched adventure with a next-door neighbor whose ideas of bicycle touring were somewhat different than mine but who somehow managed to remain a friend anyway.

By my second bicycling outing I'd become an inveterate journal writer, and it took no great leap of the imagination to decide to mail the results piecemeal to my mother, who obligingly transcribed my cramped handwriting from the sweat-soaked and travel-worn pages of a legal pad. It was on that second journey that this book was conceived, but without my mother's time and my grandmother's early inspiration, it would have been stillborn.

It is with great gratitude that I acknowledge the contribution of my mother, Patricia, my grandfather Henry, and my grandmother Gladys. My thanks also go out to a collection of other people—Kathy, Laura, Dave, Lori, Bob, Mark, John, Dennis, Ben, Jack, Robin, Paul, Trish, Ruth, Mary Ann and George, David and Debbie, my father, Richard— whose encouragement helped bring this project to fruition—to Kohel Haver for guiding me through the maze of a book contract, to Ira Heinrich for telling me the story of Turtle and Pehiepe, to Jim Babb and Pamela Benner and all the good people at McGraw-Hill's Ragged Mountain Press, to everyone I met in 5,400 miles and seventeen states, and especially to Vera for more than I could ever list. My gratitude also goes out to the many other people who will someday lead me to clap my hand to my forehead and exclaim, "My gosh, how could I have forgotten you, too!"

Getting the Nerve

I was stopped at a scenic lookout 200 feet below the crest of an 8,700-foot pass in central Idaho, straddling my bicycle, breathing deeply of the cool mountain air and relishing the play of light and shadow over the broad valley from which I'd just climbed. I was traveling alone, as I had been for most of the previous thousand miles, but loneliness was no burden. I had plenty of companionship in the alpine breeze and the slow parade of scenery, while the hospitable people of central Idaho were no farther away than the passing cars full of weekend tourists who waved cheerfully at me as they drove by.

I was talking to just such a person now, in fact, a heavy-set woman who'd driven into the mountains from her home somewhere on the Snake River Plain.

"Where are you from?" she asked, and I explained that I'd left Sacramento, California, some two weeks before.

"And where are you going?"

I shrugged. "At least to the Mississippi. From there it will depend on how much time I have left."

We chatted a while longer, then she turned to go. Suddenly she turned back. "I've just got to ask," she said, "what gives you the nerve to do this?"

"The nerve to do what?" I responded. "Bicycle across the country? Or. . . ." I glanced back at the 5 miles of six percent grade I'd just completed, "climb that hill?"

"Both," she said. But from the way she eyed the hill, I could tell she found them equally incomprehensible.

I shrugged again. "Neither takes nerve. They both just take time."

———•—•———

Anyone in good health can bicycle coast to coast. All it takes are good knees, a few months of training, low gears . . . and the will to do it. This book is not the story of an extraordinary athletic accomplishment, nor is it a tale of perseverance in the face of great hardships. It is the story of a journey across the northern half of a great country, a story of people and places that will live forever in my memory—and of one attempt to turn back the pace of life and escape the sheltered tyranny of the automobile, which deprives us all of the feel, the very taste of the countryside.

When I began this journey I was looking for spiritual truths born of physical hardships—a hand-to-mouth existence that would put me in better touch with what my ancestors called Providence by forcing me to depend on it for such day-to-day necessities as shelter and food. But except for some problems with a sore knee, the anticipated hardships never materialized. Instead, I fell into a state of deep spiritual and physical relaxation such as I'd never known before. Almost unnoticed the cares of the world sloughed away; I gradually lost interest in such matters as how far I had pedaled on a given day. I was no longer out to conquer the continent. The journey itself had become more important than the destination.

For one summer I exited the fast lane of urban society and set out to find America from the road shoulder. It was a journey that took ten weeks, zigzagging across the continent at an average pace of slightly more than 3 miles an hour. But in a greater sense it is a journey that will continue for the rest of my life.

CHAPTER 1

Beginnings

A Ten-Year-Old Dream

Saturday, June 14, 1986
Sacramento, California

On the eve of my departure from Sacramento, I was anything but relaxed. Even though this would be the greatest adventure of my life—the fulfillment of a ten-year-old dream—I was beset by fears. They were ill-defined, but they centered around loneliness. I would be away from my wife, Jane, for an entire summer, and I would be traveling mostly solo.

There were other reasons to be intimidated. I was about to embark on a journey that would ultimately cover nearly 5,400 miles. I would take millions of pedal strokes, climb untold thousands of feet, and spend dozens of nights alone. Despite my belief that the trip required no great athletic prowess, the prospect was daunting.

My mind strayed back to 1975. I had been in graduate school at the time, working on a Ph.D. in the unadventurous field of economics, when an acquaintance told me how he'd once invested a summer pedaling across the continent. I responded in what I later would realize was the classic manner, telling him—probably all too bluntly—that the very idea was insane.

But the seed was planted, and it didn't take long to germinate. I'd been a bicyclist long before it was chic, enduring the jibes of high school classmates to spend Saturday afternoons riding a balloon-tired one-speed around the gravel back roads of northern Illinois. In college I happily joined the ten-speed craze, arranging class schedules to leave at least one spring or fall afternoon a week for exploring the roads that beckoned from the outskirts of campus. I was an obvious candidate for long-distance touring.

Within a few weeks I was seriously discussing the idea with Jane. We were to marry shortly after the end of classes and were planning something adventurous for a wedding trip. Although neither of us had ever ridden a loaded touring bike or pedaled up a hill higher than 200 feet, we seriously considered flying to the West Coast and bicycling back to Michigan, where we then lived. Eventually we opted for a ten-week car-camping and backpacking trip, but the bicycle trip took on the legendary status of the one-that-got-away, and we fell to speculating on when we might have time to do it. As the years passed, I took a number of seven- to ten-day trips, alone or with friends, in locations ranging from Oklahoma to Nova Scotia, all the time dreaming of someday doing "The Big One."

By the time Jane and I approached our tenth anniversary it was clear that a multi-week bicycle trip wasn't in our joint future. Jane had completed nearly a decade of graduate school and postgraduate training and was an ambitious new college professor; devoting an entire summer to something as professionally unproductive as a bicycle trek would hardly further her career. When her first job transplanted us from the Midwest to California and left me temporarily out of work, she suggested that rather than look for employment immediately I first take the transcontinental trip I'd dreamed of so many years. We agreed on seven weeks for the trip — an average of 85 miles a day by the standard routes — which would get me back in time for a three-week joint vacation before she had to start teaching again in August.

Twenty-five hundred miles of training and a thorough bicycle overhaul later, I was finally ready to go.

———— •◦• ————

My route plans were deliberately vague and bore only a superficial resemblance to the route I eventually followed. Initially I planned to ride north through central California into southern Oregon, where I would meet a cousin who would accompany me for several days. Swinging far to the north, I would also avoid the lonely, waterless stretches of central Nevada. From Oregon I would ride alone into eastern Idaho, to be met there by an old friend who would ride with me as far as his home in Iowa. With luck I hoped to reach Iowa in a month, leaving nearly three weeks to get from there to the Atlantic. On previous solo outings I'd covered as many as 700 miles a week, so while the pace was fast by long-distance cycling standards, it seemed well within my abilities.

Still, I was overwhelmed by the many things that could go wrong. I had pedaled in mountains before, but never with fifty pounds of equipment. Did I seriously believe I could make it across the great rampart of the Cascades, where even the lowest passes rise nearly a mile above the valley floor? Did I really want to spend half a summer alone? The more I thought about it, the greater loomed the dangers.

I kept telling myself these fears were irrational, that mile-for-mile my training rides at home—rides I unhesitatingly took alone—were much more dangerous than cross-country touring; in the city I was far more likely to encounter a hit-and-run driver—or an armed robber—than in the rural areas through which I would be traveling most of the trip. But reason is a poor persuader. I was afraid of being alone, and no amount of rationalization was going to change that.

This wasn't the first time I'd had cold feet on the eve of a major undertaking. The move to California had forced me to seek a new career just as I'd begun to succeed in a previous one, leaving me rootless and vaguely depressed, unsure where I was headed. I had a law degree to go with the Ph.D., which certainly put me on the professional fast track to someplace, but I no longer knew where the fast track led, or even whether I wanted to follow it.

The trip beckoned as a refuge from uncertainty. Although it is possible to plan a bicycle trip in the same meticulous manner as too many of us attempt to order our lives, the essence of bicycle touring is spontaneity. As long as you don't have to meet a train or a plane, you rarely need to know precisely where you'll be tomorrow—or even at the end of today. If you have adequate equipment and are willing to carry enough food and water, you can spend the night almost anywhere that feels safe—a roadside park, a church lawn, even a cemetery; some planning is necessary, but too much makes you oblivious to the opportunities at hand. With the rest of my life in flux I felt the need to relearn the lessons of spontaneity, faith, and adaptability that few things can teach so well as a bicycle trip. I wanted to step aside from the schedule-driven world of Yuppie America to rediscover the simple joy of life itself.

CHAPTER 2

California

Seeing for the First Time

DAY 1 • Sunday, June 15 • CUMULATIVE MILES: 81
Sacramento to Colusa State Park

DAY 2 • Monday, June 16 • CUMULATIVE MILES: 174
Colusa State Park to Jelly's Ferry

DAY 3 • Tuesday, June 17 • CUMULATIVE MILES: 231
Jelly's Ferry to Hillcrest

DAY 4 • Wednesday, June 18 • CUMULATIVE MILES: 279
Hillcrest to Big Valley Summit

DAY 5 • Thursday, June 19 • CUMULATIVE MILES: 350
Big Valley Summit to Lava Beds National Monument

DAY 6 • Friday, June 20 • CUMULATIVE MILES: 385
Lava Beds to Tulelake

The next morning the cold feet had passed and I was ready to begin. Jane accompanied me the first mile, to a candy store near our home where we indulged in farewell truffles. "When are you leaving?" asked the proprietor, who knew us as regular customers.

"Now," I replied, picking up one truffle and handing the other to Jane. "We're just having one for the road." We turned to each other simultaneously. "Cheers," we chorused, touching our truffles together as though they were champagne glasses.

Then it was time to go. Jane would return home, then drive to my planned camp and join me for my first night on the road. As an added bonus she would carry my camping gear, allowing me to ease into my upcoming routine without having to worry about fifty pounds of equipment.

For many miles around Sacramento flat farmland unfolds in a repetitive pattern most people would find monotonous. On training rides I'd crisscrossed similar terrain many times, so I anticipated an uninspiring first day's ride.

I could not have been more wrong. As I pedaled north and began to relax into the trip, I found myself really looking at the surrounding landscape for the first time. To the right was a field of tomatoes, to my left a field of barley. On one side stretched the Coast Range, a ragged ribbon of hazy blue vanishing into the distance, north and south. On the other rose the Sierra Nevada, snow-clad peaks shimmering above a band of orange-brown smog, the outlines of the mountains becoming more distinct as my gaze roamed north, away from the polluted city.

Between these ranges stretched the Sacramento Valley, 50 miles wide, 150 miles long, a vast table-top plain flanked by parallel mountain ramparts, so flat that in the next 80 miles I would gain only 32 feet in elevation.

Other than an arching bridge over the Sacramento River, the only notable hill was a sharp climb onto a levee. There, 20 feet above the flood plain, I caught a first brief inkling of how my perceptions were already shifting toward the slower rhythms of the land, physically so close to home, yet so different in spirit.

Much of the lower Sacramento Valley is devoted to rice farming; from the levee top I could gaze across acres of flooded rice fields, the young shoots lush and green, the water reflecting blue in the late afternoon sun. Nearby a pair of irrigation canals paralleled the road, their edges lined with cattails. Cycling slowly along, I flushed first one, then another great blue heron from the cattails, while farther away snowy egrets—brilliant splashes of white amid the green and blue of rice and water—perched on the low earthen dikes subdividing the fields. Intent on searching for minnows, the egrets ignored me, allowing me to feel that I, too, was part of this magnificent pastoral setting.

For a few minutes I felt vibrantly alive, transported to a realm of peace, tranquility, and soul-wrenching beauty. Then the road surface degenerated to a loose, chunky gravel that required all my attention to negotiate.

———————————•◦•———————————

Two hours into the journey I stopped to call Jane, asking her to bring a few forgotten items to our rendezvous. It was my only stop that day except to look at scenery.

Pedaling effortlessly before a 15- to 20-mile-an-hour wind, I'd lost almost all the city traffic. Except for that short stretch of gravel, the roads were good and I pedaled steadily north, watching the Sutter Buttes rise before me.

The Sutter Buttes are the only break in the flat landscape of the lower Sacramento Valley. The remnants of a cluster of ancient volcanos, locally hailed as the world's smallest mountain range because the entire uplift fits into a circle only 10 miles in diameter, the Buttes are an island of craggy rock rising 2,100 feet above the surrounding plain, splitting the valley in half and forcing the Sacramento River into a broad detour.

The area is rich in lore and history. It was here, in 1846, that a small band of disgruntled settlers met with Captain John C. Fremont to launch the Bear Flag Revolt, wresting California from Mexico and briefly establishing it as an independent nation before it became a state.

Before that the Buttes were central to the spiritual lives of the fifty thousand Native Americans who once lived nearby. They called the peaks the Mountains in the Middle and considered them the center of the universe—geographically, visually, and spiritually.

Even their creation legends focused on the Buttes. According to one, the Buttes were formed when the Great Spirit, having created the Sierra Nevada mountains, was crossing the Sacramento Valley to make the Coast Ranges. En route he paused to gaze upon the great white sentinel of the north, 14,000-foot Mt. Shasta. As he did, a piece of the new mountains slipped through his fingers and dropped to the plain. "I'll come back when I need you," he said.

But when he finished his work, he left the small mountain where it had fallen. "It will be a sign to all my children," he said, "that with the Great Spirit there is always enough, with some to spare."

This legend, charming as it is, probably has been heavily influenced by whites. A more authentic story is the tale of Turtle and Pehiepe, who at the beginning of the world found themselves adrift on an endless sea. Everything was dark, empty, and cold.

Pehiepe and Turtle were spirit beings. Pehiepe was the Watcher, whose job it was to witness things as they occurred. Turtle was the world's best swimmer and diver. Nevertheless, they were afraid and lonely. They didn't remember where their raft had come from or where it was going. Finally Pehiepe said, "We can't just float here forever. There must be someone who can make a world for us. Let's sing and call, and maybe he'll come."

They wailed and cried and sang for a long time. All at once the sky split open and a glowing rope of feathers swished down until one end landed on the raft. Slowly, hand over hand, a great being lowered himself down the rope.

The being was dressed in a robe, but around its edges shone a blinding, golden light. He turned solemnly to Turtle and Pehiepe. "You called the World Maker," he said, "and I've come. Why do you want me?"

World Maker listened while Turtle and Pehiepe told their story. Eventually he raised his hand. "Hush, hush," he said. "I can make a world. But I can't make it out of nothing. If you can get me a little ball of mud, I can make a world."

Pehiepe and Turtle looked around at the cold dark water. "How are we going to get that in the middle of an ocean?" one of them asked with a touch of sarcasm.

But World Maker was patient. "Oceans have bottoms," he said. "There, you can find some mud. All I need is a handful."

Turtle knew what that meant. He stood up. "I'm the diver. I guess it's my job." He took a deep breath and prepared to jump from the raft.

But World Maker stopped him. "Don't be so hasty." He pulled the rope of feathers down from the heavens and tied one end to Turtle's ankle. "However far you dive," he said, "you'll be safe. When you find the mud, just tug on the rope, and we'll pull you up."

Turtle dove. Down he went, deeper and deeper and deeper, but still he couldn't find the bottom. He began to get frightened. He was running out of air, and there were miles of ocean between him and the surface.

Finally, he knew he could take only one more stroke. He kicked hard and reached out as far as he could. He thought he could feel something, but it slipped away, and then he was out of air, pulling desperately on the rope and swimming up as fast as he could.

With the help of World Maker and Pehiepe, Turtle burst from the water like the breaching of a whale. He landed on the raft, where for a long time all he could do was gasp. Finally he turned to World Maker. "I guess we're just going to have to stay here," he said.

But World Maker said, "You're being hasty again, Turtle." He took a stone knife from inside his robe and used it to clean beneath Turtle's fingernails.

When he was done he had a speck of mud the size of a tiny seed. "Turtle," he said, "you tried as hard as you could. That's all anybody ever needs to do. I said I needed a ball of mud, but this is enough."

World Maker set the tiny seed of mud on the center of the raft. "Now, we have to sing our power song," he said. "You have to help."

As they sang the little ball of mud began to quiver. With a pop it became as big as a pea. They sang some more, and suddenly it was as big as an acorn, then as big as Pehiepe's head.

"Hey," Pehiepe said, "We really are making a world." They sang louder, and the ball of mud got bigger and bigger until, with a great roar, a cluster of mountains rose from the water beside them.

The mountain that World Maker, Pehiepe, and Turtle sang into existence was the Middle Mountain. The three of them climbed to its highest peak, where World Maker made the rivers to drain the water from the land. Then he went to a secret cave, where he made the first man and first woman and sent them out into the newly made world.

———————•●•———————

Like the native people who lived in their shadow, I, too, had been fascinated by the Buttes since I'd first seen them. But for me the lure wasn't the call of myth or history. It was simply the urge to explore this mystery so close at hand, to see what hidden wonders it might contain.

It was an urge I hadn't been able to indulge. Unlike the Sierra Nevada or the Coast Ranges, the Buttes lie entirely on private land, unpenetrated by a single public road. To me they were as much terra incognita as the far side of the Moon, a great question mark looming on the horizon of my comfortable urban home. They were a symbol of the remote, the primeval, rising incongruously in the midst of civilization—a perfect metaphor for my own journey.

———————•●•———————

Eventually I reached the town of Colusa and after some searching found the state park where Jane and I would be spending the night—a few acres of camping and picnic sites along the Sacramento River, within walking distance of downtown. I was concerned about Jane. She should have been in camp more than an hour earlier—in fact, I'd expected her to bike back toward Sacramento to meet me—but she was nowhere in sight.

I called home but got no answer, so I settled down to wait. With an hour of daylight left the day was still reasonably warm, but if she didn't arrive by dark it would get chilly—and she had all my gear. I was worried she might be stranded, but I was equally worried about having to spend a night without even a sleeping bag.

Once in the Midwest I'd left at noon to bicycle to a state park about 80 miles from home. Jane had planned to meet me after she got off work, but something had delayed her, and by sunset she hadn't arrived. At nine o'clock she was still missing, and by ten o'clock, when she finally joined me, I was swatting hordes of hungry mosquitoes, beginning to shiver, and preparing to spend the night in a heated bathroom. As I waited for her on the river bluff in Colusa, that memory kept resurfacing.

Half an hour later she arrived. She'd misunderstood my directions and wound up on the wrong side of the Sacramento River, dodging RVs trailing fishing boats along 30 miles of narrow levee-top road. She hadn't figured out what was wrong until she reached a bridge across a tributary, the Feather River. "The Feather?" she'd said out loud. "But that goes through. . . ." She'd looked at a map, then set off down a farm lane, bouncing over miles of rough gravel before eventually finding a bridge across the Sacramento.

But she'd arrived, safe and before dark, and that was all that mattered.

Our tenth anniversary was four days away, and because of the bike trip we would be celebrating it separately. We'd discussed postponing my departure until after the big date, but seven weeks was already uncomfortably short for my planned odyssey; reducing it to little more than six would make a full transcontinental journey impossible without cutting into our joint vacation. So we'd had our big celebration a few nights before, planning a smaller one for that evening.

Unknown to Jane, I'd sent her an anniversary message on the radio show "Prairie Home Companion," which often airs greetings from listeners. My message—timed for the following weekend—read: "Happy Tenth Anniversary to Jane from her husband, Rick, who's bicycling across country and is now somewhere in Idaho."

The greeting, I later learned, was indeed aired, but Jane never heard it; she decided to work that afternoon instead of listening to her favorite radio program. Ironically, my message had also derived from a projected schedule that was too ambitious; on the day it was read, I was nowhere near Idaho, having barely crossed the state line into Oregon.

That night we intended to eat as fancy a dinner as we could find in that town of 4,900, but by the time we'd pitched camp and gone in search of food it was nine o'clock, and hunger was a bigger concern than atmosphere; we wound up joining the local high school kids at a hamburger stand. Still, we had a pleasant evening, rescheduling the romantic dinner as a homecoming celebration rather than a farewell. But as we snuggled into our sleeping bags and I felt her reassuring presence beside me, I felt a pang as I realized this was the last evening we'd spend together until sometime in August.

———•———

If my first day had been unexpectedly pleasant, the next was unexpectedly unpleasant.

I anticipated a continuation of a relaxing, easy excursion up the Sacramento Valley, blown along by the prevailing southeasterly winds. In part that expectation came true. The winds blew unabated from the south-southeast, often at 20 to 25 miles an hour.

It was my second day in the sprawling flatland of the Sacramento Valley, and its scale was overwhelming, especially since this is only half of California's great Central Valley, the other half being the San Joaquin Valley to the south. It seemed amazing that anything so large could be so flat, yet still be surrounded by tall mountains.

The mountains to the west grew higher and the valley gradually narrowed. I had my first sights of Mt. Lassen and Mt. Shasta, the two great volcanoes of northern California. Shasta played hide-and-seek in the clouds, but for 2 glorious miles the road ran straight toward it; 70 miles away, its glistening, snow-covered peak seemed to float high above the haze of the valley below. Mt. Lassen was visible for hours, magnificently etched against the baby-blue eastern horizon, looking close enough to touch even though it was 50 miles away.

But soon after I'd said good-bye to Jane, the day was marred by aggravations: boredom, traffic, and—worst of all—pain. The traffic I could have handled without the boredom, and the slow march of scenery wouldn't have been so monotonous without the need to keep alert enough to handle the traffic. For 50 miles there was no reason to stop—not even a town—and I rode the entire distance without getting off the bicycle, drinking all four water bottles, lathering suntan lotion, eating a lunch of Jane's cornbread. My goal was Red Bluff, near the head of the valley, and the more variegated terrain I hoped to find there.

The longer I rode in that mental state somewhere between trance and boredom, the dimmer grew the memory of the magic day before, when the Sacramento Valley had revealed itself as one of the most beautiful places on Earth. Eventually, all I wanted was to get somewhere else as quickly as possible.

Perhaps I pushed too hard. After about 40 miles my right knee was hurting. Shifting positions didn't help, nor did adjusting the seat height. Suddenly I was angry and frustrated. I'd trained 2,500 miles without pain in my knee. Now, on a flat road with a strong tailwind, it was giving out.

I wondered, as I cut back the pace and inched on toward Red Bluff, what would happen the next day, when I would have to climb—and climb a lot. Was my long-dreamed-of trip going to end in ignominy halfway up the mountains?

————————•◦•————————

After Red Bluff my spirits improved, and I dared to hope I might yet make it across the country. A stop at a bike shop for minor adjustments had delayed me long enough that I was ready to find a place to camp, and I hoped the break had been good for my knee. Pedaling north on the shoulder of the freeway—which for a few miles was the only road out of town—I was amazed by a dramatic change in the countryside. Gone was the infinite flat valley, replaced by undulating terrain. The transition was startling, more so because it was unexpected. Exiting the freeway I found myself immersed in rolling hills—acres of golden grass interspersed with clusters of silver-green oaks. Atop each hill was a vista of 10,000-foot Mt. Lassen, clearer than ever, tantalizing in its apparent proximity.

My campsite was a boat launch and picnic area by the Sacramento River. The bike mechanic in Red Bluff had told me it was a popular camping area, but I had it all to myself—perhaps because a sign at the turnoff baldly proclaimed, "NO CAMPING." I wasn't sure whether the sign was new or something that had been ignored for years, but it was too late to go elsewhere. I tucked myself into a corner, out of sight, planning to plead necessity if the police found me. I doubted they'd object.

The scenery had dissolved my boredom, but my knee had continued to hurt on the 12-mile ride from Red Bluff. That evening I thought long and hard about what to do. Previous bike trips had settled into day-by-day experiences, each day a self-contained unit imposing no need to think beyond the immediate future. Food, water, safety from traffic, and a good place to spend the night—those were the critical necessities. Some could be provided by reasonable planning, but there was always an element of uncertainty.

So it would be with my knee. All my life I'd believed in a God who cares even about such seemingly trivial matters as a sore knee. Now it was time to put that belief into practice. That didn't mean my knee would necessarily be well tomorrow—or even next week. I'd done everything humanly possible—icing it at rest stops, taking aspirin, pedaling as gently as the terrain allowed. Tomorrow was tomorrow, and the day after that was the indefinite future. They were in the realm of God, and I would just have to wait to see what would develop.

————————•◦•————————

The next morning began in high spirits. My knee felt good and my confidence began flooding back. I was indeed willing to live one day at a time.

The ride continued as it had ended the evening before, quietly winding among rolling hills along the Sacramento River. Mt. Lassen still thrust upward but no longer as the starkly detailed etching of the previous afternoon. Now it was a misty silhouette against the morning sky, with a diffuse, pearly glow from the higher snowfields adding to its aura of unattainability.

The landscape at the head of the Sacramento Valley reminded me of Alaska. The willow-lined banks of the Sacramento River and the rapids where it rushes over shoals and around gravel bars evoke memories of the glacier-fed streams of the Alaska Range, and the very spaciousness of this northernmost part of the great Central Valley mimics the grand scale of Alaska. Oddly, this rolling plain felt more open than had the previous day's vast, flat expanses, for I was no longer hemmed in by the ever-present sight of foothills. Only the tallest peaks remained visible, rising as islands scattered in all directions. My imagination filled the gaps between them, not with the lesser summits I knew were there, but with broad valleys leading to more distant mountains beyond. And that bit of legerdemain neatly converted a valley surrounded on three sides by unbroken ramparts into a vast plain interrupted by isolated peaks, enlarging it to a region of truly Alaskan proportions.

———————•●•———————

My speculations came to an abrupt halt when my knee began nagging me with reminders that all was not well. I'd only covered 8 miles when I stopped to rest. "Leave it to God," I reminded myself.

But I was depressed, and so I called Jane.

"Do you want me to come pick you up?" she asked.

I was touched. She hated long drives, especially by herself, yet she was offering to go 180 miles each way so I wouldn't have to ride back on a train or bus.

"No," I said. "I just wanted to talk to you. . . ." I recalled my wish to quit worrying about things I couldn't control. "And ask for your prayers."

Then, almost as an afterthought, I remembered the cousin who would join me in Oregon three days later. We were to meet at the railroad station in Chemult, but there was a closer alternative on the same rail line. "Call Ben," I added. "Tell him I'll either meet him in Klamath Falls, or a day later than planned." I now had a plan of action. "I'll take it easy today," I concluded, "and try to phone him myself this evening."

But after I hung up I decided to call Ben right away. And that was the answer to my prayer.

"No problem," he said. "Klamath Falls would be better for me anyway. And could we still meet on Friday rather than Thursday?"

I was thrilled. I'd gained *both* a day and 70 miles, without inconveniencing Ben. Now I could use that extra time to rest my knee rather than push hard to meet a schedule.

Although the rest had helped, the pain returned after a few minutes of cycling, so I paused frequently to enjoy the scenery and take pictures. After 10 miles I stopped for two hours beside a rushing creek, reading a book and nibbling—of all strange things on a trip where weight was at a premium—on a head of cauliflower I'd bought the day before. I was surprised and relieved to find I wasn't bored by the slow progress. I had assumed that I'd be in constant motion, but for the first time I realized it didn't have to be that way. Simply lounging by the creek was a pleasant way to spend the rest of the morning. To meet Ben on schedule I only needed to ride 55 miles a day. I vowed not to press farther even if I thought I could.

A couple of hours sitting in the growing heat exhausted my water supply, so I rode into a nearby town for lunch and a refill, then continued north to the village of Bella Vista. From there I faced what was probably the greatest challenge of the entire trip: the climb over the southern end of the Cascades.

Nowhere else in the country is there a mountain wall like that forming the eastern edge of the Central Valley. Broken only by the Feather River at its northern end, the Sierra Nevada Range rises virtually from sea level to 14,000 feet at its southern end. Near Sacramento the highest peaks are only 10,000 feet, and a hundred miles farther north they fall to 8,000, but the passes remain high. Along the entire length of the range there is no pass under 5,500 feet, and from the west, that means nearly a 5,500-foot climb. Passes in other mountain ranges may boast greater elevations, but few involve such large climbs.

The Cascades, which merge into the northern end of the Sierra Nevada near Red Bluff, are almost as impressive—lower, but longer—running from British Columbia to northern California. Although the passes aren't as high as those in the Sierra Nevada, most still force you to climb nearly a mile.

I'd initially planned to take a scenic route through the national park around Mt. Lassen, but the park road climbs to 8,500 feet, and my sore knee forced me to look elsewhere. I'd opted for state highway 299, which crosses 4,400-foot Hatcher Summit 30 miles north of Mt. Lassen. People told me it was an easy climb with a good shoulder.

For the first mile the advice was accurate, but then the shoulder ended and traffic became a problem. There was a lot of it, mostly trucks, often coming in pairs of double-trailer rigs running close together. I learned quickly to get off the road whenever I heard them bearing down from behind; there were so many that sometimes I could cover only 20 to 30 yards between the time one went by and the next hove into earshot.

My knee fared well with the frequent rest stops, and I plodded along, soon passing the 1,000-foot elevation sign. As I crawled along between trucks I had plenty of time to study the Cascade foothills. From each vantage point the landscape described a nearly perfect geometric plane, tilted southwest at an angle of about two degrees and cut by numerous parallel canyons with intervening ridges. The road followed one ridge while distant ridges appeared and then fell into line, sloping from the Central Valley to the shoulders of the higher peaks 30 miles beyond. Rising steeply above the foothills, the volcanic peaks broke the symmetry of the landscape, proving that this sloping peneplain does not continue forever.

In a few miles the route dropped from the ridges to a creek bed, and the big picture was no longer apparent. Nor were there any landmarks against which to gauge progress. Everything still slanted, but because the slope of the valley matched that of the rest of the land, the surrounding hills never grew higher. There was no sense of progress, no sense of plunging deeper into the mountains, only an endless 500-foot-deep valley tilted at two degrees.

But the riding was easy and fun, for the valley picked up the tailwind that had been following me, funnelling it into a gale that made pedaling uphill effortless. And I had entered a land of trees—big pines offering cool shade along the rushing stream that was never far away.

I passed an old mine—a piece of California history quietly rusting into oblivion, a beam and sheet-metal structure the size of a large house, its vacant windows staring blankly at me from across the creek. The walls and roof were rust-streaked to myriad shades of orange-brown, and loose pieces of sheet metal banged arrhythmically in the wind. I later learned that, in what seemed like a wry anticipation of its ultimate fate, it had been named the Afterthought Mine and had produced substantial quantities of copper and zinc from the Civil War until as recently as World War II.

Eventually the road climbed out of the valley, and I struggled up a steep 500-foot grade to the town of Round Mountain, stopping on its outskirts to refill my bottles from a spigot discharging some of the most refreshing water I'd ever tasted.

My knee was holding up well, and while the road had descended several hundred feet into the creek bed after the 1,000-foot sign, it had been a gentle but steady climb ever since. I figured I must be nearing the 3,000-foot mark, and despite my vow to take it easy I was beginning to think about going all the way over the pass before nightfall. There was still plenty of daylight.

I rounded the last bend into town. "ELEVATION 2000."

"No!" I yelled.

———————•••———————

I stopped in Round Mountain for a snack.

"Are you with those other cyclists?" a shop clerk asked.

"What cyclists?"

"Two guys stopped here an hour ago. They're heading for Boston. One had a sore knee and bought some Ben Gay."

I was pleased to discover I had company but fought the urge to try to catch them for the night. As I'd just discovered, I wasn't doing as well as I'd thought. If I gave chase, I could easily wreck my knee for weeks.

Three miles later I heard about them again.

I was sitting on a log in front of another small market in the village of Montgomery Creek. I'd met a deputy sheriff in the store and was asking him about possible camping places, when a woman pulled up in a blue pickup.

"You with those other two?"

"No, but I've heard about 'em."

"Yeah? Well, they went by my place ten minutes ago. I sent them up to Hillcrest. Told 'em to camp at the roadside park."

"You can camp there?"

"Sure. And there are bathrooms and water."

It sounded good to me. But a few minutes later I began to wonder. From Montgomery Creek, the deputy had told me, the highway begins to climb in earnest, and I soon found out he wasn't kidding.

It must have taken forty-five minutes to get up that hill. By the time I'd gone a mile, I was *hoping* that passing trucks would provide an excuse to stop, but it was well after 5 p.m. and the traffic had abated considerably, so I found other excuses to rest, grateful that I'd put mountain-bike gears on my bicycle before leaving home.

All things end eventually, including murderous hills. At the top, I looked back. "STEEP DOWNGRADE – 6½% grade next 3 miles." No wonder I'd had to work so hard.

A cafe in the aptly named village of Hillcrest provided dinner and a bag of ice for my knee. It seemed foolish to lug enough food for a whole day up a 3,000-foot hill and then elect not to eat it, but it was nice to sit indoors for a few minutes and not have to prepare dinner.

As I ate I talked with another customer. "You picked a whale of a hill to come up," he told me.

"You can say that again."

"Yeah, it's one of the five or six steepest highways in California."

"It figures. But it's also the lowest pass over the mountains."

"Yeah—that's why the truckers like it."

That explained a lot.

Later I commented about the clouds I'd seen building to the northwest. "Is it going to rain?"

"Maybe. They say it's a fifty-fifty chance. If it does, don't wait around for it to clear—it could rain all day. But it'll be dry in Burney, on the other side. That's in the rain shadow. Maybe you want to go there tonight—it won't be dark for a couple of hours."

A spatter of raindrops met me outside, and I considered taking his advice. But while the worst of the climb was behind, it was still several miles to the summit; I remembered my vow not to overtax my knee and pulled into the rest area a half mile later. If it rained I'd deal with it—I was prepared. Besides, I wanted to meet the other cyclists.

I found them at a picnic table, just finishing a multi-course dinner. They even had a tossed salad, with dressing yet. I would never have considered lugging eight ounces of salad dressing over a 4,400-foot pass, but I was impressed by anyone who would. It certainly looked better than the bagels, cheese, cauliflower, and grapefruit I had with me, and somewhat sheepishly I realized that the salad dressing was a lot lighter than the grapefruit and cauliflower I hadn't even eaten.

They were from the San Francisco area but had started well north of there, near Eureka. Their names were John and Craig, and John, in particular, had led an adventurous life, working for an Alaskan cannery one summer and solo biking one winter from British Columbia to Mexico. He and Craig had just graduated from college and were free until late August, when John would start graduate school, but they hoped to be on the East Coast in eight weeks. Like me, they'd been on the road three days.

And like me, Craig had a sore knee, but his was much worse than mine, visibly swollen and painful, even when he wasn't on his bicycle. "It works okay when I get it loosened up," he said, but I was afraid he was in for trouble.

We pitched camp near one of the picnic tables, despite signs proclaiming that camping wasn't permitted in the rest area. "Don't stay overnight," explained a sign, "because others might need your parking space." Since we weren't using any parking spaces, I hoped the no-camping rule didn't apply. Not that I was particularly worried; after all, the deputy sheriff had tacitly approved the woman's recommendation.

The next morning we awoke to clear skies but brisk temperatures. The tailwind was still present, and as soon as it was reasonably warm we were ready to hit the road.

"Did you hear my bicycle fall over last night?" John asked me as we were packing.

"No."

"Neither did I. I've always assumed that if anyone messed with my bike the noise would wake me, but it fell over last night and I slept through it. I think I need to reconsider my security system."

I agreed. I hadn't woken up either. I wondered if I should lock my bike at night, even if I slept only a few feet from it.

The three of us rode out of the rest area but soon separated, as each sought his own pace over the 7 miles and 1,100 feet that still divided us from the summit. John, uninjured and pedaling strongly, soon disappeared. Craig and I had very different ideas about how to nurse sore knees. He rode slowly at first until his knee limbered up, then quickly pulled away. I didn't try to stay with him; my goal was to reach the summit staying just below the threshold of true pain. I succeeded, but it took a while, and by that time John and Craig were gone.

I found their bicycles propped against a cafe in Burney, at the base of the pass. Like me, they'd decided to buy hot breakfasts when they could, taking advantage of the enormous lumberjack meals served by many small-town cafes. In this case, $2.85 apiece bought us "pancake sandwiches": three cakes and three sausages with an egg on top. I wouldn't have to eat again until midafternoon.

"Did you see our message at the pass?" John asked.

"What message?"

"We left a note to meet us at the first good cafe in Burney."

"I must have missed it. But when you weren't on top, I figured you were either down here or at the scenic overlook partway down. Did you stop at the overlook?"

"What overlook?"

"It was about half a mile past the summit."

"I didn't see it. I was concentrating on my tuck."

"Well, did you see the snow-covered mountain to the south?"

John shook his head.

"White-line fever," Craig muttered a bit wistfully—all he'd seen was the white line on the side of the road.

I wasn't surprised. A lot of cyclists get caught up in the mechanics of riding and see little more of the countryside than do oblivious motorists swishing by in their air-conditioned cocoons. Once, on a week-long ride in Nebraska with five hundred other cyclists, I'd spotted a sign pointing to a state park, half a mile off the route. The road was gravel, but I turned in anyway, finding a small lake ringed by low hills. A flock of pelicans burst from the shore in a commotion of splashes and flup-flup-flupping wings, seeming, as someone once told me, to need as much runway to get airborne as a flight of loaded B-52s. Watching them was the high point of my day, but that evening in camp I couldn't find another cyclist who'd even seen the park sign, let alone ventured in. White-line fever is simply the cyclist's form of speed, distance, and performance mania; I'd had my taste of it the day I'd hurt my knee, when I'd cycled all those miles without a break. I was paying for it now in knee pain, but I'd also paid for it then by losing touch with the land I'd come to see.

While they claimed to be taking it easy on Craig's knee, John and Craig were still planning an 80-mile day. So I bade them adieu, wondering if our paths would cross again before the East Coast. For their sakes I hoped not. To meet Ben I was detouring well away from the shortest route east; if I saw them again, it would mean Craig's knee hadn't been able to take the strain.

As it turned out I didn't see them again that summer, but a year later I encountered them on a one-day tour in the Sierra Nevada, near Sacramento, where Craig told me his knee had continued to plague him all the way into Idaho. Eventually he'd stopped for several days to recuperate, then he and John made it to the East Coast.

———————•◦•———————

One of the more unpleasant aspects of bicycle touring is that you are uncomfortably vulnerable to the hostilities of the people you encounter. But far more often cycling provides the opposite—the opportunity to see people at their best, partly because they respond to your vulnerability, but also because you pass by slowly enough to perceive them as individuals, and to be so perceived in turn.

Even so I was pleasantly surprised as I rode east from Burney to discover that I was entering one of the most hospitable regions I'd ever encountered. It wasn't the exuberant friendliness I'd occasionally found in
east Texas or parts of the Midwest, where passing drivers had flagged me
down just for a chat and where everyone greeted me with a friendly wave.
It was a more practical hospitality. If I asked a question, people would
drop what they were doing to answer—and if they couldn't answer, they'd
find someone who could.

Since there was only one main road I sometimes saw people more than
once. The deputy sheriff who'd helped give me camping directions the
previous night had shown up the next morning in the cafe in Burney. The
man who'd given me the weather forecast that evening appeared again in
the afternoon. I was resting by a creek reading a book when he stopped to
ask how my knee was doing and to offer a lift if I needed it, though his
small car could only have accommodated my bicycle in the back seat.
When I declined he grinned, then spent the next five minutes telling me
about the local geology.

"Are you a geologist?" I asked.

"No," he said. "I'm a chemist. But you can't live around here without
absorbing a lot of geology!"

"Aren't you scared riding alone?" one grocery-store clerk asked.

"Not around here," was my immediate answer.

"No, of course not," she replied with an obvious, I took that for
granted attitude. Nor was she the only person to take that view—people
east of the Cascades clearly saw themselves as having no big-city problems.

"Where can I put my bike so I can see it while I shop?" I'd asked a bag
boy at the same store.

"Don't worry," he'd replied. "I guarantee you nobody'll steal it around
here."

Apparently not everything is safe; the deputy sheriff wore a thick vest
under his uniform.

"Why the bulletproof vest?" I overheard someone ask him.

"You never know what you'll encounter when you get a call out into
the brush," he replied. "I go tramping around in places where people
would rather not see me."

Something told me this region might have a dual character. Near the
roads and in the towns people were friendly; I wouldn't have hesitated to

knock on any door for help. But apparently up in the hills, in hard-to-find places, lurked some unsavory characters. I didn't ask what kind. Hermits? Marijuana farmers? Survivalists? Neo-Nazis? All were possible. This was a place where people who wished to disappear could do so.

It also seemed a good place for people who merely wanted to loosen the grip of civilization. Many of those I talked to had grown up in cities but spurned the urban life, moving here to find a slower, simpler existence. Mixing with indigenous ranchers and loggers, this new wave of immigrants seemed to have built an unusual community. "Anti-Yuppies" they might be called. College-educated people retired from the rat race, who with their environmental sensibilities and desire to limit population growth have made this area culturally more similar to Oregon than to the rest of California. I wondered how people like the chemist managed to make their livings in an area covered mostly by timber and scrub rangeland. Home computers and instant communications help, of course, but the anti-Yuppies still must have sacrificed much in the way of income; average incomes in northeastern California were less than two-thirds the average for the state as a whole.

As I pedaled along, stopping frequently, I understood the sacrifice. The east side of the Cascades seemed far more pleasant than the Central Valley. Just passing through gave me a taste of the pace of life, a pleasant change from the years I'd spent in cities. Pedaling through the Central Valley at 85 miles a day I had been bored; here, at barely half the pace, I was enthusiastic and relaxed.

———————•—————

That evening I picnicked on a roadside guardrail, basking in the setting sun and listening to the happy roar of my camp stove boiling water for dinner. One thousand feet below stretched the Fall River Valley, a series of ancient lake beds now turned to broad meadows, with a few surviving lakes glinting silver in the evening sun. The traffic had died to a trickle, and in that last hour before sunset I had the scenery almost to myself.

And what scenery it was, and what a place for a picnic—perched most of the way up a dizzyingly steep mountainside carpeted in golden grass, with an unblocked view of the Cascades.

Before me stood the snowy cones of Lassen and Shasta, and between them I could see dozens of lesser volcanoes. Everything in sight was volcanic in origin. For the last 25 miles I'd been ascending a series of ridges formed by geological faults that, sometime after the last lava flows blanketed most of northeastern California in thousands of feet of basalt, had thrust some blocks up and others down. The mountain I was sitting on was almost certainly another. Each ridge was steep and high on the west, with only a moderate drop-off to the east. In combination they produced a series of steps—big climb, short drop, big climb, short drop—rising gradually toward the northeast.

I was still in the drainage basin of the Pit River, a tributary of the Sacramento that drains the entire eastern side of the Cascades between Mt. Lassen and Mt. Shasta, as well as much of the Modoc Plateau—as this wedding-cake structure of lava flows and meadows is named. The otherwise-unknown Pit, the chemist-cum-geologist boasted with obvious hometown pride, joins the Columbia and the Klamath as one of only three rivers to successfully breach the great wall of the Cascades.

———————•••———————

It had been a beautiful but difficult day. I'd climbed three hills totalling at least 3,300 feet—500 more than the previous day's climb into the Cascades. I camped that night on the highway right-of-way on top of the mountain, well back from the road where I couldn't be seen. It wasn't the ideal spot—I would have preferred a park or a campground—but there were none around, and a woman in one of the small towns had suggested it. "I'd camp there," she'd said. "No one around here will bother you."

Surprisingly, I had company. Soon after I finished pitching my tent, a large truck turned into a nearby pullout. At first I was nervous, wondering why the driver had stopped, fearful he might spot me. Then reason regained control—a truck driver wasn't going to mug me; he was probably just taking a break. Comforted, I snuggled into my sleeping bag, listening to the wind buffeting my tent and wondering at how cold the evening had suddenly become.

———————•••———————

At dawn it was still cold (I later learned the temperature had plummeted to thirty-three degrees). A light wind came out of the northeast; after four days of tailwinds even a gentle headwind was unwelcome.

I stopped for a pancake breakfast in Bieber, then pushed north on a little-used back road toward Lava Beds National Monument near the Oregon border. After only a few miles of pedaling directly into the steadily freshening breeze my knee began to hurt. I slowed down to rest it.

I had just entered a wildlife refuge, and as I crossed a low bridge over a marshy stream I was surrounded by a cloud of swallows—hundreds of them, flying around me in dizzying circles, half going one way, half the other, many only 30 feet away. They followed for a hundred yards or so, then dispersed, eventually roosting on telephone lines near the bridge or scattering across the marshes. They must have been protecting nests beneath the bridge.

I coasted to a stop to watch and listen for other wildlife and was quickly rewarded. A plover burst from the ditch beside me, its cries of "whip-it, whip-it, whip-it" fading into the distance as it fled. A pair of ducks took startled flight from a hidden pool among the cattails, then splashed into the marsh grass a few yards beyond. From deeper in the cattails came a "sploosh," then another, as a doe bounded away in a series of soggy leaps. As peace returned and the rippling caused by my arrival subsided, songbirds began a continuous twitter. I could distinguish a half dozen different calls; an expert undoubtedly would have heard more. I listened quietly for half an hour, then reluctantly moved on. I knew of no campground before Lava Beds, still many miles away.

———————•●•———————

The rest of the day the wind and my knee conspired against me—the wind forcing me to pedal harder than I would have liked, my knee making it unwise to put my head down and bull through the windiest stretches.

But except for these, the next few miles were the type of cycling I'd hoped to find. From the wildlife refuge the road wound gradually through ranch country along the Pit River, then crossed a low divide and plunged into a 15-mile stretch of open ponderosa forest, the rich scents of pine sap and sun-warmed grass drenching my senses to the exclusion of almost all else.

The quiet back road did not continue all the way to Lava Beds, eventually merging with a state highway. At first the highway was good riding, with a 2-foot shoulder giving adequate protection from the traffic. But halfway to the Lava Beds turnoff the shoulder ended, and while the traffic was courteous, with most drivers waving and many giving me a whole lane when they passed, there were too many of them for comfort.

When I'd left Sacramento I'd decided to carry a warning flag, an orange banner on an 8-foot fiberglass pole, and I was particularly glad I had it. The wind was blowing at an angle from my right and as it did so, it bent the pole as much as 2 or 3 feet to the left, forcing the cars to give me that much extra berth.

The flag unfortunately provoked the trip's only unpleasant confrontation. I was still in Sacramento on an off-road bike path when another cyclist started to pass me on a blind turn. As he pulled out, two cyclists popped into view coming toward us. Everybody swerved madly, narrowly averting a head-on collision.

"Keep on your own side of the yellow line," one of the oncoming cyclists shouted as he sped by.

"Get that damn flag out of the way," the one who was passing me snapped in turn as he again pulled even with me. "I can't pass close to you without hitting it."

My irritation was mitigated by the realization he was right about the flag; even when the wind wasn't bending it to one side or the other, the flag could definitely be a hazard to other cyclists. Later, I discarded the mounting bracket, which was raked at a forty-five-degree angle, and slid the pole into a vertical position in the corner of one of my rear bags.

But I couldn't let it go at that. "You don't have to pass on a curve," I told him. "Why not wait for a straight stretch?"

"Not when someone's going as slow as you are," he growled, then sped off.

Some people, I suppose, always need someone else to blame. But the incident was also a warning—similar to Craig and John's white-line fever: Simply being on a bicycle wouldn't necessarily insulate me from the hurry sickness I was trying to leave behind; what was required was a complete change of attitude.

I kept waiting for a motorist to react with the same vehemence: "Get that flag out of my way! I want to pass without crossing the centerline!" But so far it hadn't happened. Could it be that motorists treat cyclists better than cyclists treat each other?

———•—•———

Eventually I reached the turnoff for Lava Beds. I'd been planning to buy groceries at a little town named Perez—on my map it appeared near the turnoff—but Perez didn't exist, and the next "town," Tionesta, was nothing but a small private campground. It had a camp store, though, and I arrived just as the proprietors were restocking their shelves with a car-load of groceries they'd bought in a supermarket 30 miles away, peeling off the original price tags and replacing them with tags of their own. I wondered how big their markup was. Given the small scale of their business, I couldn't see how any markup could cover the value of their time and mileage, but as they sorted out the groceries it became clear that they handled that problem by combining business and personal shopping.

Unfortunately, they also dealt with their low sales volume by buying nothing perishable. That meant that for the next twenty-four hours I'd be eating only crackers, cheese spread, potato chips, and a pound of spaghetti I'd been carrying for the last two days.

I could have spent the night in Tionesta, but I preferred to ride on into the monument. It was a beautiful ride, especially in the evening, as the road climbed onto the shoulder of an 8,000-foot volcano. The sun settled behind the mountain, and I gradually climbed higher, with the Modoc Plateau opening behind me, a sweeping expanse of ponderosa-clad hills fading into the distance, eventually lapping against the snowy peaks of the Warner Range, 80 miles to the southeast. As I set up camp that night I paused to watch the slow June twilight gradually fade the distant colors from blue to indigo and then to dull lavender, softening the contours but allowing the sense of infinite vistas to linger long into the evening.

———— •••• ————

The next day I rested. Despite my vow not to exceed 55 miles a day I'd pedaled 71 the day before, and today I wanted to keep the mileage low. This, however, was the day I'd planned to meet my cousin Ben in Klamath Falls, 60 miles away. To buy the necessary time I'd phoned him the previous evening, telling him that instead of meeting his train — which was due at 10 P.M. — I'd meet him the following morning at a road junction east of town. That cost us half a day together, but it shortened my route considerably.

With that dilemma solved, I was in no hurry to leave Lava Beds. I took ranger-guided walks in the morning and again in the afternoon, dawdling until 4:30.

In a not-all-that-different life, I might have become a geologist. Whenever I encounter an interesting landform, one of the first questions that comes to mind is how it was formed. At Lava Beds part of the answer was fairly simple — at one time or another everything had spewed from the mouth of a volcano — but the landforms were particularly unusual, consisting of thousands of acres of lava flows, some not much more than a thousand years old, an assortment of cinder cones, and one of the world's most impressive sets of lava caves.

Lava caves are formed when the outside shell of a stream of lava cools while the molten rock within continues to move. Eventually the lava drains out the downhill end of the tube, leaving a long cave that may be accessible through breaks in its roof. Such caves aren't all that unusual, but they only form if the lava flow has just the right slope. If it's too steep, the outer shell never gets a chance to harden; if it's too gradual, the flow solidifies as a unit.

Lava Beds contains two to three hundred such tubes, some branched and interconnected, some with tunnels running several hundred yards before their paths are blocked by collapsed ceilings. An untold number may await discovery, lying, perhaps, beneath more recent flows.

Not designed for the casual visitor looking for a quick drive-through attraction, the monument is the perfect place for leisurely exploration. The rest of the Park Service could draw an important lesson from the way Lava Beds is managed—everything is designed first to lure visitors from their cars, then to encourage them to test their abilities. A few dozen caves are easily accessible, but only one was lighted with signs to explain its features and benches to convert one section into a tiny auditorium. Exploring the dark caves by flashlight, visitors are free to walk in most places, duck-walk in others, crawl if they are so inclined, with no restrictions. Undeveloped caves in the monument's backcountry allow visitors to do some real spelunking.

On one ranger-guided hike I was accompanied by two elderly ladies, retired school teachers from Los Angeles. We hiked 4 miles along a rough trail, seeking a vantage of the monument's most recent lava flow, which isn't visible from the road. We ran out of time before we got there, but not before we'd had a pleasant walk through the desert chaparral that covers the older flows, finding along the way good views of Mt. Shasta and the mountains near Crater Lake to the north.

The only time my two companions—both well past retirement age—showed their years was when the ranger talked about the Park Service's forest-fire policy.

"But you still put them out, don't you?" one of the ladies ventured.

"No," the ranger explained for the second time. "Unless there's a danger to developed areas we usually let them burn. The vegetation is well adapted to fire, and because we were so conscientious about putting out fires in the past, there's too much underbrush now. All of that stuff," he waved at a thicket of chaparral, "shouldn't be here. Without our interference most of it would have burned off years ago. But now it just gets thicker. So, as long as they don't get out of hand, we let fires burn." He grinned. "In fact, we sometimes set them."

She was aghast. "Why? That doesn't make sense."

So he explained yet again.

But it seemed hopeless. The teachers' preconceptions were too strong, steeped in decades of Smokey the Bear and other anti-fire propaganda. Living in Los Angeles for many years had compounded their prejudice;

brush fires are a major danger in that part of the state, threatening lives and property every summer. Even though southern California's brush-fire problems are also magnified by too many years of fire suppression, the solution there cannot be as simple, for too much property would be lost if a fire got out of control.

This misunderstanding didn't detract from my elderly companions' accomplishments. Even if they hadn't understood everything they'd seen they were willing to leave the stifling security of the automobile to prove that, even at eighty, they weren't too old to meet the land on its own terms, scrambling—somewhat gingerly, but scrambling nonetheless—through brambles and over rocks to find the desert stillness that can be encountered only beyond the reach of mechanized civilization.

———•○•———

California's only major Indian war, the Modoc War of 1872 to 1873, was fought in the lava flows, with fifty-two warriors under a chief named Captain Jack holding off ten times as many cavalry for three months without suffering a single casualty, until the army finally brought in a set of field mortars and began round-the-clock shelling.

On my way out of the monument I stopped to hike a short, self-guided trail through the Indian stronghold, a jumble of fractured rock that is one of the greatest natural fortresses imaginable. Even with artillery the cavalry couldn't win an outright victory—the Indians were cut off from water. When forced to retreat, they still escaped cleanly, slipping down a secret path over the lava flows and covering several miles before the army even knew they were gone.

But like so many Indian wars, this one had an unhappy ending. The escapees were tracked down, caught, and sent to Oklahoma—a fate worse than the reservation from which they'd fled. All they wanted was a reservation of their own, not the one they were forced to share with their enemies, the Klamath Indians. Their wish was never granted. Now, more than a century later, the remaining Modoc have lost their tribal identity, absorbed into the larger Klamath tribe.

———•○•———

As I left the monument the landscape changed drastically. I was entering the flat, lush farm country of the Tulle Lake valley, with irrigation sprinklers throwing glittering streamers over fields of hay, grain, and potatoes. The valley was ringed by mountains, with Shasta dominating the southwest skyline.

But there were no places to camp. The north wind had come up strongly and my knee was hurting again. As I neared Tulelake, on the north side of the valley, I knew this was as far as I would go.

In my native Midwest, farm country such as this meant clean, quiet little towns and friendly people. Not here. At its best Tulelake looked depressed. The community, much of which is house-trailers, seemed to turn in on itself, the reverse of the hospitable range country of the Modoc Plateau.

I followed a sign that read "TRAILER PARK" and found only a large gravel lot. I asked the owner where else I might go, but she could offer no suggestions.

I went on into the center of town—not far in a town of eight hundred. Eventually locating Tulelake's one police car, I asked where I could camp.

"Not in the city limits." The patrolman thought for a moment. "And if you camp in the country around here, I can guarantee you someone'll hassle you. We get a lot of wetbacks 'round here."

My remaining Midwestern illusions vanished. In California, farming means migrant labor and lots of transients, a few of whom might be rough characters, regardless of whether they are illegal immigrants or U.S. citizens.

"There's an abandoned farmhouse a bit out of town," the policeman said, giving me directions. "That's where I usually tell folks like you to go. You can get in out of the weather, out of sight of the road. Nobody I've sent there has ever had a problem."

I thanked him, and as I pedaled out of town a group of teenagers watched idly from a street corner. Suddenly I didn't like the feel of this town at all. I found a phone and looked up motels in the Yellow Pages, but the ads covered the entire northeastern corner of the state. There were at least a hundred listings, none of them local as far as I could tell. I rode back through downtown, looked at two rundown hotels, and shuddered. The teenagers on the corner continued to watch.

By then I was sure I didn't want to sleep in an abandoned house. If the wrong people saw me enter, it could be a terrible trap. Better to sleep on the gravel at the trailer park. Besides, it had a shower.

The young woman I'd talked to before was gone, but her husband was in the office. So I started over.

"Do you have a place for a tent?" I asked.

He shook his head.

"Any grassy place where I could pitch a tent or unroll a sleeping bag?"

He thought for a moment, started to speak, changed his mind, then started to speak and changed his mind again.

"How about there?" I wanted to ask, pointing to the lush grass next to the small, trim house that doubled as office and home. But I hesitated to be so direct.

Apparently he didn't realize how appealing the spot would be to a tent camper. "Only the lawn around the house," he said shrugging.

"That'll do fine. Is it okay with you?"

"Oh sure, but it's not much of a site."

I almost laughed. It would be the best bed I'd seen since Sacramento. "How much?"

We settled on four dollars, plus two dollars for the shower—a bargain, since his trailer sites went for ten.

———————•◉•———————

The next morning I woke slowly, luxuriating in the soft grass beneath me. The trailer park had a laundry, so I decided to wash my clothes before meeting Ben. Most of them were now six days dirty. The lint screens in the dryers weren't user-maintainable, however, and hadn't been cleaned in ages; it took three cycles to dry my puny load, and even then everything was damp.

Meanwhile I packed what gear I could. My luxurious camping spot and my tent were covered with white splotches from birds roosting in the tree above. I grumbled, mopped off my tent as best I could, then rolled it up.

Well after nine o'clock I left. I had 32 miles to ride to meet Ben, and the accursed north wind had already sprung up.

———————•◉•———————

Within a couple of miles my knee began to hurt. I'd been babying it for the last four days, and although the pain had never been severe—generally only mild twinges or a dull ache—it had been a constant reminder that something was wrong. It had been both the curse and the blessing of the trip. A curse because except for the first day I had been unable to pedal as hard or long as I'd wanted, and a blessing because it had slowed me down, making the journey itself much more pleasant.

The simplest blessing was merely a change in timing. Clouds hung on the northern horizon most days, and the last time I'd talked to Ben he'd said it had been raining at his home in Eugene all week. Even on the rain-shadow side of the Cascades it had been stormy; a ranger at Lava Beds had told me that for several days before I'd arrived they'd had north winds of 30 to 35 miles an hour. If my knee hadn't delayed me I'd have bicycled straight into the teeth of that storm.

But my troublesome knee was also related to other blessings more important than the good fortune of decent weather—deep blessings, connected to the reasons I'd left Sacramento in the first place.

Part of the appeal of a transcontinental journey had always been the vision of reliving the pioneer dream, even if from west to east instead of east to west. "Northwest Passage," by Canadian folk singer Stan Rogers, became my theme song, and I found myself singing it at least once a day:

> Ah, for just one time, I would take the Northwest Passage
> To find the hand of Franklin reaching for the Beaufort Sea
> Tracing one warm line through a land so wide and savage
> And make a Northwest Passage to the sea
>
> Westward from the Davis Strait, 'tis there 'twas said to lie
> The sea-route to the Orient for which so many died
> Seeking gold and glory, leaving weathered broken bones
> And a long-forgotten lonely cairn of stones
>
> Three centuries thereafter, I take passage overland
> In the footsteps of brave Kelso, where his "sea of flowers" began
> Watching cities rise before me, then behind me sink again
> This tardiest explorer, driving hard across the plain
>
> And through the night, behind the wheel, the mileage clicking West
> I think upon Mackenzie, David Thompson and the rest
> Who cracked the mountain ramparts, and did show a path for me
> To race the roaring Fraser to the sea
>
> How then am I so different from the first men through this way?
> Like them I left a settled life, I threw it all away
> To seek a Northwest Passage at the call of many men
> To find there but the road back home again

My journey would be both a physical and a spiritual passage across the breadth of a continent, a spiritual odyssey into a simpler existence, a return to an awareness of the things that mattered, things that I could hold fast once I returned home.

Pedaling north out of Tulelake I wondered what I had learned so far. I had vowed to try to learn something new each day, not only about the land through which I was passing, but also about myself and the world. And I'd been making a conscious effort to take each day separately. A familiar quote from somewhere—Shakespeare? the Bible?—kept ringing in my mind, and the application was obvious: "Sufficient unto the day is the evil thereof." Each morning since the Central Valley I'd known my knee was strong enough to carry me through that day. I might worry about whether I'd have to give up the trip the next day, but *that* was in the future, not the present. Today's issues were always simple: pedaling up the next pass, finding a campsite, water, food. Tomorrow was a separate entity, but there was nothing I could do today except take it easy. At this I hadn't been completely successful, but I was gaining. If I succeeded, I knew I would learn a lesson well worth the inconvenience.

I pedaled slowly north, crossing the Oregon border and approaching my rendezvous with Ben and the next stage of the journey.

CHAPTER 3

Ben

Of Rattlesnakes and a Dead
Porcupine

DAY 7 • Saturday, June 21 • CUMULATIVE MILES: 452
Tulelake, California, to Quartz Mountain Summit,
Oregon

DAY 8 • Sunday, June 22 • CUMULATIVE MILES: 531
Quartz Mountain Summit to Alkali Lake Roadside Park

DAY 9 • Monday, June 23 • CUMULATIVE MILES: 616
Alkali Lake Roadside Park to Burns

When I entered Oregon, I entered bicyclist's heaven.
I'd been cycling for several miles through a region of low hills threaded by a network of well-paved back roads that branched and rejoined then branched again as they wound through the gentle ranch country surrounding the little town of Bonanza, population two hundred.

I would love to return there someday to explore the surrounding hills, but more than the landscape I remember the people. On that Saturday morning many of them were gathered in the town's cafe.

I've never understood how small-town cafes can make enough money to stay in business, but as I sat and watched the farmers and ranchers talking, I realized how vital they are as places to meet friends and exchange information. In conjunction with churches, they are the news centers of rural communities.

The one in Bonanza was exceptional among its kind. As I stepped inside, everyone looked up. Two men sitting next to the door grinned at me, their whippet-thin bodies, western garb, and prematurely wizened faces giving them the archetypal appearance of the cowboys they might well have been. "Where ya ridin' from?" one asked.

"Sacramento."

There was a quiet conversation at another table, then a stage-whisper: "Go ahead and ask him."

33

"How far do ya reckon ya make in a day?" someone spoke up.

I sat down at one of the few empty tables. I had everyone's attention. "I've been doing about 60 miles. On other trips I've averaged closer to 100."

The cowboys nodded. The stage-whisper added, "I told you they can cover a lot of distance."

I turned to a woman at a nearby table. "Do you get a lot of bikers here?" I asked. "The last 20 miles have been the nicest of my trip. If I lived in Klamath Falls, I'd be out here every other weekend."

"We get a few. And there's a guy here in town who does a lot of biking, up and down the mountains, all over the place. He's about thirty-five years old. Here, let me give you his phone number. If you come back, you give him a call—he'd love to join you, and it's a lot more fun with company, isn't it?"

And so it went. I was besieged with questions, overwhelmed with hospitality. What a difference the last few miles had made. Tulelake had been the least hospitable place I'd encountered so far; Bonanza the most.

———— •❖• ————

After breakfast I went to the general store, where I'd been told I could buy stamps for my growing collection of unmailed cards and letters. No, the owner said, they didn't sell stamps officially, but she had some of her own she'd be happy to let me buy. She could also give me envelopes.

As I wrote addresses I told her of my plans to meet my cousin. "I'm going to be late," I added. "We were to meet sometime between ten o'clock and noon." It was nearly noon already, and I had 7 miles to ride and a good-size hill to climb.

A middle-aged customer spoke up from a nearby sales counter. "Is he wearing a blue helmet?"

I didn't know.

"Well, I live up at the corner, and there's a biker who's been sitting in front of my restaurant for a couple of hours. I bet he's your cousin."

"Are you going back?"

"Right away."

"Would you tell him I'll be along . . ." I thought a moment, "in about an hour?"

"Sure thing."

Bonanza. I wished I'd been there the night before, when I'd needed a place to camp.

———————•◦•———————

I was nearly an hour late meeting Ben, and my knee had begun to bother me again as I climbed that last hill. Suddenly my growing focus on day-by-day living took on new meaning. Crossing the continent no longer mattered. What did matter was a pleasant ride with Ben, not unduly hampered by my knee. A mile from the summit I stopped and prayed quietly, simply for that. I was surprised by the confidence I gained from the realization that whatever became of my knee was largely beyond my control.

———————•◦•———————

Our relatives had long said that Ben and I would be perfect companions for adventure, but this would be our first. We'd tried a weekend bicycle trip once before, when we'd both lived in Minnesota, but it had been October, and by the time we'd gone 10 miles a cold rain persuaded us to spend the weekend in town instead.

That was the first time I'd seen Ben since childhood, and I was left with one strong impression: My cousin had a remarkable ability to walk into an awkward situation and act thoroughly relaxed, so that everyone else relaxed with him. We wound up at a dinner party hosted by the dean of the University of Minnesota Law School, where I was a visiting professor. The dean had insisted that Ben come along, even though he had nothing to wear but camping clothes.

Somehow Ben pulled it off, walking into a room full of law professors, wearing a lumberjack shirt and baggy wool trousers. If I'd tried something like that I'd have spent the entire evening hiding in a corner, wishing I'd never come. But that would never have worked for Ben. With his 6-foot frame, bean-pole build, and long red hair pulled back in a ponytail, he could never be inconspicuous, no matter what he was wearing. Even though at twenty-two he was by far the youngest person in the room, he took center stage, quickly charming the entire group. For days afterward my colleagues repeatedly told me what an interesting person my cousin is.

Biking together now, several years later, I would again marvel at his ability to make friends with anyone he met. Cowboys or law professors, visiting tourists or ranchers, he could unerringly identify their concerns and listen quietly even when they expounded opinions I knew were contrary to his own, deftly changing the subject if a confrontation seemed inevitable. "You're a social chameleon," I later complimented him. "You can change your coloring to match your environment. It's a gift—I wish I could do it."

———•◦•———

On the first day our primary interest was simply getting reacquainted. After a leisurely lunch at the restaurant we started the 3-mile climb to the crest of Bly Mountain Summit, the first of three passes between us and Lakeview, 65 miles to the east.

As we rode, Ben told me about the problems he'd had reaching our rendezvous. The first had come in the Amtrak station in Eugene. The train was about to leave, but when he attempted to buy a ticket he discovered that his credit card had expired. The credit-card company hadn't sent him a replacement, nor had they notified him; he had no option but to pay cash. He was going to be on a tight budget for the rest of the trip.

But that wasn't his only problem. His train, due to reach Klamath Falls at 10 P.M., had been ninety minutes late.

"You ought to try bicycling down the main street in Klamath Falls at 11:30 on a Friday night," he told me. "All the local kids were out cruising back and forth. They'd pull up beside me and race their engines. 'You wanna drag?' they'd ask." Ben smiled and raised two fingers, in a gesture that was half wave, half salute. " 'Later,' I told 'em. 'Later.' "

Then, Ben discovered that the campground where he'd planned to spend the night didn't exist, although it was shown clearly on the highway map. And there weren't any others. After asking for advice he'd biked to the top of a butte 7 miles west of town and slept in the woods near a radio tower. "Nobody bothered me," he reported. "Nobody but the radio employees go up there because it's too steep." It was also 7 miles in the wrong direction, so in the morning Ben got to ride all the way back through town again.

Just as we reached the top of the pass, he cursed softly, then laughed.

"What's wrong?" I asked.

"I left a water bottle at the restaurant!"

We debated the issue briefly, but we were heading into drier country, and water bottles were too important to abandon. Ben stripped his camping gear off his bicycle and left me to guard it while he went back to the restaurant.

"Boy did I feel stupid," he said when he returned.

"Don't worry about it," I replied, thinking of the myriad times I'd done similar things. "Let's just say you liked the hill so much you decided to climb it again!"

———•◦•———

A few miles later, Ben added another to his list of pre-trip hassles. "Did I tell you what happened as I was cycling to the train station in Eugene?"

"No."

"I broke a spoke. I haven't broken a spoke since I built these wheels six years ago, but I lost one yesterday afternoon."

"Did you fix it?"

"No, I didn't have any spares—I shouldn't have needed any. That wheel's supposed to be strong."

But it broke during the first 2 miles of the trip. Some days that's just the kind of thing you can count on.

————•••————

The next $2\frac{1}{2}$ days proved that Ben and I had much more in common than either of us could have guessed. From the beginning we were ideally matched cycling companions. Without conscious effort we maintained the same pace and picked the same rest stops. As we rode we swapped stories about previous experiences. "I've got one for you, Rick," Ben would begin, and then launch into a description of the time he'd almost been struck by lightning backpacking in the High Sierra, or how he'd nearly succumbed to hypothermia bicycling in the rain on Vancouver Island. I would then tell him a story of my own, perhaps about my close encounter with a grizzly bear one summer when I lived in Alaska, or the time in Nova Scotia when my bicycle and I emerged unscathed after a car came up behind me and sideswiped one coming from the opposite direction. It was amazing how many stories Ben had accumulated in his twenty-seven years, and a relief that our story-telling remained free of the I-can-top-that-one competition that can ruin such exchanges.

The only issue on which we disagreed was food. While I enjoyed eating—particularly on a bicycle trip where I could consume a virtually unlimited number of calories—I viewed food preparation as a waste of time that could be better spent either riding or relaxing. My dinners were usually simple, and I seldom prepared a hot meal.

Ben, however, was a gourmet backcountry cook. To him, dinner was one of the most important parts of the day, and he didn't object to spending an hour or longer preparing it. "If you don't eat things you like," he told me, "you'll have food fantasies." I knew he was speaking from experience, for he had bicycled solo cross-country and had recently returned from trekking in Nepal. "You can spend all day thinking about what you'd like to eat if only you had it along. The way to beat that is to eat well from the start."

For the three evenings we would be together, I certainly didn't mind taking the time to prepare hot meals, especially since he was willing to cook. Our first night we made remarkably tasty spaghetti with a vegetarian sauce containing such unusual ingredients as cauliflower and broccoli.

It turned out to be the only hot meal we prepared. My stove refused to burn properly, continuously flaring up with a sooty orange flame. It had done the same thing the last time I'd used it, charring a ring on a picnic table in Lava Beds, but this time it was even worse, and we nearly set a range fire before discovering a fiery mist of gas leaking from a crack in the fuel line. The stove was an expensive top-of-the-line model with a lifetime warranty, but that was no consolation. We barely managed to cook our spaghetti, then almost threw it out uneaten, fearing that some of the fuel might have sprayed into it. After that, neither of us considered lighting the stove again. We would eat the rest of our meals cold or in restaurants.

———————•◦•———————

The next day was a pleasant blur of evolving scenery, sunshine, and laughter. We started by riding into Lakeview for a late breakfast, then headed north into the dry rangeland of eastern Oregon.

Based on a travelogue I had seen many years ago, I was expecting a stark landscape of jagged rock and sparse vegetation, but we found something entirely different, a gradually narrowing mountain valley of hayfields and horse ranches sandwiched between the flanks of tree-covered mountains, similar to what I'd been seeing since Bonanza. Twenty-five miles later, crossing a low divide, we finally left the forests behind and the landscape assumed the stark beauty I'd expected. For 15 miles the road followed the Abert Rim, proudly hailed by the locals as one of the highest fault escarpments in the nation, a 2,400-foot cliff rising abruptly from a flat basin and dwindling to the north until it disappeared from view. Below the cliff, startling in contrast to the surrounding sagebrush, was Lake Abert, fed by snow melt from the mountains we'd just left, its shoreline devoid of marshes or cottonwoods, a solemn warning that these sparkling waters were probably alkaline.

Our maps showed a town named Valley Falls on the near shore of the lake, but it was nothing more than a general store. As we approached it we were overtaken by three cyclists, decked out like racers and riding in a tight pack. A few minutes later another cyclist came into view, and then another. None were carrying camping equipment.

"I wonder where they're from," I said as we watched them pull away.

Lakeview was the largest town around, but it hadn't seemed big enough to support a racing club.

We soon got an answer. A light-brown van loaded with cycling gear and carrying a large sign boasting "Wimbledon Bike Team" overtook us, and as it passed I noted the California plates. When we reached Valley Falls we found it waiting near the general store, surrounded by the riders we'd seen earlier. More cyclists appeared in the distance as we strolled over to greet those clustered around the van.

The Wimbledon Bike Team, we learned, wasn't a racing club, but ten teen-age boys and four adult counselors (or "coaches," as they called themselves) on a cross-country journey. The youths were residents of a boys' home near Sacramento that used endurance sports to work with troubled or disadvantaged youths. Their bicycle trip seemed a marvelous idea. The boys couldn't help but learn invaluable lessons about discipline, teamwork, and self-reliance, and once they'd learned them, I expected most wouldn't again succumb to the problems that had put them in the home to begin with.

The Wimbledon riders had arranged to camp in a picnic area run by the general store, but Ben and I wanted to go farther, so we asked the store owner for advice.

"There's a highway rest stop in about 40 miles," he told us. "And yes, it has water if you need it. But watch out, that's rattlesnake country."

Shortly afterward, as though to add substance to this warning, a snake rattled at us from the ditch.

But rattlesnakes weren't the only wildlife in the area. A few miles later we found a porcupine that had tried to climb a fence and become trapped in the barbed wire. It was dead now—though only recently so—hanging from the fence with its head resting on the top wire, pathetically gazing at the freedom that had lain so close at hand.

Ben and I had been in a goofy mood all day, and the porcupine's tragedy struck us as funny, a black-humored riposte to the "Hang In There Baby" posters that were popular for several years. Both of us unpacked our cameras and stepped through the fence to get pictures from the other side. As we did, a pickup drove by, then stopped abruptly and backed up.

It's embarrassing enough to find yourself taking pictures of a dead porcupine; to be caught at it is even worse. But the rancher wasn't interested in our perverse senses of humor. "I'm sorry, but I can't have you camping on my land," he called.

"Oh," I replied, "we're not staying. We're just, uh . . ." I waved sheepishly at the porcupine, "taking pictures." It seemed so bizarre that I couldn't think of anything else to say.

He nodded as though our behavior were perfectly normal. "That's okay," he said. "Take all the pictures you want." He put the truck back in gear, grinned, and sped off.

"You know," I said to Ben later, "we're lucky that porcupine wasn't still alive."

"Why?"

"Because we'd have wanted to rescue it."

"Sure. What's wrong with that?"

"How would you have done it?"

Ben thought for a moment. "We could have lifted it with two tire pumps."

"And gotten lashed by its tail. Porcupines do that, you know."

"Hmm. . . . Two long sticks would have worked, but I didn't see any around, did you?"

I shook my head.

Ben grinned suddenly. "I've got a solution, but around here it could get you shot." He made the obligatory dramatic pause. "Do you have any wire cutters?"

I laughed, both horrified and amused by the notion of the rancher catching us cutting down his fence instead of just taking pictures.

———— •◦• ————

By the time we left the porcupine it was well past six o'clock, and our planned campsite was still 35 miles away on the far side of the next pass. But neither of us was in a hurry, so we rode slowly, watching the dying sun transform the lake to silver, basking in the sunset's reflected glory, not only from the water, but also from the escarpment beside us. It was as though we were peddling through a reflecting oven of vivid, golden light. As we climbed slowly toward the pass the valley widened below us, and the peaks of the distant Cascades appeared in sharp silhouette against the twilit sky. It was a time to talk, a time to share concerns and aspirations, to become better friends as well as cousins.

Neither of us was concerned that it would be dark when we reached camp. "There's no need to worry," I said. "Last night the moon was full, and it rises fifty minutes earlier each evening. So tonight there should be plenty of moonlight when we'll need it."

But the sun set and no moon appeared. From the top of the pass we stared into the deepening dusk of the valley beyond. "Oh, no!" I moaned. "I had it backward. The moon rises fifty minutes *later* each evening. And it'll be at least another hour after that before it's high enough to give off a decent amount of light!"

"Let's not wait," Ben said, and started down the hill.

So we rode down the pass at night without lights. There was no traffic, the road was straight, and there were no trees to block the last of the evening twilight. My chief concern was to avoid colliding with Ben. "Talk to me," I called as he pulled ahead. "I can't see you anymore. Where are you?"

"Here I am." And with nothing better to say he started reciting nonsense syllables and numbers. "La, la, la. Lo, lo, lo. One, two, three. Three, two, one."

But his voice gradually faded in the distance, and I was alone, riding my brakes more frequently as the visibility worsened, calling out like a foghorn, "Ben, Ben, are you up there Ben?" and fearing he might stop somewhere by the roadside to wait for me.

Within a few minutes we reached the park. Shortly after that the moon rose.

———————————•••———————————

That night we unrolled our sleeping bags on picnic tables, listening to mice scurrying for crumbs on the concrete slab beneath us.

"Maybe we should hang our food from something," I said, as I watched a particularly daring mouse try to climb the legs of Ben's table.

Ben yawned. "I just leave my food on my bicycle. I've always worked under the assumption that mice can't climb spokes. I've never had one get into my panniers yet."

I was dubious, remembering a backpacking trip when my wife's uncle had given similar advice, telling us that nothing would steal our food at 12,000 feet in the Sierra Nevada. He'd been wrong, and a marmot had left our party of five with nothing but three packets of instant soup and a pound of Spam. It had been a hungry evening.

But tonight the risks weren't so high. Even the hungriest mouse could eat only a little, and if we needed to replace something, three general stores were scattered along the next 80 miles.

———————————•••———————————

Morning came without incident. Ben had been right—no mouse had managed to get to our food—and the day dawned clear and cool. Although we knew it would soon be hot, we weren't in a hurry. For at least two hours we snuggled down in our sleeping bags, catnapping or just watching the morning unfold.

About the time we were ready to get up the Wimbledon riders passed by, waving cheerfully, already 40 miles into their day. At first I was chagrined, embarrassed that we'd let them catch us. Then I shrugged it off. This wasn't a race. Yes, the best times to ride are early and late, when the winds are calm and the traffic absent. But after thirty-two years I knew one thing for certain: I would never be a morning person.

As we started to pack our gear a large horse trailer pulled into the rest area.

Ben nudged me. "You can tell those are working horses—they're already saddled."

Just in time to prove the point, a cowboy disembarked and walked over to us, carrying a steaming mug of coffee. The mug was one of the tapered, ceramic, no-spill cups popular among urban commuters, an incongruous contrast to his weather-beaten face, bowed legs, and western apparel. I couldn't help but think of him as the Yuppie Cowboy.

He grinned warmly as he approached. "Where ya riding from?" Almost everybody in Oregon asked where we were from—few asked where we were going. Perhaps they simply could think of no better place to be than Oregon.

Ben told him about the previous day's ride beneath the Abert Rim.

"That's rattlesnake country," was the immediate response.

"Yeah," Ben replied, "that's what everybody says. And one rattled at us as we rode along!"

The cowboy was suddenly attentive. "Did you kill it?"

That stopped us cold. It had never crossed our minds. After all, the snake hadn't bothered us—we were the intruders in its home.

Ben recovered faster than I did. "No. We didn't have anything to kill it with."

The cowboy looked at our bikes. "How 'bout one of those tire pumps."

"Never thought of it," Ben admitted. "But it might be a bit hard on the pump."

The cowboy nodded. "Yeah, and it wouldn't give you much reach either."

We talked a few minutes longer before he decided it was time to get back to work. He wished us well and headed back to his truck. As soon as he was out of earshot, I turned to Ben. "I don't know about you, but I wouldn't have killed that snake even if I could have."

"No," Ben replied. "But I understand how he feels. After all, around here snakes are a threat to livestock. If a snake bites a steer, you might as well butcher it right then—it's not going to grow any more."

———————•◦•———————

After that, the day's ride proved relatively uninteresting. We spent most of the morning crossing a single ranch—there are huge landholdings in this part of the country, and from what we heard along the way, this one must have covered close to a million acres—then we caught up with the Wimbledon riders in time to join them for lunch at the general store in the tiny town of Wagontire.

As the afternoon wore on, the temperature pushed into the nineties and the sagebrush hills became increasingly monotonous. At midafternoon we stopped at a gas station, where we rested in the shade until there was barely enough daylight to pedal on to Burns, our destination for the evening. With several thousand residents, it was one of the largest towns in the western half of the state.

———————•◦•———————

We rolled into town just before sunset and stopped at a private campground, attracted by a spreading lawn of lush grass. The office was closed for the night, but there were instructions telling latecomers where to camp and how to pay.

As we were registering, we were interrupted by a voice from a nearby campsite. We looked up and saw a middle-aged man and his wife sitting next to a small camper.

He waved us over. "Don't worry about that," he called. "I know the owner. You can camp on our site. He won't mind, and I'll tell him about it in the morning. Come on over and have a seat. Would you like a beer?" He turned to his wife. "Bernie, why don't you get these boys a beer."

I declined the beer but gratefully accepted first one Coke and then another.

Our host was a non-stop talker. "My name's Bob," he told us. "And this is my wife, Bernie—short for Bernice. Where are you boys from? We're from just a few miles up the road, but we travel all over. I'm a striper, and this is my. . . ."

"A what?"

"A striper," Bernie interrupted. "Bob paints stripes in parking lots. We travel all around, camping, spending a few days here and a few days there. Last winter we went down to Arizona, but we're never going to do that again, are we, Bob? It's just too far away from home, and I missed being home for Christmas. Why, we got so much snow last winter that it piled up really deep on the shed over our boat, and we weren't there to do any-thing about it. But I think what you boys are doing is grand. I want to hear all about it. . . ."

"Bernie is a water-skier, aren't you, Bernie? We'd go out on Lake Shasta all the time when we were younger. Tell them about the time. . . ."

For the rest of the evening Ben and I listened as the conversation bounced dizzyingly between them, each interrupting the other, constantly changing the topic, and occasionally asking questions but seldom allow-ing more than a few words in answer. As the evening progressed Bob and Bernie quit noticing each other's interruptions, and soon both were talk-ing at once, Bernie to me, Bob to Ben, but neither of them paying much attention to what we had to say. Ben stole a glance in my direction and grinned. He clearly enjoyed watching the two of them fail to interact.

After about an hour Bob said, "Let's go over to the bar next door. I'll buy you each a drink."

"Is there food over there?" I asked. "We haven't had dinner yet."

"I don't know. They should have something. I'll buy."

"And I want to play blackjack," Bernie added. "They have blackjack over there."

"You should see Bernie play blackjack," Bob added. "She's something."

———— •◦• ————

The blackjack table was closed for the evening, but there was food, though it was typical bar food with nothing better than frozen hamburg-ers microwaved into a semblance of edibility. Afterward we were still hun-gry, but neither of us could stand the thought of another hamburger.

"What else do you have to eat?" I asked the waitress, as she brought Bob and Bernie another round of drinks.

"Potato chips. That's about it."

It sounded better than hamburgers.

"You want potato chips?" Bob asked loudly.

"Sure, but I'll be happy to get them myself."

"No. You want potato chips, you got potato chips." He rose a bit un-steadily and walked over to the bar, bringing back three bags of chips and slapping them down in front of us. He sat down again. "Eat your potato chips."

I looked at Ben, but he was still grinning. Bernie was telling water-ski-ing stories.

As I listened to Bernie reminiscing about her glory years, at the other end of the table Bob was regaling Ben with something that sounded like politics. He was becoming bellicose as he continued to drink, and from time to time he would send a remark to our end of the table, generally taking the opportunity to level a snide comment at his wife. He'd been insulting her all evening, but with drink the insults came more frequently. She was quite capable of returning the insults in kind. I was reminded of a Garrison Keillor Lake Wobegone monologue about a couple who thrived on constant bickering, even on their fiftieth anniversary. Bob and Bernie were merely a younger version of that couple; somehow, their marriage had survived years of insults, and they seemed oblivious not only to each other's reactions but also to ours.

Suddenly Bob's voice overrode all others. "I'm not paying for all this, you know," he said, waving at the drinks and the empty potato-chip bags. "Do you know what I mean by that?"

There was a long silence as Bob's gaze shifted from Ben to me. Even Bernie was quiet.

"Do you know what I mean?" Bob repeated.

I spoke cautiously. "I'm not sure I do."

"It means," Bob said dramatically, "that *I'm* not paying. The people of Burns are. When I start work tomorrow!" He slapped the table. "Drink up!" And the babble of conversation resumed.

But that was the end of the evening. I excused myself to phone Jane; I was still talking to her when the others filed out, with Bob making smooching noises at me as he passed.

When I got back to the campground I found that Bob and Bernie had invited Ben in for a final beer, but they soon kicked us out so Bob could .get a good night's sleep.

As we unrolled our sleeping bags, Ben grinned at me. "That was an interesting evening, wasn't it? Not exactly what we'd expected, but interesting."

I agreed, but with less enthusiasm. Ben was taking a bus back to Eugene in the morning, and that hadn't been the way I'd wanted to spend our last evening together. But there'd been no way to get out of it gracefully.

———————•●•———————

In the morning, both Bob and Bernie were much subdued, speaking quietly, talking a lot less, and not interrupting each other or us. I began to wonder if they'd already had a few beers before Ben and I had come on the scene the day before. "Bob's not usually like this," Bernie had told me that evening. "When he's on a job he goes to bed at nine o'clock and is up before six. But he hasn't started work yet, so tonight we're staying up late." As I watched his businesslike approach to the morning I believed her.

And they'd certainly been gracious to celebrate with us, even if it wasn't my type of celebration.

They offered us coffee, but we didn't stay long. Bob had work to do, and Ben and I needed to find the bus stop and a schedule. As we rode downtown I told Ben I'd gotten some bad news from my wife. "You remember that I was meeting a friend in Idaho?" I asked. "Well, he won't be able to make it. He has a good reason, but it's still disappointing. When I first planned this trip, four people were going to accompany me on various stages. Two cancelled before I left Sacramento. Now it looks like you're going to be the only one who actually made it."

Ben was sympathetic but encouraging. "I'd go the rest of the way if I could. I know you'll have a good time anyway."

I shrugged. Riding alone in California, I'd felt no need for company, but now that Ben and I were about to separate, I couldn't help but feel depressed. "I hope you're right."

———————•◉•———————

Ben's bus wasn't scheduled to leave until midafternoon, so we took the morning to figure out how to box up his bicycle. He'd hoped he could load it on the bus unboxed, but the ticket agent said that was flatly prohibited. Since the nearest bicycle box was probably in the nearest bike store, 60 miles away, we jury-rigged a cardboard covering from appliance boxes scavenged from a local catalog store. The resulting contrivance was diamond-shaped and wouldn't lie flat, but it passed muster.

We spent the next few hours quietly talking and waiting for the bus, the arrival of which spurred a flurry of activity to get Ben and his bicycle aboard. Almost before I realized what had happened I was on my own again, sad, a bit lonely, but ready for the next stage of the journey.

For three days I had lived not merely day by day, but moment by moment. And my knee had not given me even a twinge. I hoped both the relaxed attitude and the pain-free pedaling would continue now that I was again on my own.

CHAPTER 4

Into Idaho

Going It Alone

DAY 10 • Tuesday, June 24 • CUMULATIVE MILES: 676
Burns to Starr Ridge Summit

DAY 11 • Wednesday, June 25 • CUMULATIVE MILES: 785
Starr Ridge Summit to Brogan

DAY 12 • Thursday, June 26 • CUMULATIVE MILES: 869
Brogan, Oregon, to Black Canyon Dam, Idaho

DAY 13 • Friday, June 27 • CUMULATIVE MILES: 930
Black Canyon Dam to Pine Flat Campground

DAY 14 • Saturday, June 28 • CUMULATIVE MILES: 999
Pine Flat Campground to Stanley

DAY 15 • Sunday, June 29 • CUMULATIVE MILES: 1,073
Stanley to Sun Valley

DAY 16 • Monday, June 30 • CUMULATIVE MILES: 1,151
Sun Valley to Craters of the Moon

DAY 17 • Tuesday, July 1 • CUMULATIVE MILES: 1,227
Craters of the Moon to Mud Lake

DAY 18 • Wednesday, July 2 • CUMULATIVE MILES: 1,325
Mud Lake to Victor

I spent another hour in town, mailing my broken stove back home and buying enough groceries to get to Idaho. Earlier I'd spotted the Wimbledon riders heading east. I considered trying to catch them, but they had a five-hour head start and were probably halfway to the state line. I doubted I'd see them again.

On the map the shortest route east, U.S. Highway 20, looked singularly uninteresting, sporting as scenic highlights two low passes with the unappealing names of Stinkingwater and Drinkwater.

A few miles out of town, however, Highway 395 branches north toward the town of John Day. Earlier Ben had encouraged me to go that way, tantalizing me with stories of pine forests and rugged granite peaks, but it was at least 70 miles out of the way and I hadn't taken the suggestion seriously. As I neared the junction a thunderstorm, which had been brewing for hours in the southern sky, rapidly drew near, buffeting me with a strong crosswind and quickening my pulse with the threat of lightning. If I continued east, I doubted I'd make a dozen miles before I'd need to seek shelter.

The road north ran straight downwind. I'd ruled it out earlier because a detour would have prevented me from meeting my friend Jack on schedule in Idaho, and it would have been the first major departure from my planned route—eating up time I would need to reach the Atlantic.

But now I wouldn't be meeting Jack, and—as I'd reminded myself several times before—the purpose of this journey was the trip itself, not the destination.

I made a liberating snap decision not to pigheadedly schedule my way across the continent. I would celebrate my newfound freedom by turning north and running before the storm.

An exhilarating 25-mile-an-hour tailwind pushed me up a long, winding canyon toward a wooded 5,000-foot pass. The storm gradually gained momentum, enveloping most of the southern sky by the time I reached the top. Riding the exciting shock wave of the approaching storm, the scent of pine urging me on, I didn't stop, even when an appealing campground offered itself. I sailed over the top without pausing, down the long descent on the other side, through the barely existent town of Silvies and into a canyon that formed a natural wind tunnel through the next mountain range. All the while the storm licked at my heels, gaining strength. I counted the seconds between lightning and thunder; by the time the wind expelled me from the far end of the gorge, the gap was only five seconds—the storm was a mile away. But then I was in the open, coasting before the wind at 25 miles an hour into Seneca, having covered 43 miles and a sizable hill in little more than two hours.

I stopped at a tavern and asked the proprietor about places to camp. She chuckled and said I could probably sleep in the city park, but it was wide open to the wind. If I preferred I could sleep on the downwind side of her tavern. "You're going to John Day?" she asked.

I nodded.

"You'll love that ride. From the top of the next pass, it's my favorite road in Oregon."

We continued to talk as the southern sky turned blue-black.

"Looks like it's going to rain soon," I ventured.

She looked outside. "Yes, but not for a while. The storm's caught over the mountains. It'll take it a while to get here."

I thought of that glorious wind, still whipping northward. "How long?"

"Oh, fifteen minutes at least. Maybe half an hour."

At 20 miles an hour I could be long gone by then. "Is there any shelter between here and the pass?"

She shook her head. "Not much. It's pretty open terrain. But there are a few ranch houses."

That was all I needed, just something for an emergency if the storm should catch me. "People seem pretty friendly around here."

She nodded again and smiled. "Yeah, these are good folk."

I thought about camping on the steps of a bar, even among good folk, then thought about the national-forest campground which, according to my map, sat atop the pass 10 miles away. I decided to go for it; if the storm caught me, I'd either hide in a ditch or beg shelter from a rancher.

I outran the rain, pedaling effortlessly across a broad valley and watching the misty-blue summits of the Strawberry Mountains to the northeast, an island of 9,000-foot peaks rising far above their lesser companions. Then it was an easy climb to the pass, sheltered by woods, the storm several miles behind me.

I set up camp a few minutes before sunset and settled into my tent to await the rain, munching trail mix and writing in my journal. In the distance I could hear occasional rumbles of thunder, and a few drops of rain spattered my tent as the wind roared through the pines. But the storm never reached me, and eventually I drifted off to sleep.

———— •••• ————

The next day was a mixture of extremes: downhill grades so steep and winding I had to stop to let my brakes cool; hot, grunting upgrades; and gentle descents across miles of empty rangeland. Exhilaration, hard work, pain, frustration, lost confidence, and ultimate tranquility—all in only twenty-four hours.

It began simply enough. I rose late, breaking camp at my now-customary leisurely pace, and was on the road sometime between 8:30 and 9:30— I wasn't sure, because early in the trip I'd taken off my watch to live on solar time. Unceremoniously I crested the pass and began the 2,000-foot, 15-mile drop to John Day.

At first the road fell steeply into a shallow valley—a heart-stopping descent notched into a precipitous canyon wall but hardly living up to its billing as one of the most spectacular roads in Oregon.

But then the road bent sharply and dove through a gap in the ridge-line, and the view opened up; far below to the right lay a valley, carpeted in lush meadows, a black ribbon of asphalt stretching through it and curving out of sight—my road—2 miles and one switchback ahead. A logging truck growled by as I leaned against a guardrail, but the driver waved cheerily. Three or four minutes later the truck reappeared below, continuing its geared-down run for the lowlands and quickly vanishing around the bend.

But it wasn't the valley that first caught my attention or held it. Canyon Mountain, westernmost of the Strawberries—a looming, blue-green wall that blocked the valley ahead and towered nearly 4,000 feet above me—dominated the scenery. Its details were lost in the partial backlight of the morning sun, but hints of crags, spires, and remnant snowfields in protected hollows still were visible. The Strawberries, now set aside as a wilderness area, were beckoning—someday I'll return to walk their 20-mile length and scale their lofty heights.

But for now I was a mundane lowland creature, and remounting my bicycle, I let gravity carry me down through scrub and meadow into a deep gorge that led to the aptly named town of Canyon City. Two miles later I was in John Day.

My first stop was a bike shop where I bought a new tire to replace one that was badly worn. I usually do my own repairs, but this time I left the work to the shop owner.

As he worked, we talked. "I bet you do a land office business in tires," I said. For the 1976 U.S. Bicentennial, an organization named Bikecentennial had mapped out a 4,300-mile cross-country route from Oregon to Virginia. In the ensuing decade Bikecentennial grew to be a national touring club with nearly twenty thousand members and a large network of mapped routes. Because John Day was on the original trail, about 600 miles from the start, many cyclists would be just about ready for new tires as they came into town. Bikecentennial's detailed maps divided the route into 25-mile segments and noted bike shops along the way. I was carrying maps for much of the TransAmerica Trail, and one of the local maps had directed me to this shop.

"We do sell a few," he said.

"Get many cyclists through here?"

"We had seventy-five yesterday."

My jaw dropped. "Seventy-five?"

"Yes. Ever hear of the Wandering Wheels?"

"No."

He gave me a brochure. "They're a Christian group that takes seven weeks to ride coast to coast. They stop at churches, sing hymns, and give testimonies. They've been doing it for years. Last night they stayed in the campground in Ironside. I doubt you can catch them—that's 70 miles away. But maybe they don't ride every day."

Suddenly my attention was interrupted by a tug on my hand. I looked down to see his two-year-old daughter offering me a package containing a pair of hand grips for a child's bike.

"Thank you," I told her. She beamed.

"She's going to be a real salesman, that one," her father said.

———————•●•———————

Soon I was back on the road, following the Bikecentennial Trail to Prairie City.

Two miles later I crashed. I had no one to blame but myself. Even though the traffic was courteous, I kept shying away from it, as though back in California, attempting to ride the six-inch strip of pavement outside the fog line. I might have gotten away with it, but I was unusually close to the edge when I rounded a bend and got my first glimpse of the north side of the Strawberry Mountains. Peering at them, I veered slightly to the right.

Suddenly I was teetering on the lip of a one-inch drop-off. For two infinite seconds I balanced there; then my front wheel dropped into the gravel, twisted hard to the right, and stopped abruptly. I did a full somersault over the handlebars and wound up on my side, skidding headfirst on the gravel.

Fortunately I wasn't going very fast and, remembering my childhood gymnastics, I hit the ground in a tuck, landing initially on a shoulder instead of my head or an outflung arm. As I skidded along on my elbow, I tightened my tuck, which sent me into another head roll from which I came up on my feet, running. The scene could not have been more dramatically choreographed—over the handlebars, two somersaults, then up on my feet. Not bad for someone who'd long ago decided tumbling wasn't his forte.

But I wasn't thinking about choreography at the time. I was roundly cursing myself, even before I looked at my elbow. A strip of skin three inches long by half an inch wide was missing; subcutaneous fat gleamed pearly white in the sun. Then blood welled up everywhere—not fast, probably just enough to assure a good cleansing.

I'd hardly finished cursing myself when help arrived. A pickup full of eighteen- to twenty-year-olds slowed, stopped, then backed up, despite my attempts to wave it on.

The driver and passengers hopped out.

"You okay?"

"Yeah."

"Someone run you off the road?"

"No. I did it to myself, gawking at the mountains."

"You been here long?"

"About thirty seconds." I explained the accident.

One of the others spoke up. "Gee, if we'd come along sooner we'd have seen it! You must have been a sight!" His grin robbed his words of any offense.

The first guy spoke again. "How's your bike?"

I reached to pick it up, but three sets of hands did it for me. "At least there's a bike shop back in town if I need anything."

"Heck with that," the first guy spoke again. "I'm a good bike mechanic. I'll fix it for free."

By this time another car had stopped.

Four or five strong we gathered around the bicycle. The handlebars were twisted, but that was to be expected; they're supposed to twist in a crash so you don't impale yourself. And the brakes were out of alignment, but that could be easily fixed. The wheels were still round, the deraileur intact. The only other damage was a few minor perforations in one pannier pocket. I'd have to be careful what I put in it for the rest of the trip—nothing small, and nothing that couldn't get wet. All in all I'd been lucky.

My benefactors were slow to leave—checking two or three times before pulling away. As the bar owner had said the night before, there were good folk around here. I wondered if the difference between these country and city folk was the need to band together in this harsh, underpopulated land where a single county can sprawl over 1,700 square miles but boast a population of only 1,400. I think part of it is also that in the country, people are free of fears that paralyze even the best-intentioned urbanites. But I wondered if the slower pace of backroads life also gives people time to be more aware, encouraging their natural hospitality.

Emulating everyone who's been thrown by his steed, I remounted and pedaled on—shaky, uninterested in riding quickly, and gun-shy of the edge of the road. I had to fight off sudden waves of panic each time balance caused me to steer to the right.

———————— •◦• ————————

The day was only half over. Blown along by a northwest wind I pedaled into Prairie City, then struggled up a steep 10-mile hill, sweating profusely in the afternoon sun. Once I reached the summit the rest of the day was easy. Three more passes lay ahead, but none was steep and the wind was behind me.

I was skirting the edge of yet another of Oregon's many mountain provinces, the southern flanks of the Blue Mountains—a little-known land of pines, lakes, and granite crags rising higher than the Strawberries and running all the way to Washington. To the north, where I-84 crosses the range near Pendleton, the Blues form a well-defined ridge, one of the most difficult barriers on the Oregon Trail, but their southern end, although higher, is gentle woodland, a mile above sea level with scattered meadows allowing intermittent glimpses of nearby peaks.

The long descent toward the Snake River offered expanded views of distant mountains rising above pastures and hayfields in nearby valleys. As I dropped still lower, the hayfields diminished and the foreground became sweeping expanses of sagebrush desert. Perhaps barren and monotonous for some, the landscape was a soothing balm for my jangled nerves. Through it all the ever-present tailwind urged me eastward.

Before I left the high country I had yet another taste of Oregon friendliness. I was standing in a meadow, taking a picture, when a car pulled slowly by, its middle-aged driver studying me carefully. A moment later he returned, then swung around again and stopped on the shoulder nearby.

There are few thing that make cyclists more nervous than a driver who comes back for a second pass. He may want to curse you, perhaps physically assault you for some imagined offense. But this man meant no harm.

"Are you okay?" he asked.

I held up my camera. "Just taking a picture." I grinned in disbelief at how friendly everyone was.

"Wanted to be sure," he said, putting his car in gear. "Have a good ride!" Then he was gone.

———————•◦•———————

I'd tentatively planned to camp in Ironside where the Wandering Wheels had stayed the night before, but I discovered that Ironside had no campground. They'd slept in the community center, which was now closed. I was sure that by knocking on doors I could get permission to camp on a lawn or, more likely, the offer of dinner and a bed, but I also knew there was a commercial campground 23 miles down the road in Brogan.

My knee was still in good shape and, free to set my own schedule, I could ride long days if so inclined. This would be my longest so far—nearly 110 miles—but it was a relaxed 110, and that made all the difference.

I felt no pressure to race to Brogan before sunset; if necessary I could always find a ranch house.

So I pedaled on up a long, gentle hill, watching shadows lengthen and measuring my progress against a series of low buttes. Halfway up I stopped to photograph the light and shadow patterns on a nearby butte, not surprised when the only motorist on the road stopped to talk.

This one didn't ask if I needed help. He was a tourist from the Willamette Valley returning from a vacation, and he too was interested in photographing the scene that had caught my attention. There was so little traffic that he left his trailer parked in the middle of the road, and for five minutes we stood blocking the road but not worrying about it, talking about cameras and bike trips and proving that while cyclists and RV owners are often natural enemies, that need not be the case, at least not in the relaxed ranch country of eastern Oregon.

I reached Brogan an hour later, well after sunset, but with plenty of light to allow me to stay on the road during the final, steep descent into town. I felt strong and still had a tailwind, and for a few moments I considered riding farther, but that would have been counterproductive. It had been a good afternoon; why risk ruining it?

I probably could have stayed in the city park — many small towns allow cyclists to do so — but I chose the campground instead.

"Do you have room for a biker?" I asked when a woman answered my knock. It wasn't a particularly intelligent question — the campground was empty.

"Certainly."

"How much?"

"Well, we usually charge RVs eight dollars a night, but that seems a bit high for a biker. I expect you'll be on the road early in the morning. How 'bout a biker special of four dollars?"

That sounded fair to me, but she wasn't finished. "No, that's still high. How 'bout two dollars? And that includes the shower." She waved to an expanse of soft-looking grass. "Camp anywhere."

I could definitely get spoiled here in Oregon, I thought, as I settled into camp.

———————•◦•———————

I rose early and pedaled 24 miles into Vale for a pancake breakfast. After that, 16 more miles of fighting a strengthening crosswind brought me to Ontario, on the Oregon side of the Snake River, where I planned to do some shopping before crossing the river and tackling the mountains of central Idaho.

It was a hot day, humid by Western standards. As I approached town the hazy, stifling heat made the terrain seem inhospitable, the bleakness of the neighboring hillsides accentuated by comparison with the narrow strip of irrigated farmland near the road. A bank thermometer registered ninety-four degrees. Why would anyone would want to live here, I wondered.

I've always loved deserts, but this area was oppressive, with nothing to offer but monotonous hillsides and equally monotonous valleys. I was glad I hadn't taken the short route from Burns—it would have put me on this kind of terrain all the way.

The Snake River, hailed as the sixth largest river in the United States, was a disappointment. A surprisingly narrow stream, only about 100 yards wide and lying in a shallow valley, it hardly seemed the descendant of the mighty torrent I'd known from visits to the mountains of its headwaters in Wyoming.

What had I expected? The Mississippi? I reminded myself that in the hundreds of miles since it had left the mountains, the Snake had been dammed, diverted, apportioned, and carefully rationed to thousands of square miles of farmland. It was a wonder there was any water left at all— and no wonder the placid stream flowing through Ontario bore no resemblance to its upstream parent.

Ontario itself, however, was pleasant. With nearly ten thousand residents it was the first community I'd seen since Red Bluff whose population exceeded its elevation. Compared with the other places I'd been recently it was a metropolis, with four-lane streets, stoplights, and—as I discovered before I left—rush-hour traffic.

By the time I'd completed my errands—a bike shop, a drugstore, a camera store, and a K-Mart—it was five o'clock, and I'd been in town more than three hours. I was surprised to discover that I wasn't agonizing over wasted time; nearly two weeks into the journey I was slipping into a state of relaxation more complete than any I'd known before. I wondered if it was a function of the length of the trip. On shorter tours delays had left me champing at the bit, urging myself into a frenzied hurry-hurry-hurry until I was back on the road, trying to make up the lost time. Knowing that my ride had barely begun, I regarded such delays as necessary concomitants to the rest of the trip. Perhaps, as on the previous evening's unhurried twilight ride, I was beginning to live by the rhythms of sun and wind, casting loose the shackles of clocks, mileage, and schedules.

I also took time to talk to people, beginning with a woman I'd met on my way into town. A pharmacist from Sun Valley, Idaho, she too had done a great deal of cycle touring. She spotted me in the parking lot of a convenience store and walked over to introduce herself, asking about my planned route and offering suggestions.

"If you come through Sun Valley and need a shower," she added, "look me up. I'll be back in town Tuesday." She handed me her business card. "I'd offer you a place to stay, but I don't have room. I know how hard it can be to find a shower when you're on the road."

I thanked her but told her not to expect me. This was Thursday, and I planned to be well beyond Sun Valley by Tuesday.

———•••———

Crossing into Idaho, I had hoped to make it well into the mountains before dark, but it was getting late. I shifted my target to Emmett, 30 miles away.

The terrain became more hospitable, perhaps because there was more water for irrigation, possibly because the valleys were wider and more densely populated. Whatever the reason, much more acreage was under cultivation, and the landscape was one of broad green valleys, a pleasant contrast to the bordering hills.

Emmett was populous, 4,500 people, though not particularly attractive. It was large enough to support not one but two supermarkets, and it likely would be the last town with more than one hundred inhabitants before Ketchum, 200 miles and three mountain passes away. Since I'd spent too much money eating in restaurants, I took the opportunity to stock up on food, loading myself down with cauliflower, a pound of carrots, a large box of granola, a box of Pop Tarts, an apple, a banana, a grapefruit, and a package of chipped meat. I barely managed to fit my booty into my bike bags. Suddenly I realized I'd be lugging it up a 6,500-foot hill.

I'd been thinking about that hill for several days. Even as I luxuriated in the long descent from the Blue Mountains the day before, I resented the Snake River for making me lose more than half my hard-won elevation and forcing me to descend to 2,100 feet before tackling an 8,700-foot pass in the Sawtooth Mountains. It was a climb I could avoid by staying in the Snake River Plain, but doing so would bypass the part of Idaho I most wanted to see. As in California, I faced a major climb, greater than my ascent over the Cascades. This one would be spread out over more than 150 miles, but the prospect was still intimidating.

Immediately after buying all that food in Emmett, I impulsively stopped at a drive-in for dinner. So much for my plans to conserve money, though $1.95 for a half-pound hamburger was a bargain. Then I stopped at Emmett's second supermarket to pick up bagels—one of the few breads that travel well when stuffed into a pannier—but I wasn't hopeful. Bagels had been progressively harder to find since I'd left California.

Pulling into the supermarket parking lot I spied a familiar light-brown van. The Wimbledon riders were ahead of me! Excited conversation broke out, with a half dozen teenagers peppering me with rapid-fire questions. "Where's your buddy?" "Where've you been?" "You went *there* and caught up with us!" "Where are you camping?" "So are we! It's about 4 miles out of town."

Their story emerged quickly. They'd been caught at a swimming hole when the storm had come two days earlier. Mounting their bikes they fled east, barely getting out of its path. They'd faced headwinds the whole way and taken as long to cover 160 miles as I'd taken to cover 250—and I'd carried fifty pounds of equipment over six passes. The tailwind had made the difference, but catching them gave me a touch of macho pride. A corner of my mind filed away the fact that at 97 miles a day—my average pace for the previous two days—I could cover another 3,600 miles before my seven weeks expired. For all my efforts to live day by day, the drive to blaze a trail across the continent was as strong as ever.

———————— ·•· ————————

The campground was a roadside park. I'd barely rolled to a stop when I was again overwhelmed with hospitality.

"Would you like some soup?" Tim, one of the counselors, asked. "We've got a lot extra."

I'd already eaten, but like most cyclists I could always find room for more, especially for soup like this—far and away the best meal since the night my stove broke. After the soup came ice cream. "It used to be Neapolitan," the leader said, "but it kind of melted." It was still food fit for a king.

Camping with this group was like coming home, although I'd seen them only twice before. But they were familiar—perhaps my only acquaintances within 300 miles—and they took me in like a long-lost friend, not only giving me food, but also first-aid supplies for my elbow.

Without the Wimbledon group I might not have had a place to camp, for while my map showed a campground, the roadside park bore a prominent "NO CAMPING" sign. As I studied the map trying to figure out what had gone wrong, I realized that the campground symbol I'd been targeting was on the other side of the Payette, a river I'd been following for several miles. The Wimbledon riders appeared to have made the same mistake, but it was too late in the day to do anything about it.

"Don't worry," Tim told me, "if the police ask, you're one of us. They'll probably let us stay, and we'll just tell them you're part of our group."

As it was the police were no worry. The park superintendent stopped by shortly after dusk and gave us permission to camp. "The no-camping rule doesn't apply to groups like you," he said. "Only to transients and migrant workers who might set up long-term camps and mess the place up. Folks like you are fine."

I probably would have received the same treatment if I'd been alone, but it was nice to be included in the group. As I set up camp and drifted off to sleep, I wished I could ride with them the next day, but they were taking a rest day. Our routes would cross again in Yellowstone, though, and there was a good chance I'd see them there.

The next morning I awoke early, wondering who'd turned on the lawn sprinklers. It had happened before—a natural hazard of camping in irrigation country—but this time the rattle on my tent roof was rain. There wasn't much of it, but it was the first rain I'd encountered since that brief shower in the Cascades.

I woke again a couple of hours later, amazed by how quiet the campsite was, having forgotten about teenagers' sleeping habits. Even at 8 A.M.— late at this time of year since dawn comes early—everyone except one of the counselors was still asleep. Unable to sleep I got up and chatted with Tim as I fixed a tire that had gone flat during the night. While I was at it, I borrowed the group's impressive collection of bike-repair equipment to remove 870 miles of accumulated wobbles from my wheels.

Tim was a quiet person whom I'd liked from the moment I'd met him. Like me he'd lived several years in Minnesota, working as a policeman in a small town on the Mississippi. I particularly respected his talents as a counselor, obtaining the boys' obedience without raising his voice and instilling a sense of group purpose that did much to counteract a competitive tendency—the group's main weakness.

When I finished my repairs Tim offered a pancake breakfast. Then, reluctantly, I said good-bye. Other than the day I'd waited for Ben's bus, it was my latest start so far—already noon. The humid heat that had plagued me the day before again clamped down.

My route followed the Payette River, which drains the western side of the Sawtooth Range and provides irrigation for the valley I'd followed the day before. It also furnishes an easy route deep into the jumbled mountains of central Idaho.

Nevertheless I found it slow going, impeded by the heat, a light headwind, and countless small hills as the road bounced over the uneven terrain of the valley floor. Gradually I penetrated the mountains, alternately passing through canyons and broad meadows as the surrounding hills grew from 500 to 1,000 and eventually 2,000 feet. But other than the cold green waters of the river itself, the only indicator that these parched foothills would eventually become mountains was a fringe of pines along the top of the most distant ridgeline. Other than that the hillsides were treeless, their weathered bones laid bare under a thin cloak of green, their shoulders eroded into a series of graceful curves like pleats in an old-fashioned skirt. From a distance the hillsides were a rainbow of pastels—tan, purple, and yellow-green with etchings of deeper green showing the paths of deeper gullies where a few shrubs manage to survive. On the steepest slopes the gentle contours were interrupted by a fine network of terraces, trails left by generations of cattle.

After 15 miles I stopped for a snack in Horseshoe Bend, then turned north on a major state highway. This, too, was canyon and meadow country, with the Payette running strongly through the heart of it, flanked by scattered beaches of fine sand and occasional groves of cool Ponderosa pine.

But it was Friday and the traffic was terrible, with logging trucks, RVs, and weekend boaters from Boise strung along the highway. In California I'd never have dared to ride such a road, but everybody was polite, slowing down when necessary, passing me with plenty of room to spare, and waiting to pass until they could see far enough around the next bend. Despite my fears I never met a single rude or impatient driver.

I commented about this to a general-store owner in the village of Banks.

"We get a lot of bikers around here," he replied. "This weekend and next week we're hosting the Ore-Ida Challenge, the largest women's stage race in North America."

A stage race is a multi-day competition, like the Tour de France, with placement determined by adding up the riders' times on the individual segments. "You going to see it?" I asked.

"I'll be driving the pace car."

I grinned. Yesterday I'd met a woman from Sun Valley who'd offered her shower; today I'd met this man. Cyclists seemed to be everywhere.

———————•◦•———————

I abandoned the highway for a quiet side road to Garden Valley, a peaceful town sitting at the junction of the south and middle forks of the Payette. For the first few miles the road hugged the bank of the river, and my senses were filled with the roar of rapids and the invigorating smell of cold water. The Payette would be a superb stream for kayakers; even in its calm places it must have had a 6-mile-an-hour current, and the intervening rapids were spectacular swirls of whitewater and boulders. For 60 miles there were no dams, making the upper Payette one of the longest free-flowing streams remaining in the West.

In Garden Valley I stopped at the general store to refill my water bottles and buy a quart of chocolate milk. I fell into conversation with a man from Boise who'd just brought in a consignment of goods.

"Where're you riding from?" he asked.

"Sacramento."

"Oh! I spent a couple of years there, at Mather Field," he said, referring to a large air base on the outskirts of town.

"I know a lot of people at Mather. That's how I got this T-shirt. I ran a twenty-four-hour relay sponsored by the Air Force." I was part of a ten-man team that ran 1-mile intervals in rotation for a full day. Triumphantly, I'd done my first dozen legs faster than six minutes each.

"I did something like that a couple of years ago," my new acquaintance said. "We ran 105 miles for the American Lung Association."

"A relay?"

"No. We did 35 miles a day over the Fourth of July weekend. One day I covered 11 miles in fifty-five minutes. It wiped me out for the rest of the day, but it was fun. I used to train by running from Boise to Horseshoe Bend."

Later I looked at a map and discovered that depending on where he'd started, Boise to Horseshoe Bend was 20 to 30 miles. Moral: Don't brag to strangers.

———————— •❖• ————————

From Garden Valley my route continued to follow the Payette, but within a few miles the map showed the road turning to gravel. I wondered how bad it would be; rumors had varied dramatically. "I've sent bikers over it both ways with no problems," the bike-shop owner had said back in Ontario. "You'll have to take it easy, but no problem. There's perhaps 12 miles of gravel."

"Six to 8 miles," Tim had said last night. "We asked the State Police, and that's what they said."

But as I got closer the stories became worse—and more consistent. There were 14 to 17 miles of loose rocks and rough surfaces, the whole beaten into a washboard by a constant parade of logging trucks. It hadn't been graded for a month. "But it's better than the main route from Boise," said the store owner in Banks. "The Ore-Ida ride sags the racers over that stretch," he added, meaning they would be carried across in vans. "It's just too narrow and winding to be safe. You picked the right route. And . . ." he looked at his watch, "by the time you get there, most of the loggers will have quit for the night."

And I'd still have at least three hours of daylight, probably more. I expected it would be plenty.

I was wrong. The road was terrible. The underlying rock had degenerated into coarse white sand, and the glare was so bright that even with the sun behind me I could barely make out details. It was hard to see the bigger drifts of sand until I'd hit them. Worse, the loose sand was often two inches deep, making it virtually impossible to walk my bicycle, let alone pedal it.

It was in one of the many sandy patches that I fell again, toppling in slow motion as I tried to bull my way through in low gear, landing—despite my best efforts not to—directly on my injured elbow, reopening the scab and filling it with gritty sand.

I hopped up cursing, roundly consigning the road to Hades. The old saying holds that the road to Hell is paved with good intentions, but when it gets there, I thought, I bet it looks like *this*!

I dusted the dirt out of my wound and doused it with half a bottle of peroxide. For the first time on this or any other bike trip I probably would have swallowed my pride and accepted a ride if anyone had offered—I might even have flagged someone down and insisted. But I was alone. And even though I'd been fighting the gravel for the better part of an hour, I'd only covered 2 or 3 miles.

A mile later a driver coming from the opposite direction stopped and leaned out the window.

"How much more of this is there?" I asked, though I was pretty sure I knew the answer.

"About 8 miles. I hate to tell you, but the worst is yet to come."

I groaned. It wasn't worth it. I'd taken this shortcut to avoid 80 miles, a 6,100-foot pass, and the city traffic of Boise, but it still wasn't worth it. Going back now would cost two days, so I struggled on.

I discovered that worse by car was better by bike. The road got bumpier, with buried rocks giving it a cobblestone texture, but the surface was no longer loose, and I could ride 4, even 5 miles an hour.

Gradually I noticed that I was passing through some spectacular mountain scenery. The valley had narrowed substantially, and up ahead the road plunged into a deep, V-shaped gorge, a stark, rocky canyon common in the West but seldom accessible except by gravel. Perhaps such roads are left unpaved simply to save maintenance costs in the wake of inevitable landslides.

The road began to climb, cutting its way steeply up the canyon wall until the river was nothing but a green, foam-flecked ribbon hundreds of feet below. Then I was over the crest and dropping back toward the river, bumping over the rocks at the phenomenal speed of 10 miles an hour, keeping well clear of the edge lest another spill send me over the low mound of road-grader scrapings that was the only excuse for a guardrail and into the chasm beyond.

Shortly before the end I spied a national-forest campground. With perhaps an hour of daylight left I could see no reason to ride farther.

A car pulled out of the campground and stopped, and an elderly lady got out and introduced herself as the campground hostess—a volunteer who helped the Forest Service keep the campground clean and friendly. She and her husband were from Washington state and were staying here until October, and one of their children was visiting.

"I help them clean the bathrooms," their five-year-old granddaughter told me that evening.

"Shh!" her mother said.

"It's smelly!"

"*Shh!*"

The campground hostess had other information to convey. "There's a hot spring about a mile downriver from the campground. If you want to bathe in it, we'll watch your bike. Just leave it in the site next to ours. And remember to take a flashlight for the trip back."

I almost didn't go, but Ben had raved about the pleasures of hot springs. We'd almost stopped at one near Lakeview—probably would have stopped if it hadn't been so commercialized. At the time I'd been secretly glad; I'd have stopped out of respect for Ben, but to me it sounded boring.

This attitude soon changed. Soaking in a hot spring is the essence of relaxation, the ultimate proof that an outdoor vacation doesn't require constant motion. It is no exaggeration to say it made the frustrations of the sand-trapped gravel road worthwhile.

The spring wasn't a deep bubbling pool of the type found in Yellowstone—too hot for bathing and too fragile—but a trickle of hot water running down the riverbank. Wherever the warm stream formed a natural pool, previous bathers had been at work, enlarging the basin to bathtub size or larger, piling rocks on the downstream edge and lining the bottom with plastic, all in an effort to retain more water. The result was something like a natural hot tub.

The pool I chose was perched on a bluff 20 feet above the Payette. As I sat there, partially floating in 2 feet of water slightly warmer than body temperature, I could hear the gurgle of water coming into the pool, the louder splash of the exit stream, and the muted but powerful roar of the river below as it prepared to enter a major rapids.

All the kinks went out of my muscles and my body turned to soft, comfortable jelly. As the sun set the air got cooler, but it merely provided a pleasant contrast to the warmth of the spring water. I'm not sure how late I might have stayed, but shortly after sunset I decided to try out one of the other pools. It was fed by a waterfall, and you could stand beneath the inflow stream, letting it cascade over you.

Because the riverbank was dangerously steep, the only way to get to the other pool was by wading through a knee-deep channel of the frigid river. It was a bracing prelude to the hot water, and the waterfall provided a glorious way to warm up again, but this spring was a bit too hot. Within a minute I was sweating, and after five minutes I gave up and returned to the campground, there to spread my sleeping bag beneath the stars and record the day's events in my journal.

And then I relearned one of the great mysteries of camping: how easy it is to lose things, despite the paucity of things to lose and places to lose them. As I climbed into my sleeping bag I knew my pen was beside me on the groundsheet—I'd put it there not two minutes before. Exasperated, groping, I finally found it not six inches from where I'd first looked. Small items had been vanishing every day, either in camp or in the various pockets of my bicycle bags. I'd expected that two weeks on the road would cure the problem, but no, it seemed I always found something new to lose.

——————— •❋• ———————

In the morning I pedaled through a mile of gravel, then, reveling in the freedom, I reached pavement and let a strengthening tailwind blow me the final few miles to Lowman. I'd planned a big breakfast in town, but the only restaurant catered mostly to tourists, and its prices were correspondingly high. So I bought a large cinnamon roll and ate it on the veranda, talking with curious tourists and basking in the sun.

I was joined by a burly man with flowing white hair and a full beard. Although he must have been well into his fifties, he had a younger man's strength and agility, and walked with an easy confidence that made him

look every inch the mountain man of the previous century. I recognized
him immediately from a newspaper article posted inside the restaurant;
for years he'd been living off the land in the nearby forests, his main pos-
sessions a pickup and a black-powder rifle, earning what little money he
needed as a guide in the nearby wilderness.

"Some real pretty country around here," I said as he stood beside me.

"Yup," he replied. "But I could take you places where you'd never want
to come back. Lakes so pure and clean . . . air so clear . . . fish. . . . You'd
never want to leave."

I looked around at the hills of pine and thought of the rushing Payette.
"Yeah—I'm even going to have trouble leaving here."

"Here?" he almost snorted. "I could take you places that make this look
like. . . ." He trailed off for want of an analogy.

———————•◦•———————

A few miles outside Lowman I met a cyclist coming from the opposite
direction, the only biker I'd seen since California other than Ben and the
Wimbledon riders. He was carrying an impressive load and was headed
west toward Spokane.

Slowing to a stop, he presented a colorful sight. He was older than the
average touring cyclist—probably forty to forty-five—and his hair and
week's growth of beard were strongly streaked with gray. He wore a
floppy, wide-brimmed felt hat, and his bike was equipped with Karimoor
bags, a brand almost unknown in the U.S. When he spoke he displayed
two gaps in his lower front teeth, with a single tooth remaining in the
middle. Somehow, even before he spoke, I knew he was Australian.

I have always found Australians to be fascinating if somewhat extro-
verted. If they weren't such *friendly* extroverts, they might well be on their
way to becoming the next ugly Americans. Once, while vacationing in
Scotland, I'd struck up a conversation with a chance acquaintance who
informed me his name was Kev.

"Where are you from?" I'd asked, though fairly certain of the answer.

"Australia," he'd said with obvious pride.

"I thought so, but I didn't want to guess wrong."

Kev grinned broadly. "I don't see how anyone could be offended by being called an Aussie."

"Well, you might have been from New Zealand. . . ."

"Except perhaps a Kiwi. That might be something like calling a Canadian an American. No offense from one side, but the other might be a bit
tired of always being in the shadow."

Kev also had strong opinions about tourists. "I hate 'em," he'd told me emphatically, "always getting in the way." When I'd asked him about his present status, he'd grinned and replied, "I'm not a tourist—I'm an Australian! Anyone calls me a bloody tourist and I'll knock his lights out!" With a big grin he'd faked a few punches, "Biff! Boff! Bop!"

The Australian I met in Lowman had a lower-key personality than Kev, and like cyclists the world over we quickly got to talking about routes and places we planned to visit.

He'd been traveling $2\frac{1}{2}$ months, starting in Los Angeles, touring the Southwest, then zigzagging through southern Utah and the central Rockies. From Spokane he would ride to the East Coast, eventually completing his third American coast-to-coast trip. He'd bicycled in all parts of the world, spending four to five months a year solo-touring in one country or another.

I asked what it was like to bicycle in Australia.

"Our drivers aren't as courteous as yours," he said. "Yours are the best in the world. Ours are worse road hogs than the French and the Italians. I've been there—that's saying a lot."

"That's too bad. I'd hoped to bicycle in Australia some day."

He grinned, displaying the gaps in his teeth. "Well, don't let that stop you."

Not five minutes after he moved on I met a second solo cyclist. He was a college student who'd ridden at least as far as Yellowstone before turning back toward his home in Portland, Oregon. He, too, was an extrovert—perhaps you have to be to travel alone—but he lacked the Australian's wit and charm. Instead, he was loud and forceful, dominating our conversation and making it hard to do more than ask brief questions. He gave the impression he'd been alone so long he was bursting with things to say, aggressively launching into this, the first opportunity. As I listened I realized I had the same tendency, and resolved to beware of it. Much later I concluded that his personality represented everything I'd left the city to avoid, while the Australian's quiet manner reflected what I sought. If my quest was successful, the changes would stay with me.

———————•◦•———————

I met yet another cyclist, a middle-aged woman who whizzed by me, her husband following close behind in a pickup camper.

"How far to the top?" I shouted as she sped by. A few miles before the road had finally left the Payette and was following a small tributary toward a 6,900-foot summit. For nearly an hour I'd been climbing steeply up a long canyon, cheering each time I crossed a gully and the flow of water in the creek beside me diminished. When the creek disappeared completely I knew the summit would be close at hand.

But it would be easier if I knew how long I'd have to wait.

"Only 2 miles," she called as she disappeared around a bend.

But it turned out to be $5\frac{1}{2}$. One of the fundamental rules of bicycle touring—one I seldom remember—is never to trust anyone else's estimate of distance, especially if they're going downhill.

Eventually I crossed over the pass. On the other side was some of the best cycling I've ever encountered, in one of the most beautiful settings I've ever seen. Best of all I was in an area virtually unknown outside Idaho. I was in the high country of the Sawtooth National Recreation Area.

When God created the Sawtooth he must have had some leftovers lying around; he threw in a little bit of Yellowstone and a little bit of the Tetons, with dashes of Banff and Colorado, stirring carefully to produce a mixture that is all of these yet still uniquely Idaho. And when he was done he blanketed the foreground with meadows—big meadows stretching mile after mile, lush with that vivid spring green that at these elevations lasts all summer. Flowers—sometimes merely occasional flecks of color, but often spreading seas of white and yellow and purple spiked with brilliant flashes of red—accented the landscape. The meadows are what make the Sawtooth special, each threaded by its own gurgling stream, each offering glimpses into distant, secret places, drawing the eye toward faraway islands of gray rock and white snow, thrust against the startling backdrop of an afternoon thunderstorm.

One could walk and walk. I was grateful for this protected land; in much of Idaho wilderness is a bad word. But not here. The Forest Service has supervised this area as wilderness for years, operating it much like a national park. Appearances suggest they've done a good job, though there are a few quirks. Cattle and horse ranching are permitted in the valleys near the roads, but the usual barbed wire has been replaced by old-fashioned rail fences, zigzagging along the roadside and heightening the picturesque atmosphere.

Places such as this have always made me cry. I have never known why, but the catalyst seems to be fragile beauty that has been protected despite potential threats. I rode through the meadows, flanked by crooked rail fences, tears flowing, glad to be there and equally glad to be alone with no need to explain.

Mountains and alpine lakes also add to the splendor of the Sawtooth. Early the next morning I sat on a pebbly beach beside such a lake, gazing over sun-bleached driftwood logs across several miles of open water toward the ramparts of two peaks whose names I do not know but whose memory will remain with me all my days. A gull glided over the glassy waters, pausing occasionally to gaze across the lake toward the mountains, seeming to appreciate the morning's tranquil beauty as well.

Viewed from the lakeshore these mountains are the essence of what mountains ought to be, their fractured crags rising like flying buttresses on Medieval cathedrals, culminating in spires 3,500 feet above. The lower ridges were covered with a mantle of green, a fuzzy shag carpet that gently blanketed their slopes until they became too steep, and the trees gave way to talus, granite, and remnant patches of pearly snow, looking more pure than the puffs of clouds that decorated the baby blue above the summits.

Mountains are best viewed from these lower levels, where their rocky splendor contrasts with the gentler lowlands. Mountains need room to breathe, room to survey vast regions with the remote isolation of mythical gods. For this reason I've never had the same love for the High Sierra, where jumbles of white granite are piled claustrophobically and harsh, narrow valleys hem you in until you finally scale the highest peak, with no place between the valley floor and the summit to step back and absorb the vista. In mountains like the Sawtooth I find room to appreciate the scale of the world and to wonder that the creator of all this majesty cares for *me*, infinitesimal speck that I am, that he is not merely like the peaks, remote in holy grandeur, but also personal and intimate like the alpine lake lapping quietly at my feet.

Give me a well-glaciated mountain range and I will find these things in it. And then the irony will set in. I will want to shoulder a pack and hike along the ridge beside the lake, up to the ragged edge where trees meet talus, and beyond to the high lakes and pocket meadows of the hanging valleys. For now that I have the big picture I will not feel claustrophobic. I am ready to explore the intimate nooks and crannies, to scale the summits if possible, or stand at their base and gaze in awe on their highest ramparts.

But such a climb would have to wait for another trip; soon even the mystical mood evaporated as motorboats appeared, banishing the morning tranquility. It was time to leave, anyway. The puffs of cloud above the mountains were increasing, reminding me that I had 8,700-foot Galena Summit to cross before the inevitable afternoon thundershower either turned me back or obscured the views along the way.

I spent much of the rest of the day climbing toward the pass near the headwaters of the aptly named Salmon River, watching as the stream diminished from a rushing river to a babbling brook. This valley was the historic spawning grounds for enormous runs of salmon, and I tried to imagine those fish, drawn by instinct to swim 800 miles upstream, climbing 6,500 feet as they ran the gauntlet of commercial fishermen, Indians, and sportsmen simply to lay their eggs in the right places and then—after all that—to die. It is an awesome process, part tragedy, part holy ritual.

As I pedaled south the valley gradually rose, running between the Sawtooth range to the west and the White Cloud range to the east. The mountains rose also, but not as quickly as the valley, and the scenery grew less spectacular.

The day before I'd climbed a 6,900-foot summit starting from an elevation of 3,300 feet. This day my route began at 6,300 feet and rose slightly higher than 8,700, with much of the climb spread out along 25 miles of the Salmon River.

It should have been easy, but it wasn't. There'd been a strong wind behind me all the way the day before, even following me around a 150-degree bend that led from the upper Payette Valley into the Sawtooth. On this day, headwinds changed the first 20 miles from what should have been a gentle, 2-hour climb into a grueling $3\frac{1}{2}$-hour struggle. Only then did the climb begin in earnest: 5 miles of six percent grade.

Ben had told me I would be surprised at my strength as the trip progressed. Pedaling slowly up the pass, I realized he had been right. Two weeks ago this grade would have forced me to stop and pant every quarter mile, especially at 8,000 feet above sea level. But I stopped only twice, the second time at a scenic overlook near the summit, where I stayed several minutes saying good-bye to the Sawtooth region and letting my mind drift with the cloud shadows in the Salmon River Valley below.

From the pass I'd intended to cycle all the way to Craters of the Moon National Monument, 90 miles away. But it was already midafternoon, and the wind was still against me, ruining the 45-mile downgrade that lay ahead. I stopped for the night near Sun Valley, camping on a side road east of town.

Sun Valley and neighboring Ketchum were loaded with cyclists. With a permanent population of 2,500, Ketchum boasts not one but two bike shops, and there was another 13 miles away in Hailey. Bikers were everywhere, ranging as far as 60 miles into the Sawtooth. As I set up camp I watched a constant parade of passing cyclists of every size and shape—thin, fat, sixty-year-olds, women with young children. Some were lean and muscular, others looked as though they shouldn't be able to walk to their cars, let alone pedal a bike.

The next morning I started late, waiting in Ketchum until the bike shops opened to buy forty dollars' worth of padding for my bike seat and handlebars. I'd bought a sheepskin saddle cover in Ontario, but it hadn't been enough, so I splurged on one made by Spenco. I'd considered the Spenco cushion when I bought the sheepskin, but Spenco products are heavy as well as expensive, and I'd been reluctant to carry the extra weight. Recently weight had become less important to me; Ben had told me that would happen, adding that on his cross-country trip he'd gone so far as to buy peanut butter in five-pound tubs to save money. So far I hadn't done anything like that, but I often carried seven to eight pounds of food along with more than a gallon of water. An extra pound for a seat cover seemed minor.

From Ketchum I pedaled down the valley to Hailey, Bellevue, and Picabo. The scenery should have been pretty, but I'd spent the previous two days immersed in spectacle and barely noticed it. What impressed me was the traffic. I'd been warned about this road, and my sources were right. Were it not for the courteous Idaho drivers I'd have spent a lot of time walking. Fortunately it lasted only 18 miles; at Bellevue I turned off, and from there to Craters of the Moon I had the roads mostly to myself.

The route from Picabo to Craters of the Moon, taken in the mid- to late afternoon, was one of the most beautiful desert rides I've ever enjoyed. The road skirted the base of Idaho's rugged central uplift, at the boundary between the mountains and the lava flows of the Snake River Valley. Although I was a mile above sea level there wasn't a tree in sight. To the south stretched the lava flows, undulating mounds of black rock 10 to 20 feet high and twice as many wide, running now parallel to the road, now perpendicular to it, cut by fissures that could easily swallow a man or even a horse. On such terrain a hiker measures his progress in hours per mile rather than miles per hour and counts himself lucky to cover 5 miles in a day. And these were old lava flows, well weathered compared with the spiny jumbles closer to Craters of the Moon.

Less than a mile to the north stood equally barren foothills. With no preliminaries they rose directly from the lava flows, soaring 2,000 feet in one sudden surge, blocking the view to my left and confining the horizon to their treeless ridgelines. Like the hills along the Payette they were rounded, weathered. But unlike their cousins these hills had simpler contours without the pleated texture I'd seen before. They appeared younger, still proud and virile in their resistance to wind and rain.

The road dodged a low spur that jutted from the foothills and crossed a little bay toward another spur. Sandwiched between the road and the hills was a small spring-fed marsh, an island of greenery marking the discontinuity between mountain and plain. In front of the marsh were a few small lava flows. The late afternoon sun was almost directly behind me, lighting the slopes with a vivid glow, the absence of shadow foreshortening the ridges and gullies into a flat wall broken only by the S curve of a small stream bed, its alluvial fan looking almost glacial as it spilled down the mountainside in a broad tongue.

It wasn't the contours of the hillside that caught my attention so much as the colors. Stunningly illuminated by the six o'clock sun, they glowed back at me, an artist's palette of yellow-green and gold and every color in between, with bands of purple and tan where the underlying rocks broke through. By car I would have driven by, said, "Ooh!", sped around the next curve, and been gone. But I biked toward the hillside for nearly ten minutes, basking in its glow until almost the very end, when the illusion suddenly burst and I saw individual plants—the motes of color which, like the dots in a fine engraving, merged with distance into all shades of the rainbow, casting a glow over my mood that carried me most of the way to Craters of the Moon.

The glow was shattered when my knee began to hurt, and then received another blow 5 miles later when I arrived at the monument.

Craters of the Moon has long been one of my favorite national monuments. It occupies a region where fifteen thousand years ago the Earth's crust split open in a 65-mile-long rift like the skin of an overripe fruit. Intermittently over several thousand years red-hot magma spilled forth in a variety of forms, ranging from slow-moving basalt to fountains of lava bombs and fiery cinders that fell to form frothy black cones up to 800 feet high. Eventually an area of several hundred square miles was buried under more than 7 cubic miles of volcanic rock, some of which still looks so fresh you expect it to be warm to the touch.

Ten years earlier my wife and I spent three glorious days at Craters of the Moon. We hiked every trail and slept beneath a weathered pine, watching the most spectacular meteor display we'd ever seen. We could have stayed a week. After only three days we had made such an impression on park rangers, accustomed to passing visitors who pause only for a few hours, that the following summer one of them, who'd been transferred to Mt. Rainier National Park, picked us out of the crowd, shouting, "Craters of the Moon! You were at Craters of the Moon!"

The campground was still there, a collection of small pads of black volcanic cinders nestled in natural embayments in a lava flow. Even our pine was unchanged, a nostalgic reminder that was all the better because we'd refused to defile its gnarled trunk with our initials.

But something was different. At first I couldn't put a finger on it—the park seemed impersonal, alien. Sometimes it is unwise to return to places that were once special—all you find are the inevitable warts, shortcomings that may have been there all along but had previously been masked in the glow of memory. But that wasn't all. The ranger at the gate seemed aloof and indifferent, a far cry from what I remembered. And the campground was no longer occupied mostly by tents and small campers. It had been subtly altered—"improved for better access" is what the Park Service would probably say—its mood of cozy isolation marred by the blocky shapes of RVs rising above the intervening lava outcroppings.

As I sat at my campsite chatting with neighbors—fellow tent-campers from San Francisco—I watched the campground quickly fill as RVs pulled in from the highway and prowled in search of vacant sites. And then I realized what had happened: This place had been discovered. It wasn't simply the RVs, though they seemed out of place in the stark landscape where nothing so large and artificial could be hidden. Nor was it merely the number of visitors, though that too was a contributing factor. It was a change in mood. Craters of the Moon was the best campground along several hundred miles of U.S. 20. It had been found and, with a little Park Service modernization, converted to a trailer park, an overnight pit stop that might have been anywhere. Gone was the backwater park I had loved; in its place was this changeling, superficially similar and bearing the same name, but no longer *my* Craters of the Moon.

I wasn't the first person to have such sentiments. Edward Abbey—whose book *Desert Solitaire* is one long declaration of love for the deserts of southern Utah—expressed the same indignation over the "modernization" of his beloved Arches National Park. "Arches . . ." he wrote, "has been developed. . . .

> *Where once a few adventurous people came on weekends to camp for a night or two and enjoy a taste of the primitive and remote, you will now find serpentine streams of baroque automobiles pouring in and out, all through the spring and summer, in numbers that would have seemed fantastic when I worked there. . . . The little campgrounds where I used to putter around reading three-day-old newspapers . . . have now been consolidated into one master campground that looks, during the busy season, like a suburban village. . . .*
>
> *Progress has come at last to the Arches, after a million years of neglect.*

Surveying what had happened to Craters of the Moon, I wondered bleakly: Is "progress" inevitable?

After I'd been in camp an hour I bade adieu to my neighbors and set off to bike the monument's 7-mile scenic drive. It was the first time since I'd said good-bye to Jane that I'd ridden without bags, and as I pedaled up the steep road I was struck by how differently my bicycle handled; it was so nimble I could barely steer a straight line. I was also distressed to discover that my knee still hurt, even without the bags.

At the top of the hill I stopped, chained my bike to an interpretive sign, and walked up the short, steep trail to the top of Inferno Cone, one of the monument's tallest cinder cones, the only one visitors are encouraged to climb.

I climbed into wind and solitude. Other than the trail itself the only signs of humanity were the park road, winding unobtrusively through the lava flows and lesser cinder cones below, and the campground, the white RVs looking like chunks of Styrofoam strewn across the black lava with the nearby administration buildings equally incongruous as the sun glinted off their aluminum roofs.

As I reached the top and stepped slightly beyond the crest the campground disappeared from view. And suddenly I rediscovered the Craters of the Moon I had known and loved. I was alone on a broad, craterless summit, listening to the wind roar through the branches of a solitary pine, watching the puffs of dust that exploded whenever I moved my feet. Below me stretched the lava flows like a giant tabletop of black licorice stirred at random and left to harden, spreading east and west for 20 miles, the details blurring with distance but the impression of swirls and ridges remaining. My mind soared across this jumbled plain like a hawk gliding in the wind, swooping and diving, playing in the immense, open stretches, relishing the solitude as I was carried on imaginary explorations or climbed distant peaks.

Sometimes my attention rested on specific features of the terrain. To the south stretched a gradually diminishing string of cinder cones, marking the great rift where as recently as two thousand years ago the magma had poured forth, creating great lava flows on either side.

Beyond the cinder cones, faint on the horizon, shimmered the island mountain ranges south of the Snake River. I wished I could explore each and every one, walk their valleys and climb their passes, seeking their secrets and finding what is unique about them. For I believe no two places are alike. Each has its peculiarities, its *raison d'être*, and the joy of my explorations has been to find those differences, adding them to my memories and wondering at the sheer creativity displayed in this world, where so many things appear time and again but are never quite the same.

This is not to say that all mountain ranges are equal; some, like the Sawtooth or the Tetons, are more obvious in their beauty, speaking to more people and in clearer voices. I believe all are put there for a reason—no place is truly desolate—and all have something to teach us if we but listen to their subtle voices and approach them on their own terms. That is why even the most barren places have their advocates—people who have truly learned to hear, people who stand in the role of prophets, interpreting what these places have to say for the rest of humanity. It is a great failing of both organized religion and the environmental movement that they have missed this call—the churches from apathy, the environmental movement by all too often elevating the creation itself to the level of creator.

Only the vaguest outline of these thoughts occurred to me as I stood atop Inferno Cone. All I felt then was the call of distant blue hills—the vague desire to know what lies beyond and what beyond that—and gratitude that the changeling that called itself Craters of the Moon had so far invaded only the campground. The real Craters of the Moon had remained true, a magical place of quiet and serenity that many people pass by but few explore. It is their loss, but I am grateful they left it to me, for solitude is fragile, and the tourist-industry dream of a heavy visitor count would destroy the rest of this park just as surely as modernization had ruined the charm of its campground.

———————•◦•———————

I returned to camp a few minutes later and grabbed a bagel and cheese to take with me to the amphitheater for the evening ranger talk.

Ten years ago the evening ranger programs had attracted only a score of people. This night there must have been a hundred.

The ranger had it figured out, too. "How many of you are here to see the wildlife?" he asked.

One tentative hand was raised.

"How many are here to see some unique volcanic features?"

A scattering of hands appeared, but not many.

"How many are here because it's a national monument and you like the way the Park Service runs things so you try to collect as many as possible?"

Now he was on their wavelength. There was a murmur of assent and twenty to thirty people raised their hands.

"And how many are here because it's on the way to Yellowstone?"

There were a lot of chuckles, but well over half the group had their hands in the air.

"Well, at least you're honest about it!"

I wanted to scream—*And how many people are here because you've been here before and think it's one of the greatest places on Earth?* But I knew why he didn't ask that. Craters of the Moon probably gets few return visitors, but I could always hope that a few—perhaps only one—of the people there that night would fall in love with the monument and come to cherish it as I do.

———————•◦•———————

I returned to camp planning a good night's sleep and an early start. But as I spread my sleeping bag the family in the tent to my right fired up a gasoline lantern and began to talk loudly.

At first I grumbled to myself about how rude they were, but later I realized they were probably more ignorant than malicious. Whatever the reason they were too noisy. And sometime around 10:30, their kids—both of whom were old enough to know better—started imitating bird calls. Two younger children in the tent to my left took up the cry and their parents—the couple from San Francisco—kept trying to shush them. But how do you quiet first-graders when the neighbors make no effort to control their teenagers?

Eventually the bird calls died down and the father announced loudly, "Well, it's time for bed." He then kept talking for another fifteen minutes—his voice carrying clearly across the 30 feet between our campsites. I wasn't surprised his kids had been noisy—how could they be anything else?

When everything finally settled down it must have been 11:30. Then their dog barked—only once or twice, but it was an omen of what was to come at dawn.

At first light the dog barked at a chipmunk. I groaned, then decided that as long as I was awake I might as well go to the bathroom. That was a mistake. Until I moved the dog had apparently been unaware of my presence. When I sat up, it gave me a startled bark.

It barked again when I returned from the bathroom and crawled back into my sleeping bag.

"Shh. It's okay," I whispered, but the dog would have none of it. I was in its territory.

"Woof," it said.

I rolled away, hoping that if it couldn't see my face it might forget I existed.

"Woof."

And so it went for what seemed like hours. As long as I didn't move the dog would let me be—reversing the old proverb about letting sleeping dogs lie. But whenever I twitched it came to attention.

"Woof."

"Woof."

"Woof."

A plaintive voice came from the other tent. "Daddy, I can't sleep."

"Well, I never promised you a rose garden," Daddy quipped with aggravating cheerfulness.

"Woof."

————— •• —————

I gave up trying to sleep. Most of the RVs were getting ready to leave, and the entire campground was astir. By eight o'clock it was mostly empty, with little left but tents—a sudden and miraculous return to the way I remembered it. I was astounded to discover that most of the RVs left without taking the scenic drive. As far as I could tell, most of the campers had arrived late, attended the ranger presentation, and left early, having seen pictures of the monument but not much of the monument itself.

————— •• —————

I had planned to leave early, too, but changed my mind. The strong southwest wind that had tried to blow me off the top of Inferno Cone had become a fitful easterly breeze, so I waited to see what would develop. With a good tailwind I still hoped to cover a lot of miles, but just moving around camp made my knee slightly sore, and I didn't want to push it.

This was the first time it had hurt when I wasn't on my bicycle. Yet the previous day had been easy, with a raging tailwind blowing me all the way from Picabo to the monument. As on the day when I'd first hurt it in California, I must have pedaled too hard, trying to keep pace with the wind. How ironic that only two days before I'd been congratulating myself about how strong I'd become. And just before the pain began I'd planned as many as 160 miles for the day, hoping to ride that lovely wind most of the way to Yellowstone.

I realized I'd become complacent. Earlier when my knee had hurt I'd turned it over to God, finding the freedom that comes with accepting the unknown. But I seemed to have forgotten the lesson as soon as the pain disappeared. Scheduling 160-mile days was only the beginning; if I wasn't careful my trip would become an exercise in "If It's Tuesday, This Must Be Wyoming," as I counted off days and distances in a continual effort to schedule my way to the Atlantic.

Deep within I was still unable to let go. I had detoured twice from the fastest route east: once to John Day and more recently by venturing into the Sawtooth, an excursion that had delayed me by nearly two days. The dream of reaching the Atlantic at all costs still sang its siren song, and try as I might I couldn't ignore it. I had lost the relaxation I'd found in eastern Oregon. "You've had your fun," an inner voice seemed to say. "Now turn and run for the East while you still have time." It was my own case of the white-line fever that had afflicted Craig and John, the two cyclists I'd met in the Cascades. No matter how many times I tried to subdue it that voice always came back, conditioned by a lifetime of goal-driven behavior. I might be covering fewer miles a day, but I was little different from the RVs I criticized so harshly.

I was also looking for companionship, and that, too, was pressing me to hurry, to see if I could catch up with other cyclists. A few evenings ago my wife had told me about a group that was riding from Portland, Oregon, to Washington, D.C., to raise money for world hunger. They'd received a lot of publicity, and she told me they were scheduled to leave the Tetons in three days. At my present rate I'd be a day behind, and I kept trying to figure out how to catch up.

With my sore knee it looked unlikely, but maybe that was as it should have been. I wanted companionship primarily across a long stretch of Wyoming that had an unfriendly reputation. As I'd supposedly learned in California, when possible it is best to take the problems of the trip one day at a time. If I needed company, perhaps it would materialize later.

———— •• ————

As I scribbled these thoughts in my journal, I ate a cold breakfast of bagels, grapefruit, and Pop Tarts, then spent the morning at the monument. I'd have to leave in the afternoon, because I was nearly out of food.

I soon learned that there were sources of food other than what I was carrying. Half an hour after I finished eating, the couple from San Francisco invited me over for oatmeal, the first hot breakfast I'd seen in days. I joined them without hesitation.

These neighbors were as wonderful as my other neighbors had been obnoxious. Self-described ex-hippies, they retained much of the social consciousness of The Sixties and were concerned about raising their children to be considerate, not only of other people but of the environment as well. They favored backpacks over RVs, tents over televisions and radios. The husband was an economist working for the government; I didn't find out what his wife did. They were on a relaxed three-week vacation, with a full week scheduled in Yellowstone and another in the Tetons. Best of all, they were staying two nights in Craters of the Moon.

After a second breakfast I decided to take a walk and biked to the lower end of my favorite trail, which meandered $1\frac{3}{4}$ miles over a crater and through the lava flows. I chained my bicycle and hitchhiked to the starting point, getting a ride with a woman and her ten-year-old daughter who were taking a week to drive the scenic route from Washington to Minnesota. They weren't stopping everywhere along the way, but they were spending the time to really see the places they did visit.

I ambled through the lava flows, taking time to get reacquainted with another portion of the Craters of the Moon I'd always loved. When I got back to my bicycle, I was startled to encounter one of the Wimbledon riders. I'd known they were visiting the monument, but when I hadn't seen them the day before I'd assumed they were still a day behind.

"We got in late," he explained. "Our van broke down, and we didn't have any gear. We had to borrow sleeping bags from a park ranger!"

He led me to the rest of the group, who were camped near the entrance station, well away from the main campground.

"Look who I found!" he shouted as we approached. Everyone waved, but the adults looked tired and flustered so I didn't linger. The van had been fixed, but I had a feeling it had been a long night.

Back at my site I munched on some peanuts, talked with the couple from San Francisco, and slowly broke camp. It was downhill most of the way to the next town, and while the breeze was going to be against me, I thought I could make it without overtaxing my knee. I was sure they'd have offered dinner if I'd needed it, but as long as I could ride I preferred not to ask. Besides, it would be fun to leave with the Wimbledon riders when they rolled out in an hour or two.

I was vaguely aware of a rhythmic clink, clink, clink coming from behind me—like the sound of someone driving tent stakes. It had been going on for some time before I glanced back and identified the source: the daughter of the loud family from last night—which had surprised me by not leaving with the RVs—was industriously attacking the adjoining lava flow with a geologist's hammer. Her father was sitting next to her reading *National Geographic*.

"Hey! Don't do that!" I shouted.

She looked up. Everyone in the vicinity looked up. I was aghast, as my shout echoed around the campground.

"This is a national monument, and that's against the rules."

"Are you sure?" the father asked.

"Absolutely. You can't do that in any national monument."

"Oh," he said, and without another word his daughter put the hammer away. Maybe, I thought, there was hope for them after all.

———————•◦•———————

When I finished packing the Wimbledon group was still getting organized. "I'm sure you'll catch me," I called as I pedaled by. "And if you don't,
I expect I'll see you in Yellowstone." Unfortunately, from there they
weren't going my way across Wyoming.

But they didn't catch up when I stopped at the first town for a leisurely
lunch, nor had they caught me by the time our routes diverged a few
miles later, with theirs turning east to Idaho Falls and mine continuing
northeast to Rexburg. I never saw them again.

———————•◦•———————

For the next few miles I followed the discontinuity between the mountains and the Snake River plateau, but the lava flows were much older
than those around Craters of the Moon, and the lowlands had weathered
to a sprawling sage-covered plain dotted with a scattering of volcanic
buttes. The mountains had also become less jumbled, settling into a series
of parallel ridges and valleys, running down from the northwest to end
abruptly as they encountered the Snake River basin. The road alternately
skirted the foothills and crossed the valleys, proceeding northeast in a series of gentle swells.

I stopped for an evening snack at a small store at the mouth of one of
the valleys. A few minutes later a pickup pulled into the parking lot, and
a burly man climbed out.

"You travelin' alone?" he asked.

I nodded. "For the moment."

"Where do you spend the nights? You just camp by the road?"

I'd been asked that question a number of times before, and I'd never
liked it. By this time, I had a standard response: "No, I stay in private
campgrounds. Or in the national parks or forests."

"You had any problems? Anybody give you any trouble?" Something
in his manner indicated that he hoped the answer would be "yes."

Not yet, I wanted to reply. *Are you planning to be the first?* But I answered, "No, everyone out here's been really friendly."

"Oh," he said, sounding a bit disappointed. "That they are." Probably
he wanted to hear an exciting story, but his questions made me nervous,
and suddenly I was aware of just how deserted the road had been. As I
rode out of town I kept an eye out for his truck and was glad not to see it.

———————•◦•———————

Evening was approaching, and I began to contemplate where to spend the night. There were only two towns in the next 58 miles: Mud Lake and Rexburg. Mud Lake was closer, but there were nearly $4\frac{1}{2}$ hours of good daylight left, my knee was feeling strong again, and the wind had become a light tailwind. The conditions were perfect for a return of my twin nemeses, complacency and scheduling. I thought of pushing all the way to Rexburg by nightfall.

I was startled back to the present by a change in the wind. In less than five minutes it shifted 180 degrees, increasing from 5 to 30 miles an hour. My speed fell to a crawl, and I began to worry about my knee.

If I could have I would have stopped right there, but there was nowhere to camp. I had entered an Atomic Energy Commission reservation, and "No Trespassing" signs were everywhere. It might have been legal to sleep in the ditch along the main highway, but that was too exposed— after my recent questioning, I was especially wary of camping within sight of the main road. There was nothing to do but inch along as my dreams of reaching Rexburg vanished, and I began to wonder whether I could cover the 20 miles to Mud Lake.

———————————•◦•———————————

It took three hours, but I got there, exhausted and nearly incoherent, wondering where to spend the night. I was trying to decide whether to ask to use someone's lawn or camp on the open range—the reservation ended on the outskirts of town—when I spied a commercial campground.

Remembering my experience in Oregon, I knocked on the office door. "Have you got a biker special?" I asked.

"Certainly," the proprietor replied. "How about $3.50? And I'm sure you'd rather not sleep on the gravel we use for the trailer sites—how about the grass behind the garage?"

It was almost too good to be true.

———————————•◦•———————————

I was too tired to fix my own dinner, so I biked down the street to a hamburger stand, then stopped at a bar for a wine cooler and a table where I could work on my journal. I didn't get much written, because people kept asking about my trip. "Where are you coming from?" one young man asked.

"Sacramento."

"How long have you been out?"

I stopped to think. "Two and a half weeks."

He didn't say much more, but a few minutes later, as I stood outside packing my writing tablet into my panniers, I could hear his voice drifting loudly through the window.

"Sacramento, in $2\frac{1}{2}$ weeks. That's only about 800 miles. I could *walk* 800 miles in $2\frac{1}{2}$ weeks!"

I'd encountered many reactions to my cycling vacation, but this one was new. Since my goal was to relax, I should have taken it as a compliment. Instead I felt mildly offended and fought back an urge to shout, "*Twelve* hundred miles by the route I'm following!"

———————•••———————

The next day was a day of decision. I'd been planning to ride northeast into Yellowstone and then turn south toward the Tetons, but the roads in Yellowstone are narrow and winding. With the Fourth of July weekend approaching, the traffic would be terrible. Pedaling into Rexburg late that morning, I crossed the main route to the park and noted that there was already a continuous stream of cars and RVs heading north for the long weekend.

I stopped for lunch and considered my options. I wanted to ride through Yellowstone, but I didn't want to fight the traffic to do it. And I wasn't sure it would be safe to leave my gear unattended while I hiked through the geyser basins. I could lock the bicycle, but there was no way to protect my tent or sleeping bag. And Yellowstone—like many major national parks—is notorious for thefts.

I was still thinking about teaming up with the hunger riders—whose official name was "Bike Aid"—for the long, empty stretches of central Wyoming. It would be difficult to catch them if I looped through Yellowstone, and far too rushed to be enjoyable. The logical decision was to leave Yellowstone to the RVs. If I headed straight for the Tetons I could cross Teton Pass by the next morning, spend a relaxing day in the park, and catch the hunger riders as they left the following day.

It was obviously the best decision, but I found it hard to pass up Yellowstone, and I agonized for at least an hour before finally deciding to head east for Teton Pass.

Almost immediately I entered a land of gentle beauty—a pastoral landscape where sagebrush, which had been my constant companion since Craters of the Moon, was replaced by sweeping panoramas of lush, rolling rangeland, the thick grass rippling before the wind in ever-changing patterns of light and shadow. Long, low buildings dotted the landscape, giant root cellars still holding remnants of a potato harvest so bountiful it had flooded the market, leaving the farmers with more potatoes than they could sell. In the spring the farmers had dumped many of them outside to rot, and as I passed downwind the stench was overwhelming.

I was also passing through a land that had once experienced a front-page-headline disaster. A few miles out of Rexburg a sign reminded me that this had been the site of the Teton Dam, which burst in 1976, only eight months after completion. Caused by an engineering flaw, the flood had covered hundreds of square miles, claimed eleven lives, and driven twenty-five thousand people from their homes.

Neither the memory of a decade-old tragedy nor the occasional aroma of spoiling potatoes did much to mar the beauty of this tranquil landscape, set before the dramatic backdrop of the west side of the Teton Range.

Viewed from the west the Tetons do not look as impressive as in the classic view from Jackson Hole, but they present an uninterrupted front of pine-covered slopes that rise steadily — almost implacably — until the pines yield to gray granite and scattered snow atop an uplift that soars 6,000 feet in less than 10 miles. Sitting atop this otherwise uniform slope are the spires of the three Tetons themselves, the highest rising to nearly 14,000 feet, looking uncannily like three teats, explaining why the French trappers gave this mountain range a name that means "breasts."

The gentle beauty of the Tetons' western slope may not be as spectacular as the rugged escarpment that plunges into Jackson Hole, but the lush ranch country at their base, threaded by quiet rural roads and the blue waters of the Teton River, gives this area a charm of its own, making it ideal for cycle touring. While I regretted bypassing Yellowstone, I knew I'd made the right decision.

CHAPTER 5

Wyoming

Doing Time on the Frontier

DAY 19 • Thursday, July 3 • CUMULATIVE MILES: 1,371
Victor, Idaho, to Jenny Lake, Wyoming

DAY 20 • Friday, July 4 • CUMULATIVE MILES: 1,438
Jenny Lake to Falls Campground

DAY 21 • Saturday, July 5 • CUMULATIVE MILES: 1,550
Falls Campground to Lander

DAY 22 • Sunday, July 6 • CUMULATIVE MILES: 1,597
Lander to Sweetwater Crossing

DAY 23 • Monday, July 7 • CUMULATIVE MILES: 1,696
Sweetwater Crossing to Rawlins

DAY 24 • Tuesday, July 8 • CUMULATIVE MILES: 1,764
Rawlins to Riverside

After spending a night in a national-forest clearing at the base of Teton Pass, I began the climb into Wyoming.

It was not a long climb. Although the summit of Teton Pass is 8,400 feet above sea level, the ascent from either side is only 2,200 feet—no more than I'd come to expect from any major pass. What made it memorable was the grade, which is steep enough, as someone had told me the day before, "to keep out the riffraff."

I got my first taste of what lay ahead as I crossed the Wyoming border, where I was greeted not by a "Welcome to Wyoming" sign, but by "STEEP MOUNTAIN PASS AHEAD: 10% GRADES." Welcome to Wyoming, indeed!

I had barely crossed the state line when the road began to climb in earnest, culminating in an ascent of 1,300 feet in only $2\frac{1}{2}$ miles. I quickly discovered I didn't have the right gearing for such a sustained grade. I couldn't sit and pedal comfortably in any gear, but when I tried to stand up, the lowest gear provided too little resistance, while the next higher provided too much. So I alternated between standing and sitting, occasionally shifting to the higher gear, stopping every half mile or so to huff and puff as I measured my progress against the alpine meadows toward which I was climbing.

About a mile from the top I met two cyclists coming the other way. A pair of brothers from Connecticut, they were heading toward Portland and planning to follow much of my route in reverse. While they cooled their brakes I told them about the route ahead. "And if you have time," I concluded, "detour through the Sawtooth. It's worth it!"

"Is it on the Bikecentennial route?"

"No, the route's north of here." I hadn't been on it since eastern Oregon, but I would rejoin it the next day. "You left it in the Tetons."

"Yeah, we meant to. We came this way because we'd had enough of it. We want to go somewhere where people are friendlier."

I was startled. "Things were fine in Oregon."

"Well, I'll tell you, they don't like cyclists in Wyoming. The merchants won't look you in the eye. They'll take your money okay, but it's clear they don't want you around. We've had enough of that."

That was a new one to me, and it rekindled my nervousness about Wyoming. I'd been fearful of harassment by teenagers, not an entire populace.

––––––––––•◦•––––––––––

My worries faded at the top of the pass as I paused to sit on a grassy hillside, surrounded by wildflowers, relishing the view across the south end of Jackson Hole to the snowcapped summits of the Gros Ventre Mountains beyond. Ahead, the road wound steeply down toward Jackson, falling 2,200 feet in only 5 miles. Inching my way down, I was cautious lest the heat from my brakes melt the brake blocks or burst a tire. A stiff wind blew toward the pass, and with each switchback I had to take care not to be blown into a ditch or over an embankment.

Then the road straightened, and I could risk picking up speed, flying down toward the open, level expanses below. Within minutes the pass was only a memory, lost behind a bend, and soon I was fighting a steady stream of traffic on the outskirts of Jackson.

Resort towns such as Jackson are unpleasant outgrowths of our country's love affair with its national parks. Congested by stoplights, souvenir shops, and masses of tourists, they defy the very concept of the parks they serve. Our love of the outdoors is touched with an acute schizophrenia; each summer we run to the hinterland to seek renewal—only to bring the worst of the city with us.

My goal had been to reach town by 9:30 A.M., buy a tire (the one I'd

bought in Oregon was already showing wear), and depart as soon as possible, but I'd underestimated the time necessary to cross the pass. It was
closer to noon when I arrived, and nearly 1:30 by the time I'd eaten lunch
and bought supplies. While I had the chance I bought two tires, coiling
them into double loops I could carry out of the way, beneath the sleeping
bag, tent, and tarp already lashed to my luggage rack.

From Jackson I turned toward the park, contending with a continuous
stream of traffic and spending most of my time staring in the rear-view
mirror rather than watching the scenery. Along the way I was passed by a
flat-bed trailer bearing the name "Bike Aid." It was my first sign of the
hunger riders, who I knew were camping that night at Colter Bay, the
main Teton campground, where I hoped to catch them in the morning. I
was surprised by how small the trailer was—not much bigger than the van
accompanying the Wimbledon riders—and I later learned there were only
thirteen cyclists in the group. Given the publicity, I'd been expecting a lot
more.

A few miles later I stopped at the visitor center to ask about camping.
Having traveled in the Tetons twice before, I knew the campgrounds
tended to fill early; I was afraid I'd have to go all the way to Colter Bay to
find an opening and was happy to learn that wouldn't be necessary. Jenny
Lake Campground, only a few miles down the road, had a designated
bike site, and there was a good chance it wouldn't be occupied.

With that news I relaxed. It was time to *see* the Tetons. In Jackson I'd
noticed advertisements for scenic raft trips on the Snake River, and I'd
been thinking about the river ever since. I picked up fliers for several of
the raft companies and made a few phone calls.

The first was full for the day, but they could schedule me for the next
morning. Would I be interested? I dithered a moment, then decided it
would be too inconvenient to come back.

The next was also booked, but the third surprised me. They had an
opening on their last raft trip of the afternoon, leaving in a little over an
hour. I made a reservation, then prepared to spend an hour in the visitor
center.

I began by attending a ranger's lecture about the park. The ranger,
who'd obviously polished his presentation to a fine edge, led us outside to
the visitor center patio. "The most important thing about your park visit,"
he told us, "is to get out of your cars and walk. That's the only way you'll

really get to know the place." Here was a man after my own heart. The
one drawback to bicycle touring is that it isn't convenient to leave the bicycle for a few days and go backpacking—especially if you have limited
time to cross the continent.

The ranger continued. "A lot of people say the Tetons don't have much
wildlife, but that's because the wildlife here is shier than that up in *Jelly*-
stone." He emphasized his corruption of the name. "Up in *Jelly*stone the
animals just stand around next to the road. Here you have to keep your
eyes open to see them, but we've got everything they've got—moose, elk,
buffalo—they're all here." He went on to describe the ideal time of day for
viewing wildlife, suggesting a few locations. "But you have to treat the
wildlife with respect," he said, turning toward the woman next to me. He
took a couple of steps toward her. "Wild animals don't like it when people
come too close." He took another step, then another. "They need space,
just like us." He was within an arm's length of her now. "If you get too
close, they get nervous." The woman was leaning backward, almost toppling into the shrubbery. "They feel cornered and try to get away. Only
they're bigger than we are." He grinned and stepped back. "So give them
space. Don't run right up next to them the way they do in *Jelly*stone!"

The rest of his talk was interesting but not so dramatic, and my mind
wandered, contemplating possible detours. Although I'd decided against a
trip through Yellowstone, the ranger's mention of it called it to mind
again; instead of heading southeast toward Colorado, I could ride north
into Yellowstone and then turn east across Montana. When the ranger
finished his talk, I asked him about the roads in Yellowstone.

He answered without hesitation. "At this time of year they're terrible—
narrow, winding, and full of RVs. It's not a good time of year to be there
on a bicycle."

I knew he was right, but I was still unsure about it a few minutes later
when it was time to meet the rafting party. Putting thoughts of Yellowstone aside, I chained my bicycle in front of the visitor center, where one
of the rangers promised to keep an eye on it. "Of course we're not respon-
sible if something happens," she told me, "but we'll keep an eye out."

The raft trip was a marvelously relaxing experience. Routed for scenery
rather than whitewater, it took us along a relatively peaceful stretch of the
Snake, sweeping around bends and gravel bars beneath the 6,500-foot escarpment only a half dozen miles to our west. The river was high and the
current swift—in many places it must have been flowing 10 miles an
hour—and we bumped effortlessly along as our guide explained ecology
and geology and kept an eye out for wildlife. "With luck, we might see a

moose," he told us, but I was only half listening. I'd seen a moose only that morning, browsing in a stream bed next to the road, and now the mountains held my gaze at every turn.

The river also piqued my curiosity, and I wondered how it would measure up as a canoe stream. One of the other members of our party had the same idea and asked the guide if many people canoed it.

"The Park Service discourages it," the guide said, "but a lot of people do, and a lot of them get in trouble. This current is strong. If you hit a rock, it can dump you easily. It seems as though every day this week I've met someone out here whose canoe capsized."

He could not have spoken more prophetically. Only a few minutes later we were hailed by two young men standing on the bank. "Who are they?" someone asked.

"Canoeists," the guide said. "See, there's their canoe, wrapped around that rock."

"What do they want?"

"They want us to help them get their canoe, but the current's too strong—I'd run a risk of capsizing on a snag if I got close to shore." He cupped his hands to shout above the roar of the current. "I'll tell the rangers."

One of the canoeists nodded. The other gave a thumbs-up sign.

I was still wondering about the canoe. "How can that canoe be worth anything? It's bent into a U!"

"They can pound it out again. It's amazing how well you can straighten out these modern canoes. They're made for it."

That was news to me, but another member of our group was several steps behind me. "Why don't they just wade out there and get it?" he asked. And as our guide explained that the current was far, far too strong for that, I went back to gazing at the mountains.

———————————— ◦•◦ ————————————

The float trip was over much too soon. Within less than an hour we were back at the visitor center, and a few minutes later I turned onto the quiet side road leading to Jenny Lake.

As I pedaled along the base of the mountains, peering up each canyon, looking for landmarks from a long-ago backpacking trip into the high country, I met a cyclist coming from the opposite direction. A young college student who looked remarkably fresh and clean, he struck me as the archetypal Yuppie-to-be. "Which way are you headed?" I asked.

"East," he replied, and my heart gave a leap. "Over Togwotee Pass?"

This was the route to Colorado followed by the Bikecentennial Trail after it dropped south from Yellowstone.

"Yes. I'm going over it tomorrow. Tonight I'm heading to Jackson."

I was thrilled. "Where are you coming from?"

"Seattle. I'm taking the Bikecentennial route to Virginia."

"How were conditions in Yellowstone?"

"Oh, it was great! Yellowstone is fabulous!"

That wasn't what I wanted to hear. "How's the traffic?"

"There's some, but it's not too bad. Particularly in the mornings."

So I had two pieces of advice—totally contradictory.

"Where are you going?" he asked, inadvertently voicing the question that had become paramount in my thoughts.

"I'm not sure. Maybe through Yellowstone, but probably over Togwotee. I'll decide tomorrow, but maybe I'll wind up seeing you along the way."

———

I reached Jenny Lake shortly thereafter and cycled around the campground looking for the bike-only site. I found it easily enough but discovered that cyclists had to share it with hitchhikers. That in itself presented no problem, but there were camping spaces for only two parties, and there were already two tents.

There was still enough daylight to ride on to Colter Bay, but I didn't want to leave. Because it's a tents-only campground, Jenny Lake is a quiet backwater, isolated from the congestion of the park's larger facilities. Not only that, but I didn't want to hurry along the scenic drive leading to Colter Bay; that was a ride to be taken during the warm, lazy sunshine of morning, not under the pressure of impending dusk. Well, I was quiet, and if I slept without a tent I wouldn't be very visible. The hitchhikers probably wouldn't object, and no one else was likely to notice. I felt vaguely guilty, but just this once I wanted to camp somewhere nice, and by bicycle that's difficult to do in parks like the Tetons, where prime campsites often fill by 10 A.M.

———

That night I rediscovered the Tetons. I'd enjoyed the first part of the day, but through it all I'd been overwhelmed by the people whizzing by— whether in giant RVs or imported compacts—stopping briefly at overlooks but seldom lingering, seeing an endless succession of parking lots without ever really seeing the mountains. And much of my own visit had been superficial, constrained by the need to keep my attention focused on the rear-view mirror. It wasn't until evening, as I sat by the lake feasting on a crude dinner of carrots and peanut butter, that things began to change.

The Jenny for whom Jenny Lake is named was Jenny Leigh, the Shoshone wife of an early outfitter (a lake named for him lies nearby). As I sat in the fading twilight, I thought that if she were anything like her lake she must have been quite a woman—deep and serene, seldom ruffled by storms, backed by a silent, overwhelming strength like the granite of the mountains.

It is the height and nearness of these mountains that makes Jenny Lake special. A bit of rough surveying using my thumb and a carrot told me that the peaks rose more than fifteen degrees into the western sky, towering 6,000 feet above me, with their summits only 5 miles away. The Tetons, viewed from Jenny Lake, are undoubtedly one of the most dramatic mountain escarpments in the world.

At twilight this drama faded into tranquility. Because the nearby campground was for tents only, it was remarkably quiet. Nobody was running generators, nobody was watching TV. Many people were backpackers or climbers, and like me they were operating on solar time. By sunset the campground was nearly silent—there weren't even many campfires. I could hear water cascading into the lake from a waterfall 2 miles away, a dull roar that occasionally rose or fell in volume with changes in the wind, an ever-present backdrop to other sounds—the occasional "plop" of a jumping fish, the giggle of children playing in the distance, and the purr of a low-power outboard motor carrying a pair of fishermen toward a distant cove.

The next morning I wandered back to the lake again. The previous evening a band of high clouds in the west had warned of approaching rain, and as I sat by the shore, mentally tracing climbing routes on the highest crags and fantasizing easier hikes below, I watched scattered puffs of white drifting in from the south. The day before I'd hoped the mountain rampart of the Tetons might hold the approaching storm at bay—diverting it northward into the unguarded approaches to Yellowstone—but as the clouds rapidly accumulated, I was certain there would be storms by midafternoon.

And storm it did, right on top of me, halfway up Togwotee Pass. All through the trip I'd been crossing passes too late in the afternoon, and eventually I knew I'd pay the penalty. This would be the day.

On other occasions my late pass climbs had generally been due to circumstances beyond my control—headwinds or simply the time it took to reach the summit. This time I had dawdled, first sitting by the lake, then accepting an invitation to join a party of climbers for breakfast, but most of all as I slowly pedaled the scenic drive to Colter Bay. I was no longer trying to catch the Bike Aid group; I'd decided to either head for Yellowstone or try to team up with the Yuppie-to-be when he came north out of Jackson.

Later I got as cold and wet as I'd ever been on a bicycle, but the scenic route was worth it—a fabulous ride, alternately slipping through meadows filled with bright yellow flowers or winding over lightly forested glacial moraines, with the spires of the Cathedral Group—the highest peaks of the Teton Range—drawing the eye up and up until it might hope to behold God. But if the Almighty were to select a throne among the peaks of the Tetons, he would be unlikely to choose the Gothic spires of the Cathedral Group. A more suitable throne would be the blocky summit of nearby Mount Moran, where a glacier has scoured a deep, hanging valley, flanked on both sides by armrest-like ridges that give it the appearance of an ancient high-backed chair, a 12,600-foot throne suitable for God himself.

By car the road presents an impressive view of the mountains as they rise abruptly only 2 miles away. But from the unhindered viewpoint of a cyclist they are a majestic presence, powerful even if you close your eyes, a wall of granite streaked with snow, shutting off the western half of the world, close enough to change rapidly, almost from one pedal stroke to the next.

I took my time on that ride, regaining the sense of awe that has long made the Tetons special to me, a sense that noisy crowds and harried traffic can never completely drive away.

It was well after noon by the time I reached the grocery store and restaurant at Signal Mountain, scarcely a dozen miles from my starting point.

———————— •◦• ————————

I dawdled again at Signal Mountain, eating an overpriced fish-and-chips lunch, buying groceries, and still agonizing over whether or not to turn north to Yellowstone.

Logic said, don't do it. Not only had I already decided two days earlier to avoid the park, but it was July 4, and the traffic would be worse than ever. Further, the wind was fair for Togwotee Pass, I could see storm clouds in Yellowstone, and even if the weather were acceptable, once I'd finished with Yellowstone I'd either have to come back to the Tetons or leave the mountains permanently.

I asked everyone I met for advice. A pair of cyclists coming south out of Yellowstone said the traffic was manageable—but they'd left the park before the holiday weekend crunch and had been careful to cycle only in the early morning or late afternoon. A park ranger was less encouraging, speaking of constant streams of RVs on narrow, winding roads and recommending that I come back some other year in June or September.

Eventually I forced myself to make the only reasonable decision—the one I'd always known I'd make: I turned east onto the Bikecentennial route, toward Togwotee Pass, the Wind River Valley, and the towns of Lander and Rawlins. But even as I left the park I sought yet one more reassurance from the ranger at the gate.

"You chose right," she said. "And Togwotee Pass is beautiful. Just on the other side is Brooks Lake, where you can camp if you don't mind cycling some gravel to get in. I think it's the most beautiful place in the whole area."

Suddenly there were no more regrets, no more "Should I's?" I had a destination. I was going somewhere rather than avoiding something. It made all the difference in the world.

Unfortunately, there were growing rain clouds between me and my destination. At first they seemed to be on the far side of the pass, presumably moving away, but as I pedaled up the long valley leading to the Continental Divide, another storm closed in from the right. There were no storms behind me in the Tetons, though, so I concluded these were isolated showers that I could easily dodge, especially since I had a 25-mile-an-hour tailwind.

Confident, I stopped for a cola at a small lodge a few miles beyond the park boundary. When I came back outside, the sky was distinctly menacing.

"There's another lodge 8 miles up the road," the proprietor told me.

I nodded. With the tailwind, I could cover that distance in only twenty-five to thirty minutes. It looked as though I had at least that long until the storm would strike. But I forgot to look at the contour lines on the Bikecentennial map. If I had, I would have learned that while the second lodge was only halfway to the pass, it came after the bulk of the climb; the road rose more than 1,300 feet in those 8 miles. Equally bad—and what the map wouldn't have told me—was that there was road construction during the first half of that distance, with two gravel detours that slowed me to a crawl.

The first shower caught me within 3 miles, but it was light, so I pedaled on. The only alternative would have been to turn back. More showers were gathering behind me, and I realized I might soon get very wet. I set my thoughts on the lodge and the joys of getting over the pass, into the rain shadow on the eastern side of the mountains.

The second shower caught me a few minutes later. It began as a gentle rain but grew stronger with each peal of thunder, as though the thunder were the rattle of plumbing as the founts of heaven opened wider.

I was in little danger from lightning—the road followed a shallow valley between tree-covered ridges—but I was soaked and distinctly chilly.

I reached the lodge just as the rain ended. It was still midafternoon, and the restaurant was closed, but the tavern was open so I went inside to warm up. I wanted a cup of hot tea, but dressed in cycling tights in a western bar on the Fourth of July, I didn't have the nerve. Wondering what it would do to my cycling abilities, I ordered a wine cooler—another sissy, urban drink, but I've never liked beer—and sat down among the cowboys.

The bar was dark, lit only by a couple of candles. "It's not that we're weird here," one of the cowboys told me as I peered around the dim interior. "It's just that the storm knocked out the power."

The bartender was struggling to light a small gasoline lantern, encouraged by the kibitzing of his half dozen patrons. Once he got it lighted, though, he wasn't able to coax much more light out of it than the candles already provided, and he was unsure where to put it without scorching his woodwork. Eventually he set it on a table behind the bar, where what little light it cast was useless.

The patrons asked me where I was from and where I was going, and speculated on whether or not the next town down the road, Dubois (which they pronounced Du-boys), was the dullest place in Wyoming or only the second dullest. I asked if the storm was likely to blow over or whether it might linger all night.

"It's supposed to snow tonight," someone said. "Down to the 8,000-foot level."

"What?"

"Yes, this storm system is general—it could be cold and snowy for a couple of days."

"How much snow?"

"Oh, I've seen five or six inches this time of year."

I was aghast. I wasn't equipped for that. I began to wonder how far I could ride before it got dark.

"Which way does the wind blow on the other side of the pass?" I asked.

The bartender pondered. "You'll probably have a tailwind. But we have a story about the wind here in Wyoming. One windy day a tourist asked a rancher, 'Does it blow this way all the time here?' And the rancher replied, 'Well, sometimes it blows this way—and sometimes it blows t'other way!' "

"Yeah," said one of the cowboys. "Usually every direction in Wyoming is upwind. That's why we say that the wind in Wyoming doesn't blow—it sucks!"

I left the bar and tackled the remaining 10 miles to the summit. The sun was shining on the nearby hills, but storms were moving in again both ahead and behind. I was wearing almost my entire wardrobe, but a lot of it was damp, and I shivered as I started out. It was only 5:30 P.M.; it was going to get *cold* before the evening was over.

Even through the cold I could tell that Togwotee was a lovely pass. Spacious meadows lined with pine trees covered the valley bottoms, with 11,000-foot peaks catching occasional rays of sun in the distance. Even the storms added to the beauty, freshening the green of the meadows and casting a blue-black backdrop behind the peaks.

I pressed on, munching a bag of cookies I'd bought at Signal Mountain. I felt a bit giddy, needing to concentrate to steer a straight line. Was it the alcohol, the sugar from the cookies, the 9,600-foot elevation? Or all three?

At the pass I paused briefly to take an I-made-it picture of my bike propped against the sign marking the Continental Divide. Then, with little ceremony, I started down the other side, taking momentary shelter at a cozy lake nestled just beyond the crest to let a rain squall drift clear.

I had only one thought—to get below the predicted snow line of 8,000 feet. With a tailwind and at least two hours of daylight I could cover a lot of ground if necessary. I prayed I wouldn't get a flat—my hands would be too numb to fix it, and I would either have to camp on the spot or hitch a ride to a warmer clime. At least there was enough traffic that I could get help if I needed it.

A mile down the pass I stopped, shivering from the cold wind of my 35 mile-per-hour descent. I needed warmer clothing, but my winter vest was in the bottom of the stuff sack that held my sleeping bag. I unpacked along the roadside, gathering curious stares from passing motorists. They must have wondered if I was planning to camp in the ditch, but nobody stopped to ask if I was okay. This wasn't eastern Oregon; these were out-of-state tourists, hesitant to risk appearing foolish and probably fearful of talking to a stranger. If I got in trouble I might have to be aggressive to get help.

Properly bundled up I resumed the descent, dropping below 9,000 feet and then 8,500, stealing glances at the scenery I could find through gaps in the clouds. Mostly I tried to get lower, regretting what I was missing and further regretting that I couldn't camp at Brooks Lake.

Eight miles from the pass I encountered a national-forest campground and stopped at the entrance road to admire the view toward the Divide. A Jeep wagon pulled out.

"Excuse me," the driver asked, "where's the nearest place I can buy cigarettes?"

I stopped to think. I hadn't seen any signs of civilization since I'd left the tavern 18 miles earlier, but he could probably get cigarettes there.

"That's okay," he said. "I know somewhere closer on this side of the pass. Where are you staying tonight?"

I said I wasn't sure. I was considering trying to get all the way to Dubois, but I hated to miss the scenery. "Are there any other campgrounds down the road?"

"No. This is it." I glanced at the sign, trying to place the name, which was simply "Falls Campground," on my map. I found it near a stream called Brooks Lake Creek. A nearby road followed the creek up to the lake.

"Why don't you stay with me?" the driver continued. "You're welcome. I've got a brand-new tent—a large one. I'd love to have company."

I didn't hesitate. "Sounds wonderful."

"Good." He told me his site number. "My name's Esam. I'll be back in about half an hour. See you then."

———————•◦•———————

The next half hour went quickly. I pedaled cautiously down the bumpy gravel road into the campground, then propped my bike against a tree and strolled along a gorge overlooking the 50-foot waterfall that gave the campground its name. On the trail I talked with two motorcyclists who'd just come over Togwotee Pass.

"Is that your buddy we saw on the other side of the Divide?" one of them asked.

I shook my head. "No, I'm riding alone." I wondered if it was the Yuppie-to-be. I'd assumed he was ahead of me, but maybe I'd been wrong. "Where was he?"

"Oh, about 15 miles the other side of the pass. Just starting up the steep part."

Perhaps he'd gotten a late start from Jackson. In this weather that meant he might have trouble getting over the pass before the next day. It looked as though I wouldn't have company for the next few days after all. Perhaps, I thought, I should make another attempt to catch the hunger riders—they were scheduled to camp in Dubois tonight, and I could be there in an hour or two once it warmed up in the morning.

———————— •••• ————————

The motorcyclists soon continued on their way, and I pedaled slowly through the campground looking for my new friend's site. I was hailed by a middle-aged couple.

"You got a place to camp?" one of them asked. "You can join us here if you'd like." I propped my bike against a tree and walked over to their campfire. "Thanks, but I've already accepted another invitation. I'm just waiting for him to get back from the store."

"Well, warm up here by the fire. It must be cold riding that thing."

"Right now, only my hands. I forgot to bring gloves. My fingers get so stiff it's hard to use the brakes. That'll probably decide when I can head out of here tomorrow. I'll have to wait till it warms up enough so my hands don't freeze."

"Well, that's easy to take care of. I've got an extra pair of gloves. Why don't you just take them with you." He walked over to his trailer and rummaged around for a moment. "Here." He handed me a pair of worn but usable driving gloves. "I'm a truck driver," he added. "I've got lots of these."

I stayed by the fire several minutes, warming my hands and enjoying the hospitality until it was time to meet Esam.

Esam hadn't returned when I found his site, but another camper greeted me. "Come on over by the fire and warm up!" Like the truck driver who'd given me his gloves, he'd brought his family up for the long weekend. "We go into the mountains every weekend in the summer," he said. "But unless it warms up I think we'll go back tomorrow. This is too cold for my wife."

A few minutes later Esam returned, and the three of us huddled around the fire, enjoying the bracing contrast of intense heat and biting cold and watching the flames flicker against the surrounding darkness. A chill breeze stirred the branches of the pines above us and sent drafts through my layers of shirts and jackets.

It took an effort of will to leave the warmth and climb into a cold sleeping bag. Esam's tent was large and roomy, and soon after leaving the fire we were established inside, listening to the rustle of the wind and wondering whether the snow would descend to our elevation.

Esam was Lebanese by birth and spent nine months a year teaching school in Indiana. In summers gone by he'd wandered around the West, driving, camping, and backpacking until the new school year called him back to civilization. Then he opened a Lebanese restaurant, and managing it kept him busy year-round—doubly so during the school year. The stress had been bad for his heart, and after a bypass operation the previous winter he'd taken his doctor's advice and sold the restaurant. For the first time in a decade—perhaps longer—he was again free to wander the West. He'd bought a Jeep, loaded it with camping supplies—more, he admitted, than any one person could ever use—and left for three months. "A friend and I were in this part of Wyoming years ago," he told me, "There's a beautiful lake up there, Brooks Lake, I think it's called. Tomorrow or the next day I'm going up there again. I've got my pack and plenty of gear, so maybe I'll hike in for a few days."

"What about your heart?" I asked. "Can you do that so soon after a bypass operation?"

"My doctor gave me the go-ahead." The darkness was total, but I could hear the grin in his voice. "I'm clear to do anything I want."

"Well, watch the elevation." It was my turn to grin. "But I'm sure you know all that!" There was a long silence. "Where are you going from here?" I asked. I could sense his shrug. "Wherever I get. I'd like to wind up in Alaska."

Esam, I thought, might be fifteen years older than I, but we had a lot in common. Both of us were refugees from the urban rat race. Hopefully it wouldn't take a bypass operation to help me remember why.

The next morning dawned cold, with a light frosting of snow decorating the tent, Esam's Jeep, and my bicycle. Neither of us was in any hurry, so we stayed in the tent until at least nine o'clock before finally venturing outside.

The weather was still unsettled. The storm clouds were no longer continuous, but cold-looking puffs of white cloaked most of the sky and hung above the higher peaks, letting sunshine through only in broken patches. There easily could be more snow before the day was over, but when the sun was out it rapidly warmed up.

As I forged my way across a meadow to an adjacent island of pines—where I hoped to find some much-needed dead wood for a fire—my feet were quickly soaked with melting snow. By the time I returned with my burden, warmth was an urgent necessity, and I was grateful when our neighbor again offered us a place by his fire.

"Boy, was it cold last night," he said, voicing the thought foremost on all our minds. He nodded to the Coleman stove sitting atop his picnic table. "When I went to make breakfast this morning I found out my eggs were frozen solid." He held out a translucent oval. "It was easy to get the shell off—you just peel them. Do you think it'll cook okay?"

Esam and I shrugged. "Only one way to find out. They'll probably come out scrambled, though."

"This is just too cold for my wife and kids," our host continued. I'd already noticed there had been no other signs of activity from his tent trailer. "We're going home when it warms up. We can always come back some other weekend."

"Where's home?"

"Riverton. I'm a school superintendent there."

The trucker who'd given me the gloves was also from Riverton. I began to think the rumors of Wyoming's inhospitality were greatly exaggerated.

Somewhat warmer, Esam and I returned to our site. "Would you like breakfast?" he asked.

"Sure."

"Well, to start with, try some of this." He opened a packet of reddish brown powder. "It's not exactly traditional, but think of it as something like Lebanese breakfast cereal. Try dipping a piece of bread in oil, then in this."

I complied. "Hey, this is good!" It had a strong flavor, unlike anything I'd ever experienced before, but it reminded me of taco spices, without the cumin and with another flavor I couldn't identify. As a seasoning for the bread it worked extremely well.

As we quickly devoured the powder—and most of my bagels—Esam fired up his stove and began heating oil in a large skillet. "Now for the main course. Let's see what I've got." He took an assortment of freezer bags from the back of his truck. "A lot of this is left over from the restaurant. I must have fifty pounds of it." He pulled out a packet. "Have you ever had falafel?"

I shook my head. "No. . . ."

"Well it's not a traditional breakfast, either. But on a morning like this. . . ."

He busied himself at the stove. "And we'll just add some pine nuts. Have you ever had pine nuts? And cheese."

In a few minutes, we had a skillet of red-brown paste that looked a lot like refried beans with cheese melted over the top, and a scattering of pine nuts poking through the surface. To my middle-American eye it didn't look appetizing, but I was too hungry to care, especially since it was my first hot breakfast in a week.

I sampled it and was again surprised. I set to work with vigor, wishing I knew the names of all the ingredients so I could try it again at home. Halfway through my second plate I hesitated. "You know, I'm not sure I can eat all this."

Esam agreed. "Yes, I think we went a bit overboard. Falafel is filling— as are the other ingredients. We don't have to eat it all."

I munched away, relishing the difference in texture between the pine nuts and the paste. "But where do we get rid of the leftovers?" I looked around. "If we bury it or throw it in the fire it'll just draw animals." Manfully, I tried to surmount the remaining portion but couldn't do it. I was amazed. In volume, this meal was only half the size of the stacks of pancakes I'd devoured each morning in Oregon.

"Don't worry," Esam said. "There's got to be somewhere to throw it away. I'll take care of it."

I set down my plate. "Okay. Maybe I should be thinking of packing up. Let me help with the dishes."

Esam waved me off. "No, let me. I'm not going anywhere—at least not for a while."

"Well, can I split the cost of the campsite?"

"No, the company was payment enough. I've got all this stuff," he waved at the Jeep and the tent. "It's nice to have someone to share it with."

———— •• ————

Slightly saddened by yet another parting, I pedaled out the gravel road to the main highway. Within moments my wistfulness passed as I became immersed in the beauty of the high country. The clouds were clearing, the air was warming, and a perfect summer day was descending on the mountains. It was a day of freshly watered meadows and crystalline blue skies— skies that made me want to sing for joy and never descend to the valleys, where blankets of unneeded atmosphere soften the colors and stultify the senses.

Reaching the road, I turned back for a farewell glance at the campground, disappearing from view in the shelter of the woods.

As I watched, another cyclist pulled out behind me, one I didn't recognize. I waited for him to catch up. "You come in last night?" he asked.

"Yes. I came over Togwotee Pass in the storm."

"Me too. I didn't get to the top until 10 P.M., and then I had to ride down here. I almost froze to death. When I got to the campground it was full, but someone let me share his site."

This was the rider I'd heard about the night before. I wondered how he'd managed to stay on the road after dark, in a storm.

"Where are you going?" I asked.

"East. What about you?"

"The same. Want to ride together? I'm thinking about taking the Bike-centennial route at least to Colorado, perhaps all the way to Virginia."

"I don't want to go that far south," he said. "I'm going to Riverton to-night, then straight east to the Missouri. There's a ride in Iowa I want to catch."

"RAGBRAI?" RAGBRAI—short for *The Register*'s Annual Great Bicycle Ride Across Iowa—is a 7,500-rider week-long tour that travels from the Missouri to the Mississippi. It's sponsored by the Des Moines newspaper, and traditionally is held the last week of July.

He nodded. "Right."

"But that must not start for a couple weeks. The way the winds blow once you turn east, you'll be there in a week."

"It starts July 20th, and I want some leeway. If I'm a few days early I have friends I can visit."

It suddenly struck me that if I followed his route, I'd be on the Great Plains in less than three days. The prospect of company was appealing, but I wasn't sure I wanted to leave the mountains so soon, especially just to race for Iowa. It would be fun to ride together for the day, though, so I voiced a thought that had been on my mind ever since the sun had come out. "There's a side road that leads to what's supposed to be a nice lake. Want to go up there? We've got lots of time, and it's downhill most of the way to Riverton. Or we could always stay in Dubois."

"How far's the lake?"

I'd asked Esam that same question earlier. "Six miles of gravel."

"Gravel? No way. Besides, I don't want to be late for RAGBRAI."

I'd also been trying to decide whether I really wanted to tackle that much gravel, but his response tipped the scales. I didn't want to be infected with his version of white-line fever. "Maybe I'll see you tonight," I said, "if I head that way." If I did, though, I'd be more likely to team up with the hunger riders, who were following the same route at a more sedate pace. Soon I'd have to choose between company and Colorado.

I quickly found the road to Brooks Lake—it was well marked and nicely graded, and didn't appear particularly difficult to negotiate by bicycle. But after a half mile or so it began to climb steadily, and I realized it was heading for a broad bowl at about the same elevation as Togwotee Pass. It would take at least an hour—probably more—to climb up there on gravel. Coming down would also be tricky. It was time to reconsider.

I remembered the lessons I'd learned in Lava Beds and John Day; the times when I'd had the most fun were the days I'd made the least progress toward the East Coast. I reminded myself that my primary interest was the trip itself, that the ultimate destination was secondary.

A moment later I realized there was another way to get to the top. A steady succession of campsites was scattered along the road, and several pickup trucks had already passed me, carrying fishermen and campers toward the lake. When the next truck rumbled up behind me, I hopped off my bicycle and stuck out my thumb. This was merely a sightseeing excursion, and my cross-country trip would be complete even if I didn't pedal all the way to the top. If I got lucky I might even be able to hitch another ride down.

The truck pulled to a stop and someone leaned out the passenger-side window.

"Could I have a lift to the lake?" I asked.

"We're only going another half mile or so," was the reply, "but you're welcome to come that far."

"Thanks," I said and heaved my bicycle over the tailgate—no easy task when it and my gear weighed more than eighty pounds. I climbed in, the engine rumbled, and we jounced away.

I remember little of that trip except the bed of the pickup truck. On one side I caught glimpses of gray cliffs beyond open pine woods, while to the other I had an impression of a valley unfolding below. For the most part my attention focused on keeping my bicycle in one piece as we bounced along. The road might be well graded, but it was a lot bumpier at 30 miles an hour than it had been at 5. And the trip seemed to last far too long.

After at least eight to ten minutes we slowed to a halt. "This is it," said the driver as he stepped out to give me a hand with my bike.

"That was a lot farther than half a mile!"

"Yeah. We missed our turn, so I figured we might as well take you all the way."

It was typical of what I was coming to expect of Wyoming—contrary to its reputation.

Brooks Lake was everything I'd been told it would be and more. Its south shore is occupied by a large national-forest campground, but the sites are spacious and well engineered, and it was not obvious that this setting served as weekend home to at least a hundred people. The lake itself is an azure gem. About a mile in diameter, it sparkled in the midday sun—cold, blue and aloof, as mountain lakes are meant to be. Charmed by its tranquil beauty, I walked onto a spit of land jutting into the water.

To the east and west the lake was flanked by odd cliffs of a crumbly-looking material known as breccia, cliffs that showed deep horizontal bedding planes and fractures that made them look like giant piles of masonry decorated with patches of snow.

Some cliffs are awe-inspiring to gaze upon, but these were not, even though the Continental Divide runs along their western crest. They sit well back from the lake, and while they are probably 1,000 feet high, their flat, spacious summits are easily accessible via meadows that slope like gentle ramps into a broad valley feeding the lake's northern end. The breccia discourages climbing, leaving the cliffs to stand guard like ancient, sleepy sentinels, shutting out all traces of the outside world, making the lake seem remote and timeless.

I could understand why Esam remembered this place so well. There could be no better gateway to the wilderness than this quiet lake, with its weathered cliffs and inviting thoroughfares into an imagined hinterland. It would be easy to shoulder a pack and disappear for a week, heading north or east into the Absarokas or northwest toward the headwaters of the Yellowstone River, deep into the heart of one of America's largest remaining wildernesses.

As I wandered the lakeshore, wishing I could stay but knowing that at a minimum I needed to get to Dubois in time to buy food for the evening, I met a group of hikers preparing for just such an expedition. They were a youth group modeled on Outward Bound, two dozen teenagers and a half dozen counselors, organizing packs for a week in the wilderness. They were celebrating their departure with a watermelon feast, and one of the counselors waved me to join in.

"We can't take it with us," she said as we stood talking and spitting seeds. "Have as much as you like." Between that and Esam's breakfast, I wouldn't need to eat again until dinner.

I asked about the road leaving the lake. According to my map I had two choices: I could return the way I'd come, or I could take a crude, four-wheel-drive track that cut across the hillsides back to Togwotee Pass. Most cyclists would probably have elected to return on the graded gravel of the main road—especially since the counselor informed me the other road had been badly rutted. But, like my acquaintance that morning, most cyclists would never have come to Brooks Lake in the first place. I elected to take the high road back to the pass. Within 200 hundred yards I knew I'd made the right choice. The road surface was well packed and already dry, so it actually presented easier riding than the gravel. It did have foot-deep ruts in places, but I could keep away from them as long as I didn't get too immersed in the scenery.

And what scenery it was. The road climbed quickly from the lake, rounded the shoulder of a mountain, and burst out of the woods to traverse a steeply sloping meadow. Behind me, towering over the pine forests that girded their flanks, rose the breccia cliffs. To my left the view swept across flower-strewn meadows and scattered clumps of pine to the forested valley below the previous night's campground. Beyond that stretched the upper reaches of the Wind River Valley—a natural highway I would soon descend—4,000 feet in 70 miles. And in the distance, flanking the valley and forming a backdrop that would remain in sight for the next 150 miles, gleamed the snow-clad heights of the Wind River Range—the highest and most remote mountains in Wyoming.

My road was so narrow it barely seemed to exist. It slid unobtrusively across the hillside, with small cuts where its uphill side occasionally dug into the shoulder of the mountain, blanketed in large patches of purple lupine. Twice, pickup trucks inched up behind me, patiently waiting until I'd found a place wide enough to get out of the way, but other than that I had it to myself—6 miles of mountain splendor that eventually deposited me near the small lake where I'd sheltered from the rain squall the night before.

Since I was within a few hundred yards of Togwotee Pass, I climbed back to the top to see what I'd missed, emerging into another landscape of pine-dotted meadows and rounded peaks. Like the terrain around Brooks Lake, this too is a landscape that invites hiking, beckoning me to strike out toward the approaches to the Wind River Range 20 miles to the south, a wild land of glacier and granite, where Wyoming's highest peak rises 13,800 feet above sea level and enough snow falls to form the largest ice field this side of Canada.

But this wasn't a hiking trip, and it was already 3 P.M., so I didn't linger. I'd given up catching the Bike Aid group—a worthwhile trade for my side trip to Brooks Lake—but I was getting hungry, and the nearest food was still 31 miles away.

For the second time I dropped away from Togwotee Pass, stopping briefly to say farewell to my tiny lake, and then began the long descent to Dubois.

I made good time, stopping occasionally for pictures but mostly just coasting, letting my heart sing to the music of tires on pavement, the sweet taste of warm mountain air, and the rare combination of a long downgrade and a freshening tailwind. Within an hour I was most of the way to Dubois, thoroughly relaxed, unconcerned about the fact that I would probably not go any farther that evening. It had been a marvelous day—literally and figuratively one of the high points of the trip.

Then, without warning, everything changed. I was midway down a short, steeper-than-average hill, cruising at an effortless 35 miles an hour, when I saw a cowboy leading a horse toward the fence ahead of me. *Keep that horse back from the road!*—I wanted to shout, remembering a previous bike trip when my sudden apparition, flapping in the wind, had spooked a horse into bolting frantically. But shouting itself could spook a horse, so I braked slightly and veered to the left, trying to give it as wide a berth as possible. The cowboy looked directly at me and kept walking toward the road. Then, in one quick motion, he cocked his arm and hurled a potato-size rock at me. "Another m__f__ing bicyclist!" a detached part of me heard him exclaim. "Think you own. . . ." But I wasn't paying much attention to his words. I started to brake hard, then changed my mind and swerved sharply, heedless of whatever traffic might have been behind me. The cowboy had underestimated my speed, and the stone passed harmlessly.

I looked back and saw him shaking his fist at me. *What did I do to you?* I wanted to go back and ask. *I was just minding my own business.* Instead, I twisted around to face the driver of a car that had been following me. "Did you see what he did?" I shouted. "Did you see?" But the driver merely gazed at me, expressionless, as I moved out of the way to let him pass. He'd probably missed the whole episode and wondered why I'd been swerving all over the road.

A mile later I pulled to the side and stopped. I was still shaking. Whether the cowboy had realized it or not, he could have killed me. Not only could I have crashed and been run over by a car, but being hit by a large rock at a relative speed of 50 to 60 miles an hour would have been no joke, even though I was wearing a helmet. And from the look of hatred on his face I had a feeling that, at least at the moment, he wouldn't have cared.

What did I do to you? I thought again. Ranchers and farmers were the last people from whom I expected such a response. They had always been friendly—people who relish the wind and the sun, who realize that life from the road shoulder can be more meaningful than life in the fast lane. But the most dangerous physical assault I'd ever received in my bicycling career had just come from a ranchhand. It was as though the order of the universe had been turned upside down.

Pulling onto the road, I memorized the landmarks so that once I reached town I could tell the police where the assault had occurred.

———————•●•———————

I encountered the police earlier than expected, when a deputy sheriff drove up behind me. Before I had time to think about flagging him down, his bullhorn crackled to life so loudly it nearly startled me into the ditch. "RIDE ON THE SHOULDER, NOT IN THE TRAFFIC LANE," came his impersonal voice. Without a second glance in my direction, he hit the gas and sped by.

I complied with his directive until he was out of sight, then pulled back onto the main portion of the road. Normally he would have been right— the road had a full-width shoulder—but it was strewn with rocks and other debris, and traffic was light enough that most of the time it was safer to be in the traffic lane.

I began to doubt the wisdom of reporting my assailant to the police. I wondered if they'd take it seriously, anyway. If the deputy I'd just encountered represented the local attitude toward bicycles, I'd probably be wasting time.

———————•●•———————

When I reached Dubois I became even more convinced the matter was best left alone. Dubois seems to hate cyclists. I felt it the moment I started looking for dinner. The downtown cafe was closed for the evening, and all I could find was a bar that also claimed to serve meals. The place looked a bit rough, and I was reluctant to go inside, so I turned to a teenage boy sitting on the front steps.

"Where can I find some dinner?"

He glanced up incuriously, but his bland expression turned surly as he saw my bicycling attire.

"Dunno. Maybe up the street." He waved vaguely, back the way I'd come, then looked away again, dismissing me.

I pedaled slowly back the way he'd pointed, looking for food, but couldn't find anything. I stopped a tourist on the sidewalk and asked for suggestions. She smiled—a marked contrast to the teenager's reaction—but could offer no help. I thought about asking another of the local residents, but no one looked friendly.

I sighed. There was a convenience store nearby; it would stock enough junk food to carry me through the evening. I'd wanted to relax over a hot meal and give my shaken nerves time to recover, but obviously that was not to be. I went inside and collected an armload of pastries, candy, and potato chips, depositing them on the counter beside the cash register. The clerk rang up the purchase sullenly, seldom letting her gaze stray beyond the counter and the cash register. I had the feeling she would have preferred not to sell me anything at all. She obviously didn't want to talk, but I questioned her anyway. "Is there a place where I can fill my water bottles?"

"Not in here." She still refused to meet my gaze.

"Anywhere nearby?"

"Maybe around the corner. In the laundromat." She waved vaguely to an adjoining building. "They've got water."

I wondered if this was a small taste of what it's like to be a racial minority, but while filling my bottles I realized that, unlike a minority member, I could simply ride away from this societal stigma. The idea was foolhardy, since it was already five o'clock and there were no other significant towns within 75 miles. Since most of that distance was across the Wind River Indian Reservation, where camping wouldn't be allowed, I would be committing myself to covering the entire distance.

Whether I went to Riverton or Lander, it was downhill most of the way, and that marvelous tailwind blew unabated. If I averaged 15 miles an hour, there would be barely enough daylight. It was worth the attempt.

Of one thing I was sure: I wanted *out* of Dubois. In fact, I wanted out of the entire state of Wyoming; for the moment all other goals were secondary. If I stayed on the Bikecentennial route and pushed hard I could be in Lander that night, Rawlins the next day, and Colorado the next. Or I could abandon the route and camp in Riverton, off the beaten path, where people might be friendlier.

I decided to postpone that decision for 45 miles until the two routes diverged. For the moment, I made sure all my water bottles were full, including a two-liter pop bottle I'd been carrying since Northern California. That gave me a little over a gallon of water. Shortly after 5 P.M. I hit the road, planning more mileage before dark than I usually did in a full day.

I was pedaling into the Wind River Valley, a scenic mixture of sweeping mountain panoramas, red-rock badlands, and intimate glimpses of rushing water, but I was in no mood to enjoy the view. I had too far to go to stop for more than an occasional picture, and I was too nervous to appreciate the beauty of the rapidly changing scenery. Every time I heard a car behind me I tensed and stared in my rear-view mirror, wondering if the driver would share the sentiments of the cowboy who'd thrown the stone. I began to hope the traffic would consist mostly of tourists, and I preferred the approach of an RV to a pickup truck.

About 15 miles out of town, just before I reached the edge of the Indian reservation, the deputy sheriff who'd scolded me earlier appeared behind me. As before, I was coming down a hill, riding on the road itself, and again his highly amplified voice was the first thing I heard.

"BICYCLISTS SHOULD RIDE ON THE SHOULDER OF THE ROAD."

It is a fundamental axiom of bicycle travel never to argue with the local constabulary. You may know bicycling law better than they do, but it does not pay to antagonize them—especially on a Saturday, when the courts won't be open the next day.

But I'd had too much for one day, and something snapped. "It's full of rocks!" I yelled, pointing.

The deputy couldn't possibly have heard me, but he'd seen my gesture, and as he braked I berated myself. There was nothing to do but see it through, so I stopped beside him—carefully staying on the shoulder now that it was too late—and repeated my previous comment.

"It's full of rocks," I explained. "On a hill like that, I *can't* ride on the shoulder. The rocks probably don't look like much from a car, but if I hit one at 30 miles an hour I'll crash. I've also got to worry about crosswinds. When you saw me I was coming out of a road cut." I waved at it, behind me. "I've got to have room to wobble if I catch a gust."

He listened quietly, but when he spoke, it was clear he still didn't understand. "Which would you rather do," he asked, "skin yourself up occasionally or get run over by a car?"

I tried again. "At that speed, a crash would do more than skin me up. It might kill me—or at least break bones."

He almost shrugged. "With all you bicyclists coming through here, and all this traffic, it's a miracle no one's ever been hit."

I decided it wasn't a good idea to tell him I had no real worries about the traffic. There was very little of it, and what there was had been extremely courteous. Instead, I tried a different tack. "Look, I've got a rear-view mirror. I *know* what's going on behind me. That's why I didn't pull out of your way—I could see you were going to give me a lot of room." I didn't say that I hadn't realized he was a policeman until too late. "If you'd been coming too close, *then* I'd have risked the shoulder."

He seemed to be listening. He didn't say it, but his manner seemed to ask, *you can see all that?*

I pressed harder. "When I hear a car I spend almost as much time looking behind as I do looking ahead. I can tell within a foot how much room someone's going to give me. I'm less likely to get hit by a car than I am to crash from forgetting to watch where I'm going."

I had him now. For the next several minutes I explained the bicyclist's point of view—why some of the things we do, even aggressively riding far out into the lane on narrow roads, are actually safety precautions. "It's to keep drivers from trying to squeeze by without crossing the centerline," I said.

Eventually I changed the subject, asking the question that had been topmost on my mind ever since Dubois. "Why is it that people around here hate bicyclists?"

I expected him to dispute the use of the word "hate," but he accepted it without question. "Because they go through in large groups," he said, "blocking traffic and riding three-abreast up and down the passes."

I nodded. I'd seen such behavior far too many times on club rides. "We don't all do that," I noted, "especially when there's only a few of us." But in large groups many cyclists hog the road, abusing the safety that comes with numbers and arrogantly refusing to get out of anybody's way. I could understand why people were angry, and I thought of the Wandering Wheels, who'd probably passed this way a few days before. Even if they'd behaved courteously a group that size would present a major traffic obstacle. I wondered if I'd been suffering fallout from their passage.

I continued on my way, somewhat mollified but still determined to leave Dubois as far behind as possible. An hour later the deputy returned from the opposite direction, and as he passed, he honked, smiled, and waved. Maybe I'd made a convert.

———— •◉• ————

I had reached the Wind River Reservation, home of the Shoshone and Arapahoe Indians.

The Shoshones were famous for their enduring friendship with early whites. Sacagawea—the Indian woman who as a teenager, from 1804 to

1805, served as guide and interpreter for the Lewis and Clark expedition—had been a Shoshone; when the party returned east she'd left the expedition to live with the Wind River tribe, the people whose descendents live on the reservation. According to the map she was buried nearby.

Washakie—commonly mentioned with the phrase "The Great Chief" appended to his name—is another famous Shoshone born in Wyoming in about the same year that Sacagawea joined Lewis and Clark. Chief Washakie was well known for his friendship with whites, even helping early pioneers ford streams and track stray cattle.

But Washakie's efforts to maintain peace with whites went deeper than simply befriending travelers. In 1865, when the Crows, Cheyennes, and Sioux banded together to wipe out the invaders, he volunteered to help the U.S. Army, a decision that cost him the life of his son when the enraged Sioux raided his camp.

Three years later the government pressured Washakie's people to move onto the reservation from their ancestral lands a few miles to the south, where they were in the path of the transcontinental railroad.

In ensuing years Washakie's friendship was not kindly rewarded. In 1878, despite Shoshone objections, the army deposited 938 starving Arapahoes onto the reservation, indifferent to the fact that the two tribes were traditional enemies. Chief Washakie agreed to let the Arapahoes stay for the winter, but they became a permanent fixture. Years later the Shoshones successfully sued the federal government for, in effect, giving part of their reservation to the Arapahoes. They won $4,400,000—an astronomical award in 1938.

A dozen miles before I reached the turnoff for Riverton I passed 1,000-foot Crowheart Butte. Its name comes from a near-legendary story about Chief Washakie that says a good deal about his character.

In 1866 Chief Washakie's Shoshones found themselves in conflict with the Crows, led by Chief Big Robber. At stake was control over the hunting grounds of the region, but Chief Washakie saw no reason to continue the bloodshed of a full-scale war. He persuaded his adversary to meet him in single battle, resolving that the winner would eat his opponent's heart. The two chiefs met atop the butte and, as its name indicates, Washakie triumphed. Years later, well into his 90s, he was asked if he had truly eaten his adversary's heart. His reply was doubly interesting since he was probably in his early sixties at the time of the battle: "Youth does foolish things."

———————•❀•———————

Twilight caught me still on the reservation, about 15 miles from Lander. An hour earlier I'd decided to remain on the Bikecentennial Trail and mentally waved good-bye to the unseen hunger riders as I passed the turnoff for Riverton. I was still determined to get out of Wyoming as quickly as possible, and as I struggled up a long hill, my imagination populated the surrounding countryside with hostile eyes, watching from behind sage-covered hummocks or waiting at the end of the next road cut. My fear was irrational, especially since I felt no threat from the people of the reservation, but it added power to my pedal strokes, and within minutes I crested the hill and set off across the series of long undulations that lay between me and Lander.

For the first few miles I strained my eyes against the gathering night and forged ahead, riding the wide, smooth shoulder—now less cluttered with debris—and grateful for the thin traffic. But passing the village of Fort Washakie I encountered a steady flow of traffic from Lander, and the constant succession of headlights ruined my night vision. It became increasingly difficult to see where I was going, and eventually it was impossible to dodge the occasional stones or pieces of trash blocking my path.

A flat tire would be difficult to fix after dark, and even at slow speed a large rock could make me crash. It was only a few miles to Lander, and according to the Bikecentennial map there was a campground on the near side of town. I dismounted and began to walk. As long as there was a shoulder I could walk all night, if necessary. I'd be in town long before that.

The campground was less than a mile away, and I rolled in quietly, a little after 10 P.M. A few minutes later I had a site, and shortly after that I was lying in my tent, physically relaxed by a hot shower, too emotionally drained to even think about recording the day's events in my journal. Other than the deputy and the brief encounter necessary to register as a camper, I'd met no one, talked to no one, since I'd left Dubois. I fell asleep that night staring at the map, planning how to get out of Wyoming in two days. I still had at least 260 miles to go, with two Continental Divide crossings, but the contour lines on the Bikecentennial map indicated that neither pass would be difficult. I'd done 112 miles that day. On the next I'd try for 130.

———————•◦•———————

The next day, however, proved to be a day of delays. The safe, comfortable atmosphere of the campground left me in no hurry to get on the road, and I suddenly realized it had been more than two weeks since I'd done laundry. But even as I pulled dirty T-shirts out of my panniers, I noticed that the morning breeze was out of the northwest—a tailwind. *Maybe*—I thought—*maybe I can make it even with a late start.*

As I sorted my clothes I noticed that my woolen tights—which I'd needed at some point almost every day since Oregon—were beginning to split a seam. They'd never survive the washer and probably wouldn't tolerate many more wearings.

"Is there a place in Lander where I could get these mended?" I asked the campground proprietor, who was working nearby.

"Not on Sunday. But if you take them up to the office, maybe my wife would do it for you." He smiled. "Just don't tell her I sent you."

I thanked him and went to find her, wondering how I would broach the subject. I decided on an indirect approach, letting her bow out gracefully if she wanted. "Do you know where I can get these mended?" I asked, just as I'd asked her husband.

Her response was the same. "Not today. But maybe I can do it." She held out her hand. "Let me take a look." I handed them over, trying to figure out how to express my gratitude. I couldn't act surprised—after all, this was the offer I'd been hoping for. "Sure," she said, interrupting my thoughts. "I can fix that in a few minutes."

A few minutes was closer to an hour, and I had a feeling that with the heavy fabric the job wasn't quite as simple as she'd thought it would be. By the time she was done I'd finished my laundry, packed most of my gear, and replaced a worn tire with one of the spares I'd bought in Jackson.

"Here," she said, as she handed back the tights. "That should do. There were two layers of fabric, and it was a little hard to get at, but I think it'll hold."

The result was a thoroughly professional job, probably stronger than the original seam. I wasn't surprised when she shrugged off payment—this was the type of hospitality I'd found that cold night in the mountains—only thirty-six hours before—and it was the first indication that I'd returned to a region where bicyclists were not *personae non grata*.

———————•◦•———————

While waiting for the tights, I asked her husband about road conditions between Lander and Rawlins. "You've got a big climb coming out of Lander," he said. "Right up the Beaver Rim."

I looked at the Bikecentennial map. "Where? I don't see it." He ignored the map and pointed to a bluff blocking the southern horizon.

"See that. That's it. The road goes right to the top. It's a tough climb."

I looked at the map again. From the contour lines I could easily find the bluff, but the top seemed only about 500 feet above Lander. How hard could that be? I started to say as much, but then I looked back at it, distant, but sharply real in the morning light. It definitely looked higher than 500 feet. I studied the map again and realized I might have miscounted the contour lines at the break between two map segments. The bluff could easily be 1,500 feet rather than 500. If so, I'd never make Rawlins by nightfall, nor would I get to Colorado the next day. Maybe the extra time in Wyoming wouldn't be so bad.

As I packed I began thinking it might be nice to join the people of Lander for an early church service, but with all the delays it was 11:00 A.M. by the time I left camp and nearly 11:30 when I reached town. Since it was too late for church, I opted for an all-you-can-eat buffet. While looking for a restaurant, I met a pair of cyclists headed the other direction.

They were riding across the country and, having spent the last two nights at a hostel in Lander, were headed for Dubois.

I warned them about my run-in with the rancher, then asked the question that had been on my mind, off and on, for days. "Is there anyone ahead going my direction?" The Bike Aid group and my acquaintance from yesterday morning had both branched off for Riverton, as had the Wandering Wheels. Here on the Bikecentennial Trail, though, there was still hope I'd find other cyclists.

"Yeah," was the reply. "Two women, both riding alone. One's probably uncatchable—she's doing about 95 miles a day. The other was leaving town just as we rode in, two days ago. You might catch her in a week or so."

"Nobody else?"

"Nope, they're the only ones we've seen for a week."

And the "catchable" one had a two-day lead. It looked like the next few days were going to be lonely.

After lunch I pedaled out of town toward South Pass, the historic low point on the Continental Divide once crossed by the Oregon Trail and the Pony Express and now relegated to a little-used state highway—bypassed by the interstate in favor of a shorter but steeper route to the south. It seemed as though even the prairies and mountains were saddened that nature's own highway had been superseded, and the sage-brush hills and brick-red arroyos seemed to whisper with the echo of hooves and flapping canvas.

But soon I'd forgotten the Oregon Trail, for my route turned away from South Pass and began the long climb toward the Beaver Rim. Pushed along by the third tailwind in as many days, I pedaled easily for the first few miles, then paused to gaze back at the snow-clad summits of the Wind River Range, crystal-clear through 35 miles of intervening atmosphere. As I unpacked my camera for a photo, a car coming from the opposite direction stopped as well.

The driver, a trim man in his middle forties, climbed out while his wife waited patiently inside. "Looks like you've got a good one there," he said as he opened his own camera case.

I nodded. "Fabulous country, isn't it."

"Yeah. We're supposedly heading for the Tetons tonight, but it's so pretty, I don't think we're going to make it. Are you cycling all the way across the country?"

"If I don't run out of time."

"I admire people like you," he said. "You've really got the spirit of the pioneers." Then he waved and climbed back in his car.

———————•◦•———————

A few miles later the road began to climb in earnest, traversing the steep, sage-covered bluff I'd seen from the distance. Near the bottom I spotted a family attending to a broken-down car. I know nothing about automobiles, but I felt moved to return the generosity I'd received that morning. "Anything I can do for you?" I called as I drew near.

"No," the man began, then changed his mind. "Yeah. I've got friends in Lander. Would you call them . . ." he scribbled a number on a piece of paper, "and tell them I'm broke down out here? Just tell them . . ." he added his own name to the paper, "tell them I need a fuel pump." He fished out a handful of quarters. "For the phone." I started to wave away the money, then realized I might need the change. I looked for the nearest town on my map. "I'm not likely to see a phone till I get to Sweetwater Station," I said, "which I think is about 12 miles away. I've got to climb that hill first," I pointed to the Beaver Rim, "so it'll take at least an hour, maybe longer."

It took considerably longer, and it was nearly four o'clock when I finally stopped in front of the general store/cafe that was the only noteworthy structure in Sweetwater Station. I phoned Lander immediately and was glad to learn that the stranded driver had also given his message to a passing motorist and that his friend was on the way. Just as I was getting ready to move on, another cyclist walked into the store.

"Hi," she said. "You camping here, too?"

I shook my head, calculating how far I might still be able to go before dark. "No, I'm trying to get to Lamont. With that wind behind me, I think I can make it." Lamont was about halfway to Rawlins.

"There's not much there," she said. "My husband and I came that way this morning. This place is the nicest thing between here and Rawlins. There's a campground around back."

I hesitated, my resolve fading. Company for an evening would be nice, but so far I'd covered only 47 miles. At that rate I wouldn't get to Colorado for four more days.

"It's up to you, but if you want to stay, I just bought a big package of hamburger for dinner. We can't eat it all, and we certainly can't take it with us. You're welcome to join us."

That made my decision. I had no reason to hurry, unless my goal was to catch one of the mysterious women ahead of me. Since I already had company, that seemed silly; if I wasn't careful I could waste the rest of the trip chasing other riders.

My new acquaintance had finished her shopping and was leaving. "We're camped in back," she said. "You can't miss it. Look for the tandem."

I followed a few minutes later, walking my bicycle to the campground office behind the general store. "Special," read a sign:

WORMS $2.00/doz.
BIKER $3.25

I chuckled. So long as I wasn't going to be fed to the fish, this was my kind of place—more of what I'd found everywhere but Dubois.

I set up camp near the tandem. To the north the view swept away across lush rangelands, up the gentle hillside that was all there was to this side of the Beaver Rim. Behind me rose a range of low mountains, their slopes a mottling of pines and meadows, while nearby a pasture held a small group of horses. The campground itself was a lush meadow of soft grass, cut by a single road and sprinkled with picnic shelters, home to only a half dozen or so other campers. Settling down with a book, I knew I'd made the right choice.

Our communal dinner was a leisurely affair to which I added cheese and cauliflower in exchange for Sloppy Joe's and companionship. My new friends were Mark and Mary Lou, from Boulder, Colorado. They were riding to the Willamette Valley in Oregon, where Mark would soon start a job as a mathematics professor. This trip would combine vacation with house-hunting.

Their tandem was a miracle of packing organization and customized gadgetry. "We try to go out for a month every summer," Mark explained, "and each year we add something new. This year it was the folding chairs." He nodded toward a pair of small lawn chairs set up in front of their tent. "They weigh surprisingly little, and we can pack them so there's no wind drag."

Eventually I asked if they'd seen anyone heading in my direction. "Only one," Mary Lou said. "A woman. But she must be three days ahead of you."

"Yeah," said Mark, "She was really moving. I doubt you can catch her."

So much for that idea. It looked as though I'd be going it alone all the way to Iowa.

Dinner was punctuated by the unmistakable whine of mosquitoes and the frequent sting of their bites. It was the worst mosquito attack I'd encountered in years, and I was amazed to find them in the dry rangeland of southern Wyoming. Eventually they became so thick that casual conversation was impossible, and there was no recourse but to zip ourselves into the safety of our tents, abandoning the evening to the bugs.

------·•·------

Several hours later I was awakened by the sound of running hooves in the pasture next to the campground. The horses had been active all night, but the pattern of their hoofbeats had become louder, faster, more urgent.

Braving the mosquitoes I unzipped my tent and peered outside. The air was cool and damp, with the aura of thunderstorm. Off to the northwest, low on the horizon, was the telltale flicker of lightning.

At first I thought it was miles away in the Wind River Mountains, but it soon became apparent it was much nearer than that and drawing closer by the moment.

I stuffed all my loose gear into a waterproof bag, checked my tent stakes, then ran to the bathroom so I wouldn't have to worry about outlasting the storm. By the time I returned the wind was gusting and the first drops were pelting the tent fly.

I've always enjoyed a good thunderstorm. Many times during my youth in the Midwest I would wake up, step outside to a spring morning already unseasonably warm, and announce that it "smelled" like tornadoes. Later in the day I would stand in awe as the sky turned green and the rain slanted nearly horizontally, as chain lightning ran in circles over my head or the wind peeled full-size sheets of plywood from a stack, scattering them like so many playing cards.

Storms remind us how small and frail we are. The accomplishments of

modern technology are rendered meaningless by nature unleashed. All
that remains is a sense of primitive awe as the powers of the universe pour
forth, while we snuggle deep within our little caves.

But a wild storm isn't enjoyable in a tent. The awe quickly turns to
terror, the frailty is all too real, and the spectacle becomes an ordeal to the
spread-eagled camper trying to keep the tent stakes in the ground and the
tent from collapsing in a tangle of flapping nylon. Prayer comes easily beneath the double threats of lightning and—if there are trees nearby—falling branches. Even under the best of circumstances bicyclists live close to
Providence, but seldom is the desire for protection more overwhelmingly
real than in the midst of a storm.

When it is all over, and nature's fury abates, all too often another thing
becomes clear. Thunderstorms are wet. The storm in Sweetwater Station
was small as thunderstorms go, but it thoroughly drenched me. My tent
had given out. Facing its first real test, it had failed miserably. The floor
had leaked, soaking my sleeping bag from beneath, and water was also
reaching me from above, through the fly. If it had been colder—or if I
hadn't had woolen clothes—I would have been miserable. As it was, I was
merely uncomfortable. Long before the morning sun had dried the tent I
was ready to pack up and move on.

———————•◦•———————

I said good-bye to Mark and Mary Lou and bicycled 18 miles to Jeffrey
City before breakfast.

According to the map, Jeffrey City is a town of one thousand people—
perhaps not deserving the title "city," but definitely the largest community
between Lander and Rawlins. Ben had remembered it from his cross-
country trip, describing it as the dullest place in Wyoming, a uranium-
mining boomtown where the only thing to do is watch ore trucks shuttle
back and forth into the mill. Not all that many years earlier it would have
been worse; before the mill opened in 1957 there had been no town at all,
only an isolated post office called "Home on the Range."

Jeffrey City is also a place where Ben could have gotten in trouble. "I
stopped on the edge of town," he'd told me, "to buy a pair of sunglasses.
The store owner asked me a few questions about bicycling, then added,
'By the way, I'd change that shirt before you go into town.' "

Ben, who after a few weeks on the road had been choosing his wardrobe based only on cleanliness and the relative importance of bright, visible colors, had to look down to see what he was wearing. "No Nukes," it
proclaimed. He took the owner's advice.

But when Ben had been there the town had at least been alive. When I passed through, only a single subdivision showed any signs of prosperity, and even it was a sad reminder of grand dreams reduced to a cluster of ranch-style homes, all stamped from the same cookie-cutter molds and huddled together against the wind and cold, flanking the swirling subdivision roads with well-manicured lawns and brave, colorful facades.

Those colors were the only cheerful things in Jeffrey City. The rest was rapidly becoming a ghost town, with overgrown yards and grass sprouting through breaks in the pavement. A scattering of cars indicated that a few people remained, most likely those too poor or stubborn to move when the town died.

The wind whipped through deserted streets, scattering pebbles and rattling the aluminum siding of the school buildings. Jeffrey City must have sprouted overnight from nothing, and now its acres of trailer parks and prefab homes seemed to have died equally quickly. The culprit, of course, was the uranium mill.

"WESTERN NUCLEAR, INC. – WYOMING'S FIRST URANIUM MILL," proclaimed a once-proud sign in the center of town. Some wag had spray-painted the word "NO" in front of the word "URANIUM" – probably the same comedian who had defaced the "population 1000" sign outside town, changing the number to "3." As I sat in the Split Rock Cafe eating breakfast, I could count a few more people than that, but not many. The whole populace could probably fit in the spacious cafe or in the lobby of the modern post office, monuments to a town that was gone, left to the ranchers who'd been here before the mill opened and who remained after it closed.

———————————————

Outside Jeffrey City the wind freshened behind me, and soon I was humming along at 25 to 30 miles an hour, my spirits lifting by the moment as the ghost town fell farther and farther behind. Ever since Sweetwater Station I'd been following the Sweetwater River, route of the Oregon Trail and the Pony Express, a region where Buffalo Bill once rode 325 miles on a single shift. I tried to imagine how this country must have looked to the 350,000 people who crossed it, heading for Oregon and northern California. Was it just a wasteland lying between them and the promised land of the West, or did they appreciate its subtle beauty? I knew one thing – their evenings, too, were plagued by mosquitoes. According to the campground owner in Sweetwater Station, the pioneer's journals made frequent reference to the bugs. Their only defenses, she said, were to smear themselves with axle grease, make smoky fires, and do a little dance similar to what some of my Midwestern friends have called the "Minnesota Wave."

Mosquitoes, I'd been told, were not the only threat to my sanity on this stretch of the Bikecentennial Trail. Several of the west-bound cyclists I'd met had warned of boredom. "There's nothing," they'd told me, "all the way from Lander to Rawlins."

But they were wrong. The Sweetwater River—which according to legend acquired its name due to an ill-timed stumble by a mule carrying one explorer's sugar supply—followed a wide, grassy valley flanked by mountains. The mountains to the south were unimpressive, though fairly tall, rising in a gentle swell to form the backbone of the Continental Divide. Those on the north were lower but consisted of a dramatic series of granite outcroppings—collectively known as Rattlesnake Ridge—beginning near Jeffrey City and extending east for at least 20 miles. Near Jeffrey City the ridge was low and broken, a collection of granite domes barely exposed above the younger sediments of the valley floor, like a series of half-mile-long loaves with crusts of bare, weathered rock. Farther on the outcrops became larger and more prominent, many rising 1,200 feet above the valley. One of the tallest was Split Rock, whose notched silhouette had been an important landmark along 30 miles of the Oregon Trail, and whose base marks the ruins of a Pony Express station.

The federal government has built a small interpretive center near Split Rock, at a vantage point looking north across meadows where wagon trains once paused to rest their animals on the good forage near the river. The passage of countless iron-rimmed wheels left a path that can still be seen, although it is not easy to distinguish from the more recent scars of four-wheel-drive vehicles. But the spirit of the Oregon Trail lingers, and when I walked away from the interpretive signs and scrambled over the granite slickrock I could almost hear the crack of bullwhips, the creak of harness leather, and the rumble of wooden wheels.

What would the Oregon pioneers have thought of the modern highways that have turned their pilgrimage into a three-day journey? Many, I bet, would find such conveniences too civilized and head elsewhere. And what would they think of people like me, repeating their journey in reverse simply for the fun of it? They'd probably shake their heads in utter disbelief.

I wondered if I really had the pioneer spirit, as I'd been told the day before. The risks I took were far smaller than theirs. As many as one in ten of those who braved the Oregon Trail died en route, while I was safe from many of the worst threats they'd faced: cholera and Indians, starvation and thirst, the total absence of medical facilities. The most serious risk I faced was the carelessness of hurried drivers. Even muggers—the modern-day equivalent of frontier outlaws—pose less danger in Wyoming than in Sacramento.

And what was I seeking? The pioneers had gone West pursuing the dream of a new life. I was a sightseer, covering as many miles in a day as they covered in a week. The new life I pursued was more spiritual than physical, partly a release from the time pressures of urban civilization, partly a return to a life of simple labor, where problems could be met one day at a time. Maybe the pioneers would have understood after all.

———————•◦•———————

From Split Rock the road angled away from the Sweetwater and approached the 500-foot climb toward the Continental Divide. Before beginning the ascent, I stopped at a gas station and trading post glorified by the roadmap into a "town" named Muddy Gap. There, I dried my sleeping bag in the sun while I waited for an afternoon thunderstorm to drift across the pass ahead. More showers were forming all along the Continental Divide, but with luck I thought I could slip between them without getting wet. After that I'd probably be dodging storms all the way to Rawlins.

Leaving Muddy Gap I discovered that the next few miles weren't going to be easy. The road forked, with my route bending ninety-degrees to the south. For the first time the Wyoming wind was a headwind, swirling between the peaks on each side of the pass to blast me at 30 to 35 miles an hour, turning what should have been an easy climb into a grueling two-hour struggle. Wyoming, I thought wryly, was punishing me for wanting to leave—first with rain the night before and now with wind. By the time I crossed the pass and rolled into Lamont I was prepared to give up for the day, even though I'd covered less than 60 miles.

I stopped for dinner in a small cafe.

The Bikecentennial map indicated a place to camp in town, and Mark and Mary Lou had thought it lay in a vacant lot near the cafe. But I didn't like the look of the site. Lamont had a population of only a hundred, but it was an oil town, and the empty lot was highly visible from the road. Although everyone I'd met had been friendly, waving cheerily as they headed home from the oil fields, there were bound to be roughnecks, and I would be an easy target for a belligerent drunk.

When I stepped outside after dinner, I still hadn't decided what to do. The wind had abated considerably. Perhaps I could still make it to

Rawlins. There were at least three hours of daylight left, and it was only 32 miles; if I couldn't make it, I'd rather seek the hospitality of a rancher than camp in town.

Barely out of town, I came across a real campground, an RV park with scores of bulldozed, gravel campsites. But camping on gravel, surrounded by RVs, looked only marginally more attractive than the vacant lot. Since I'd already made the decision to press on to Rawlins, I didn't even slow down.

The road from Lamont to Rawlins traverses a 25-mile stretch of Wyoming's Great Divide Basin, 3,500 square miles of rolling sagebrush, sand dunes, and mud flats straddling the Continental Divide, draining neither to the Atlantic nor the Pacific. In all directions the horizon is ringed by mountains, though some of the passes — like the one I'd crossed coming into Lamont — are so low they are little more than hills.

By now most of the higher peaks had snagged thunderstorms, while smaller showers drifted across the basin, mottling the sky from horizon to horizon with colors that ranged from cottony white to the gun-metal blue of heavy squalls. Montana chose "Big Sky Country" as its nickname, but that evening it would have applied equally well to Wyoming.

I had crossed the basin many years before on a vacation with my parents and been singularly unimpressed, finding nothing but monotony in the patterns of sagebrush and low hills. But as I pedaled toward Rawlins, the leisurely pace of a bicycle and the dramatic skies made a tremendous difference. The rains had turned the mud flats to shallow ponds, the fickle breeze had suddenly become a tailwind again, and far in the distance fragments of rainbow arched over the eastern ramparts, gleaming in joyous counterpoint to the blue-black sky behind. I could no longer perceive this landscape as drab and uninteresting.

I also knew that these scrub lands hold a great secret, a secret whose discovery overjoyed conservationists and proved yet again that no land is a wasteland, that there is a purpose for every acre on Earth. The secret is a small weasel-like animal called the black-footed ferret. Once relatively abundant, ferrets used to be found throughout the West, but they were dependent on prairie dogs, hunting them ferociously and living in their abandoned burrows. For a hundred years ranchers had systematically poisoned the prairie dogs, and the ferrets had suffered even more than their prey. By the middle of this century they were believed extinct. Then a biologist discovered a colony on a Wyoming ranch — the rancher cooperated, apparently adopting the animals as a special concern, and the colony survived. In Lamont I'd seen a poster telling ranchers who to call if they'd seen any ferrets, and I wondered if there might be other colonies hiding nearby.

All too soon I neared the edge of the basin and began the short climb to the Continental Divide. A final rain squall passed in front, dragging lacy tendrils across the hilltop to my left. For a brief moment the late evening sun turned the hillside to vermilion and drew forth yet another rainbow from the shower above.

A moment later, nearing the Divide, I stopped to look back. *Good-bye,* I thought, addressing myself not only to that beautiful landscape of wind and clouds, sagebrush and puddle, but also to wished-for faces with quivering noses and bright, beady eyes. *Good-bye and good luck. May the next century be kinder to you.*

With sunset drawing near, I slipped over the Divide and began the long, gentle descent into Rawlins, with the great arch of the 12,000-foot Medicine Bow Mountains rising before me, flanking the North Platte River 35 miles away and showing me the gateway to Colorado, the exit from a Wyoming I was no longer sure I wanted to leave.

That night I camped west of Rawlins in a large, commercial campground tucked against the side of a rocky butte. The location looked familiar, and I decided I'd camped there with my parents on that trip many years before, when the West was new to me, and both the campground and Rawlins seemed smaller. Now the campground appeared to sprawl forever, and Rawlins, with its eleven thousand people, felt like a metropolis. I felt out of place, but it was only the third campsite I'd stopped at since Oregon that had hot water, and I appreciated the luxury of my second shower in as many days. Picking my way through rows of travel-trailers, carrying my towel, I watched flickers of lightning on the northern horizon, a reminder of the Great Divide Basin only a few miles away. Down here there would be no rain.

The next morning, fully expecting it to be my last in Wyoming, I pedaled into town looking for breakfast. There my attention was caught by a fortress-like building occupying an entire block just outside the main business district. I detoured for a closer look and discovered the original Wyoming State Penitentiary, which opens for tours at 10 A.M.

I had an hour to wait—just long enough for a leisurely pancake breakfast—so I found a nearby cafe and settled down to catch up on my journal.

Forty-five minutes later I tipped the waitress, pedaled back to the penitentiary, and—joined by a west-bound cyclist I'd met at breakfast—chained my bicycle next to the ticket booth, where the watchful eye of the attendant might discourage pilfering. Then the prison gates swung open, and I joined a small tour group accompanied by a cheerful guide who looked barely out of high school.

The moment we stepped into the dank, gloomy interior, I knew the detour was going to be worthwhile. Through these portals, during eighty years of prison operation, 12,500 criminals had stepped, ranging from rapists, murderers, and hardened incorrigibles to juveniles and such colorful outlaws as William "Gentleman Bandit" Carlisle, last of the great train robbers. Early in the prison's history there had even been a few women, the most famous of whom was Annie Bruce, incarcerated at age seventeen for poisoning her father with a plum pie spiced with strychnine. The prison, which at its peak had crowded 520 inmates into an area no larger than a city block, had been in service until 1981, but its electrical system had failed or been removed, and the only light was that which filtered through the windows.

Waiting for our tour to begin, our group had been excited, talking animatedly about what we might find inside. But as we crossed the threshold a hush fell, and except for a couple of young children we walked slowly, trailing our fingers along the walls or pausing to touch the cool metal bars.

Sunlight streamed through a bank of windows occupying the entire south wall, but the brightness failed to penetrate the interiors of the four tiers of cells, whose bars and walkways loomed like a surrealistic movie set above the hallway that separated them from the windows.

The most famous inmate had been Carlisle, who robbed three trains in a ten-week spree in 1916, proving that train robbery no longer paid by netting only $937. Three years later he escaped by hiding in a shirt crate, then robbed another train. This time he got only $86 and was shot, captured, and returned to the prison, where he remained until his release in 1936.

Over the years there were hundreds of other escapes, but like Carlisle's, few led to long-term freedom. One of the most intriguing escape artists was John McDaniel, about whom it has been said that "no prison in the country could hold him." McDaniel was a show-off; once, he was found calmly sharpening a knife he'd stolen in the kitchen and brought back to the cellblock. Another time he broke into the warden's office to deliver a list of complaints. The easiest way for him to have accomplished this, the guards realized with awe, was to have escaped and then broken in again.

From the cellblocks we proceeded to the cafeteria. On first impression it was a bleak, institutional room, with row upon row of steel tables and massive columns supporting a low roof that created a cave-like atmosphere. But compared with the cellblocks it was a realm of windows and spaciousness. It was also a realm of color, for between the windows—on nearly every available patch of wall—an inmate artist, serving a life term for forgery, had painted a series of pictures, primitive in technique but bold in color and brush stroke, pictures so glowing they seemed to jump off the walls in vivid 3-D.

The paintings told a heart-wrenching tale of yearned-for freedom and the agony of confinement, symbolized through the lonely beauty of trees, meadows, mountains, and a road that appeared to begin at the cafeteria wall and lead outward to infinite spaces, just out of sight and around a bend.

From the cafeteria, our guide led us to the gallows and the gas chambers. J. P. Julien, the architect of the gallows, believed no one should be given the terrible responsibility of taking another's life. He designed the gallows so the condemned man would be his own executioner.

The mechanism was nearly as complicated as Julien's logic, but the principle was simple: When the prisoner stepped onto the gallows, his weight tripped an apparatus that pulled a plug from a bucket of water. The bucket served as counterweight to the mechanism that sprung the trap, and after enough water had drained out—in about ninety seconds— the balance would shift, the trap would open, and the prisoner would drop to his death.

The prisoner had to stand and wait, listening to the last seconds of his life trickle away; nevertheless, of the nine men executed in this fashion, only one had to be forcibly placed onto the trap. The others, wrote the newspapers of the time, "met death bravely."

Julien was so concerned with satisfying his personal scruples that he failed to pay adequate attention to the mechanics of hanging, and didn't design the gallows with sufficient drop to execute the prisoners cleanly. Prison officials had to resort to fastening weights to the condemned men's ankles, and even then executions were botched. One prisoner had to be hanged twice, and even the second time he needed thirteen minutes to die.

The designers of the gas chamber were less squeamish. The prisoner was strapped to a chair, the doors were sealed, and the executioner pulled a lever, dropping a tablet of cyanide into a bucket of acid beneath the chair. The resulting hydrogen cyanide fumes quickly permeated the sealed metal chamber, and the condemned man was unconscious in seconds, dead soon after.

"You can sit in the chair if you like," our tour guide told us. "Go ahead.

Most people find there's enough light to take pictures."

I was appalled at the idea, but the other bicyclist and I were the only ones who didn't participate. When everyone else had left, I turned and snapped a quick picture of that unholy chair staring out of the chamber. I tried to imagine the men for whom that view had been their last. How many followed the executioner's final advice, listening quietly for the pellet to drop, then calmly counting to seven before drawing the slow, deep breath that would lead to oblivion? And how many clung desperately to life, holding their breaths until their eyes bulged and stabs of brilliance flickered at the corners of their vision, only to draw eventually that final breath in an explosive gasp of searing lungs and thundering pulse, not knowing the cyanide was already killing them by absorption through the skin?

The condemned prisoner is one of the few people who truly knows his appointed hour, but as I stood there, I knew that ultimately he meets his Maker on the same terms as anybody else, perhaps repenting at the last instant or maybe screaming defiance to the end.

———— •●• ————

Later I stopped at a hardware store to buy something to re-waterproof my tent. "I'd recommend Thompson's Water Seal," the salesman said, "but we're out of stock." He offered me a spray can of a competing brand. "This ought to work. It says it's good for nylon."

Happy to have that problem solved, I pedaled out of town onto Interstate 80, the only road leading east out of Rawlins. The Wyoming wind was gusting behind me, and I made good time, covering a rolling 20 miles in the next hour. I was momentarily tempted to continue running before the wind, with the possibility of covering as many as 200 miles a day, maybe catching the hunger riders somewhere in western Nebraska. But I wasn't ready to leave the mountains so soon; hopefully, I'd still have tailwinds when I hit the Plains after visiting the Colorado Rockies.

As I turned south toward Colorado, the wind became a crosswind. My speed dropped from 20 miles an hour to 10, and I spent the rest of the afternoon dodging thunderstorms that continually swept across the valley.

I remember little of that afternoon except the constant battle with the wind, the occasional play of lightning along the ridgelines, and a brief pelting of rain that caught me just as I entered Saratoga. By the time I reached the village of Riverside, still 30 miles shy of Colorado, I was worn out. Although it was only midafternoon I followed a sign to the city park, where camping was permitted along the bank of the North Platte.

It was not a pleasant place to camp. The trash cans stank with rotting garbage, a noisy dog was chained to an unattended picnic table, and trash was strewn all over the lawn. The mosquitoes were even worse than along the Sweetwater, and the riverbank was covered with dense underbrush that stopped the wind and gave the bugs plenty of places to hide.

I attempted to waterproof my tent, but the spray can refused to work; apparently it had been sitting on the shelf so long it had lost pressure. Disgusted, I threw it away, then fled the mosquitoes and pedaled downtown for dinner.

I was planning to eat at Riverside's one cafe, but as I pulled into the parking lot I found a sign ordering cyclists not to lean their bicycles against the front of the building. I looked around for somewhere else to put my bike, but nothing came to mind. There were no convenient trees or fences, and I wasn't about to put it out of sight behind the building or leave it in the parking lot where it might get run over. There were plenty of unobtrusive places to prop it on the front porch, but the message seemed clear. Bicyclists weren't welcome. I would dine at the general store across the street.

Before sitting down to a meal of crackers and Twinkies, I called my friend Jack in Iowa. He had been unable to join me in Idaho, but I'd been thinking for several days that we still might be able to meet somewhere in the Midwest if his schedule permitted. It was time to find out.

He was interested, but we decided to wait a couple of days to settle the details.

Excited by that news, I chatted with the store owner and his customers until twilight forced me back to camp. Soon after I got there it began to rain, with drops splashing through my tent fly as though it were so much tissue paper, spraying my face with a myriad of fine droplets—a fitting end to an unpleasant afternoon.

———— •◦• ————

The shower was brief, and I spent the rest of the evening trying to plan my route. I had reached a critical juncture in the trip and couldn't decide what to do next. Was I heading coast to coast? Or was I simply going where the spirit beckoned? If I had had all summer it would have been easy—I'd wander gradually east until I bumped into the Atlantic.

But I didn't have all summer. I'd used nearly half my allotted time, and while I'd covered 1,800 miles, my circuitous route had taken me barely a third of the way across the country. If I stayed with Bikecentennial's TransAmerica Trail, there were still 2,500 miles to the Atlantic—nearly 100 miles a day. I could shorten that by leaving the trail, visiting only a corner of Colorado, and taking a straight, flat route across the Plains. The East Coast would then be within easier reach so long as I didn't loiter.

But that sounded like the persistent, goal-driven voice I'd been battling all along. *Go for it*, it prodded. *Be able to say, "I pedaled across the country."* All afternoon it had been returning, with increased urgency, telling me to count the miles, push each day to the maximum, because I was gradually, inevitably running out of time. If I wasn't careful the next stage of my journey could easily become nothing but a long, tense race against the clock, as I struggled to gain the two or three days' grace that might make the difference.

As I headed out onto the Plains the opportunities for sightseeing, which until now I'd used to counterbalance that urge to draw the longest possible line on the map, would become less frequent. Soon I would have to confront that goal-driven voice directly and defeat it, once and for all.

Wanting to cross the country wasn't all bad. The Wimbledon counselors had been using the same objective as a much-needed exercise in discipline. Without some drive I would still be in Sacramento, wondering what it is that impels people to make such journeys. In fact, I'd often been asked just that question. My standard reply was shallow almost to the point of flippancy: "Because it's fun, even if it doesn't always look it." A better answer would be the classic mountaineer's response: *Because it's there.* It may seem superficial, but it's the only answer that truly works. *Because it's there.* If you have the drive to explore, to find what lies beyond, then the logical endpoint is to reach for the limit of what can be explored. If you don't have that drive, any answer to the question is meaningless.

But discipline is a two edged-sword. It is frighteningly easy for the pursuit of goals—or more precisely, the pursuit of achievements—to dominate all else. It is how we build careers, plan finances, and, all too often, run our lives. It is the mindset of competition carried beyond usefulness. It is the difference between being goal motivated and goal driven.

Setting a destination would give my trip a measurable sense of progress and a definable endpoint. Fixing my sights too strongly on that destination would undercut my real purpose, which was to relax and discover the land I was passing through—and myself.

A more relaxing option than targeting the Coast would be to follow the Bikecentennial Trail through Colorado, then cut northeast into Iowa to meet Jack—possibly in time for RAGBRAI. That wouldn't get me to the Mississippi until late July, nearly a week later than if I traveled a more direct route. My chances of seeing the Atlantic would not be good.

The competitive, goal-driven part of me responded to this idea as a mountaineer might to the thought of climbing to within 1,000 feet of the summit of Mt. Everest only to turn back, saying, "Oh, well." But another part of me wanted to be able to do exactly that. I needed to regain the spirit I'd found in northern California, when I wasn't sure I could pedal more than the next 100 miles. As I'd told myself on other occasions, I wanted to live for the journey, not the destination.

RAGBRAI certainly seemed like the best way to go. I had plenty of time to meet it without dashing across the Plains, and since it would set my itinerary in Iowa, I'd have no reason to worry about scheduling until I reached the Mississippi. And I knew Jack would have no trouble getting both of us registered.

But joining RAGBRAI might only succeed in postponing the problem. When it ended, I would be within 800 airline miles of the Atlantic—perhaps 1,200 by the back roads I'd have to cycle. I would have one week remaining, maybe a bit more depending on my wife's work schedule. Reaching the coast might still be possible—at least by a Herculean effort—and unless I changed I'd be primed to try, racing the clock all the way. For all my rationalization I wasn't fully ready to commit myself to RAGBRAI and thumb my nose at that demon drive to reach the Atlantic. I'd been dreaming of a cross-country trip for a decade, and I'd be disappointed if I didn't make it.

I fell asleep that night still wanting to cross the continent but also praying that somehow I would learn to live one day at a time, not driven by schedules and goals.

CHAPTER 6

Vera

Hail and Friendship in Colorado

DAY 25 • Wednesday, July 9 • CUMULATIVE MILES: 1,814
Riverside, Wyoming, to Walden, Colorado

DAY 26 • Thursday, July 10 • CUMULATIVE MILES: 1,899
Walden to Green Mountain Reservoir

DAY 27 • Friday, July 11 • CUMULATIVE MILES: 1,977
Green Mountain Reservoir to Frisco

DAY 28 • Saturday, July 12 • CUMULATIVE MILES: 2,011
Frisco to Fairplay

DAY 29 • Sunday, July 13 • CUMULATIVE MILES: 2,074
Fairplay to Salida

DAY 30 • Monday, July 14 • CUMULATIVE MILES: 2,177
Salida to Colorado Springs

Part of my prayer was answered early and in an unexpected form: a cyclist from Portland, Oregon, named Vera. I'd barely covered a half mile when I saw her bicycle in a private campground, sharing a site with a car. I almost pedaled on by, assuming the bicycle belonged with the car. But as I rode in indecisive circles near the campground entrance, I noted that the bicycle was rigged for touring, and remembering how I'd shared a site with Esam, I biked into the campground to introduce myself. "Which way are you headed?" I asked.

"South," she replied, pointing. Then she introduced me to the owners of the car—her parents, who'd been vacationing in the area and arranged to meet her for a couple of evenings.

"Have you had breakfast?" someone asked, and a couple of minutes later I was staring at a plate of potatoes, eggs, and toast—the meal I'd have ordered in the cafe if I'd felt more welcome.

I assumed Vera was one of the women I'd been hearing about since Lander. "Would you like company?" I asked after breakfast, as she prepared to load her bicycle.

She hesitated. Later I learned that because of a couple of mismatches she'd had with other cyclists, she'd nearly said, "No." Instead she replied, "If you don't mind going my pace. I'm not all that fast, and I tend to get tired by midafternoon."

I assented, and half an hour later we were pedaling out of camp, having told her parents that if all went well we'd be at a wayside park in Walden, Colorado, at 1 p.m, but more likely at 4. Then we rolled out into a dismal, gray morning, a portent of almost certain afternoon showers. Within a few miles a headwind sprang up, and we settled into the hard slog of a 50-mile trek into the wind.

Such obstacles are more easily overcome with company. When the traffic is light you can ride side by side, chattering away to take your mind off your slow progress and the drab weather. When the traffic is heavier, or the wind stronger, you can ride single file, taking turns in the lead and working together to save energy—a technique known as drafting.

At first I was reluctant to suggest drafting, even when the wind slowed our pace to a painful crawl. Any woman who'd bicycled alone across the empty stretches of Wyoming was obviously the independent sort, and Vera radiated an aura of competence and self-sufficiency that seemed to say, "I know how to handle myself in any situation." I was afraid she might take my offer as a masculine put-down: "Hey, baby, let me break the wind for you." But the wind was affecting her more than me, so eventually I made the suggestion.

It turned out she'd never drafted before. "Wow," she shouted, "that really makes a difference! I'd never have believed it. I'm barely pedaling."

We rode that way most of the day, alternating between drafting and conversation, gradually ascending the North Platte valley, flanked by mountain ranges that might have been scenic on a better day but were uninspiring under the morning's dull skies.

We were well on our way to becoming fast friends, and while we didn't know it at the time, we would travel together for five days and 300 miles, detouring far south of my planned route. During those days we would celebrate three "last" evenings together, then change our plans and continue for "just another day," until eventually our routes irreconcilably diverged.

Vera was thirty, dark haired and dark complected, with a tan many Californians would kill for. It was a biker's tan, a functional tan that, like mine, was darkest on the face, back of the arms, calves, and front of the thighs, where the afternoon sun gets its best shot. She wore her hair straight, at a length that used to be called "medium" but now would be considered longer than average, and she gave the impression of being taller than the 5'4" she claimed.

She was riding from Portland to visit a cousin in Santa Fe, and she amazed me by admitting she'd planned the trip on only three weeks' notice, buying her bicycle and her gear and doing all her training during that short period. She'd gotten the idea from her housemate, Peggy, who was cycling across the country—Vera had decided it would be nice to travel with her until their routes separated.

She and Peggy had started out on June 15—the same day I'd started—pedaling 80 miles their first day, much of it in a driving rain. Over the next few days they'd traveled up the Columbia River, then biked through eastern Washington and Idaho, into Montana.

Peggy was the "uncatchable" woman biker I'd heard about earlier, and she and Vera proved to be ill-matched, with Vera dragging into camp each evening and Peggy chafing to put in even more mileage. Before they strained their friendship they decided to part company earlier than planned; by the time I met Vera, Peggy must have been nearly to Kansas.

Although Vera had planned her trip on the spur of the moment, she had powerful motives for doing it. As she told me during snatches of conversation between drafting stints, she was trying to whip herself back into shape after a four-year battle with acute leukemia and the concomitant chemotherapy. "Those chemicals take a terrible toll," she said. "My doctor tells me not to be surprised if I never get my full strength back. And since my legs got used to it that first week, I haven't made much progress."

I asked her about the leukemia.

"After four years they consider me well on my way to recovery," she said. "But originally they gave me only a twenty percent chance of getting through it."

Later we would discuss her illness and what she'd learned during her convalescence, and while she never said so, the battle had undoubtedly required the same strength of will needed to undertake a 2,000-mile bike trek with almost no training. Fighting her illness had left her with an almost tangible aura of self-assurance.

———————— •❦• ————————

As we neared the Colorado line we met a pair of cyclists coming from the opposite direction, a brother and sister named Ruth and Steve. Like everyone else I'd met in the past several days, they had a Peggy story. "Yeah," Steve said when Vera mentioned her. "We met her a few days ago. She was riding with a guy who told us he let her set the pace and the distance. 'It's all I can do to hang on,' he said."

I was glad I'd met Vera rather than Peggy. I had no doubt I could keep up with almost anyone if I set my mind to it, but that wouldn't have been the type of trip I needed, and I might well have been too stubborn to admit it.

———————•••———————

Eventually we crossed into Colorado, then climbed a small hill and descended into a vast meadow known as North Park. The skies cleared, treating us to the best scenery since the Wind River Valley. Fifteen miles to our left rose the west side of the Front Range of the Rockies, a tilting slab of green forest topped by gray rock, completely cloud free and seeming to bask in the slanting illumination of the afternoon sun. To our right were other mountains, their summits hidden behind scattered dark clouds that were beautiful to watch but threatening harbingers of unpleasant weather. Ahead stretched North Park itself, hundreds of square miles of sagebrush and rolling hills, a chunk of Wyoming transplanted to Colorado.

A few miles later, as we were nearing our planned meeting place, Vera's father drove toward us, then stopped to ask how things were going. It was probably 3:30, and he and her mother had been waiting at least two hours.

I suppressed a grin as Vera gave him a revised ETA. "I knew he was going to be there early," I said as we resumed pedaling. "I knew it as soon as you said, 'If all goes well.' "

———————•••———————

I wasn't impressed with the roadside park when we finally reached it — a large gravel parking lot beside the river, with a few picnic tables scattered among the willows and a crowd of bloodthirsty mosquitoes to rival any in Wyoming.

The four of us sat at a picnic table to consider our options. Though neither of us had said anything, Vera and I seemed to have tacitly agreed that whatever we did, it would be together.

"Would *you* stay here on your own?" her mother asked.

Vera nodded. "I've seen worse."

Her mother turned to me. "What about you?"

I looked at the food scraps lying around the picnic table and the litter blowing through the parking lot. With a single swat I dispatched a dozen mosquitoes. "Yes."

"Then we'll stay."

"Well, there may be other options." There was a lot of daylight left, and for the last several miles Vera and I had been talking about the possibility of continuing. "Let's look at the maps. . . ."

Between us, Vera and I had three different maps, and we pulled them all out, comparing them to see if any showed other camping places nearby. If the storms held off there was enough daylight to pedal at least another 30 miles, possibly more.

Before we got organized we were hit by a blast of cold wind that stung us with sand and threatened to tear the maps out of our hands. Behind us, rapidly bearing down from the northwest, was a blue-black cloud with heavy rain blocking the view of the peaks behind.

"Let's adjourn this discussion to the first cafe in town," I suggested.

"Good idea," Vera replied, already packing up.

She was ready quickly, but I was faster—there was lightning in that storm and I wanted to get to town . . . fast.

I think my haste confused Vera's parents. They were new to camping and had always lived in New York City, where it is easy to get in out of a storm. I, on the other hand, had accumulated a number of unpleasant experiences with lightning and preferred not to add another to the list.

The wind was so strong it was a struggle pedaling back to the road, but once we got there it blasted us into town so quickly that we beat Vera's parents. It was our only tailwind of the day.

In the cafe we again pooled maps, adding another that Vera's father had picked up at the chamber of commerce across the street. We now had four, and we huddled over them with the intensity of explorers trying to learn all they could about unknown terrain.

One showed a wayside park 15 to 20 miles down the road.

Vera and I were too experienced to blithely accept the only map that promised what we wanted. But Vera's father said he thought he'd seen two other bikes at a hamburger stand a couple of blocks away, so after wolfing a piece of peach pie à la mode, I ambled up the street to see what the owners knew.

If there'd been bikers around, they were gone. I asked the cashiers if there were any camping places before Muddy Pass, 34 miles up the road. None of them knew, but some of the customers overheard me, and soon there were a half dozen people leaning over my map.

"There might be room at the Grizzly Creek bridge," somebody said. "That's where we back the water truck down to the stream, and there's probably room for a tent. But that's all I can think of."

I thanked him and left. The trouble with "might be's" is that they don't always work, and then you're stuck. Also, I didn't want to camp that close to the road.

I suppressed a smile as I thought about how Vera's parents would have reacted to the suggestion that we camp beneath a bridge. They wanted flush toilets, and there wouldn't even be a pit at a place like that. I had a feeling Vera wasn't leaving town tonight. If nothing else, she and her parents were likely to play "After you, Alfonse" until the decision was made by default.

With that in mind, I stopped at a motel across the street and asked the price of a single room. I hadn't stayed at a motel all trip, and maybe it was time to treat myself.

Twenty-five dollars. For that I'd brave the mosquitoes by the river.

A block from the motel was an open hardware store, so I stopped to see if I could replace the silicone spray that had frustrated me the night before. When I told the shopkeeper what I wanted it for, she steered me to Thompson's Water Seal, the very product I'd been trying to buy in Rawlins.

I read the instructions. "For any natural fabric," I said. "Nylon isn't natural. Will it work on nylon?"

She nodded. "We use it on snowmobile suits. They're nylon."

"How long does it take to dry?"

"Not long. We spray the suits as we wear them, then go right outside."

It sounded good. Once the rainstorm passed—it had proven to be mostly threat, with only a little rain and no lightning—I could waterproof my tent in preparation for future storms.

"Let me test it before I leave the store," I told the clerk, "to make sure there's pressure." I didn't want a repeat of the previous night's fiasco.

———————•———————

As I carried my purchase back to the cafe, I suddenly heard a whir, and two bicycles shot down the main street, running downhill before the wind, which had returned to the southwest.

"Hey," I shouted, running after them. "Hey, wait!"

One of them looked back, saw my cycling attire, and braked to a halt, with the other following suit.

We exchanged the usual run of "where are you from's" and "where are you going's." They were the vanguard of a twenty-rider group of teenagers run under the umbrella of an organization that sounded similar to the one I'd encountered at Brooks Lake.

By the time I got around to asking them about camping, four or five others had arrived and we had a second round of introductions. Eventually they told me there was no camping before the pass. There wasn't any at the pass either—they'd camped at a national-forest campground 7 miles off the route, on the far side of a 650-foot hill. "But there's a friendly rancher 20 miles out of town who gave us water and let us picnic on his lawn. You could probably camp there."

I thanked them and watched as they rode on toward the wayside park, their destination for the night. Then I returned to Vera and her parents, wondering if the rancher's hospitality would be strained by two groups of cyclists in one day and knowing her parents would be hesitant to camp on a stranger's lawn.

Back at the cafe Vera pulled me aside before I could say anything. "We're staying in the motel," she said. "We'll get a room for four if that's okay with you."

"Sure," I said, "That would be great." It wasn't until much later that I realized it was only the camaraderie of the road that made it seem so natural to share a motel room with people I'd known less than twelve hours.

"What would you have done on your own?" she asked as we walked across the street.

"Gunned it for the pass." I remembered walking the highway shoulder toward Lander. "And quite probably not have made it." I grinned. "This is a lot better."

———— •◦• ————

The motel did its best to thwart our plan. The clerk said the charge would be forty-three dollars plus tax and wanted to put us in two beds, not three.

"What about one bed and two people on the floor?" Vera asked. She turned to me. "I don't mind that, do you? I've been sleeping on harder surfaces than that for weeks."

Since this arrangement wasn't on the standard fee schedule, we dickered. Vera's parents wound up paying $29 for the bed and Vera and I split the price for the floor—$4.50. At $2.25, it was a bargain.

While Vera and her mother cooked dinner on a Coleman stove on the sidewalk, I unrolled my tent and sprayed it, planning to let it dry in the warm evening sun.

I was immediately glad I'd tried it under controlled circumstances. Contrary to what the shop clerk had said, the spray did not dry quickly. In keeping with a warning on the label, it reeked of petroleum distillates, but I didn't discover that until I'd sprayed a large segment of the tent floor. Figuring I was already committed, I sprayed the whole thing and crossed my fingers, hoping I wouldn't have to wait all night before I could bring it inside without rendering our room uninhabitable.

While waiting for the tent to dry I was joined by an elderly gentleman staying in the adjacent room. He was curious about bicycle touring, and as I answered his questions he suggested that cyclists have a lot in common with the hoboes of the Great Depression.

"Well, yes and no," I said. "A lot of the concerns are the same, and a few bicyclists are bums, but most of us are simply ordinary folk on long vacations." But one of the great things about touring is that people assume you are on a tight budget and do everything they can to help you keep expenses down. The opportunities to mooch are tremendous, and it is a thin line between accepting hospitality and begging handouts. A few minutes later dinner was called, just about the time my tent had dried enough to be rolled up. I was again overwhelmed by the hospitality of people I'd just met.

———————•••———————

Dinner was catfish, vegetables, and tortilla chips. I'd never had catfish before and pronounced it good, as did Vera's father. Vera and her mother were less certain and ate with less gusto. "You didn't see it before we cooked it," Vera said. The fish had spent all day in an ice chest and was on the margin of edibility.

But between us we rapidly polished off most of the tortilla chips. "Salt," explained Vera, echoing my thoughts.

I enjoyed that evening with Vera's parents, and I was intrigued by her mother. She obviously loved her daughter, but in some ways she was a classic, protective mother—it was fascinating to watch her in operation. She found it difficult to tell Vera what she really wanted, and the two of them played out endless verbal games of, "What do you want?" and, "Well, I'll do what you'd prefer." They'd been doing the same earlier over the question of where to spend the night, and they continued to do so now over such questions as priority in the showers and what time to get up in the morning. Vera's mother was also a worrier, and when her daughter was in the shower she plied me with questions. As with the thunderstorm she was either unsure of the real dangers or unwilling to face them, so the questions focused on trivia—things she could worry about but not uncontrollably. "Is she getting enough vitamins?" "What's the matter with her eyes? They're all bloodshot." "Is she wearing suntan lotion? She shouldn't be that tan." She never asked—or at least didn't ask me—about the dangers from cars, or the obvious risks to a woman traveling alone. Similarly, she never noted that while Vera carried a helmet strapped to her luggage rack, she never wore it except in heavy traffic or on long descents.

Just before Vera came out of the shower her mother changed the subject. "Why do people do these things? What's the reason for taking a trip like this?"

Vera had a very specific reason, but I didn't want to answer for her, especially since she must have explained it before. I answered generally, telling Vera's mother about the Wimbledon riders. "How many of those kids," I asked, "are going to wind up in reform school after accomplishing a goal like that? That's part of what these trips are about—setting a major goal and maintaining the discipline to see it through."

But as I retired to the shower I wondered why, after pondering the same question only the night before, I'd given an answer that applied to neither Vera nor myself. Apparently I felt out of step with the goal-driven ideals indoctrinated during ten years of college and graduate school, and didn't want to voice my reasons too openly. The answer I'd chosen was oriented toward a personality directly opposite my own.

On the road with Vera it had been different. I already knew her well enough to realize we were kindred spirits. We both suffered, on occasion, from excessive scheduling, and we'd both turned to cycling, in part, to learn to relax into one-day-at-a-time schedules. Riding with her was going to be good.

While I was in the shower, Vera and her mother talked about me, just as her mother and I had talked about Vera.

Later, Vera told me that her mother had said, "You know, I'm getting just as adventurous as you, inviting a total stranger in like that! But why is he doing this without his wife?"

"I don't know," Vera had said. "Some people take separate vacations. Or perhaps she doesn't have enough vacation time."

"It's mostly the time," I later told Vera with a tinge of sadness. Jane would have enjoyed the trip, and the lessons in patience and day-by-day living could have been as valuable to her as to me. As a professor just beginning the long battle for tenure, however, she'd decided to reserve her summers mostly for research. "When I finish this trip," I told Vera, "we're scheduled to take a three-week vacation. I'm holding the time open, but I'll be surprised if we use it all. We used to take long trips together, but recently she's felt she can't leave her research for more than a couple of weeks at a time."

Afterward it hit me that what I'd just said meant that my wife's career was placing her under the very live-only-for-the-future pressures I was trying to avoid. At the time it seemed so normal I barely noticed.

The next day was one for the journal, as one of my previous cycling companions used to say. And as I lay that night beneath cold, starry skies in a tent that still smelled of turpentine, I could hear Vera scribbling in her own journal, 10 feet to my left, presumably recounting her version of the day's adventures. After only two days she was becoming a good friend as well as a pleasant traveling companion, and I knew without asking that she, too, had found the day a joyous mixture of adventure and companionship.

Like the day before, this one dawned partly cloudy with scattered showers already visible in the mountains. We said good-bye to Vera's parents—who would no longer be joining us—and left early. Even so, by the time we'd been on the road an hour the accursed southeast wind had sprung up again, at first gently, then stronger, impeding our progress across the 34 miles to Muddy Pass—my second crossing of the Continental Divide at a pass with a variation on that unpleasant-sounding name.

Colorado's Muddy Pass is one of the few places where the Divide can be reached from three directions. Our road climbed it from the north, ending at a T-intersection just at the crest. To the right the crossroad continued to climb, following the Divide for a few miles before dropping toward Steamboat Springs; to the left it descended into Kremmling.

As we approached the junction I saw a series of bright-colored motes moving downhill from the direction of Steamboat Springs.

"Bicycles!" I yelled, pointing, then sprinted the last 400 yards, leaving Vera—who probably hadn't heard what I'd said—to wonder if I'd taken leave of my senses.

Two of the cyclists had already gone before I could reach the pass, but four others stopped to talk. "Where are you from?" I asked, and after the initial babel settled down I learned that the six riders actually represented three groups who'd left San Francisco, Berkeley, and Sacramento in mid-June, and whose routes, by coincidence, had converged in western Colorado just as Vera's and mine had met in Wyoming. On this day they were riding 90 miles, from Steamboat Springs to Grand Lake, and the next day they would brave Trail Ridge Road in Rocky Mountain National Park, the highest paved road in the country. From there their routes would again diverge as they pursued separate paths across the continent.

"We're planning to eat lunch at the bottom of the hill," one of them said. "Care to join us?"

Vera and I had intended to picnic at the pass, but we didn't mind going a few extra miles, and as the others remounted we agreed to meet below.

After documenting our crossing with a few photos of the Divide, we pulled back onto the highway and followed them.

Five miles later we hadn't caught up. Two other cyclists came from the other direction, riding with the wind that Vera and I had been fighting on the long, gradual descent.

"Your friends are just ahead!" one of them shouted.

"That either means they've found a lunch spot," I told Vera, "or they're running for town." "Town" was Kremmling, 22 miles away.

Two miles later we still hadn't seen them, so we abandoned the chase and stopped in a turnout to fix our sandwiches, too hungry to go farther. Besides, the weather—which had never been promising—was degenerating, and a heavy shower was drifting across our path.

As we ate, a large pickup camper pulled into our turnout—actually a rancher's driveway—and without a word the driver opened the hood and bent over the engine.

"We've got a clogged fuel pump," his wife explained as she rolled down the passenger-side window. "We didn't have any power going up the pass."

It was disturbing to have them park right in front of us, only 5 feet away and almost completely blocking our view, but they obviously meant no ill. It never crossed their minds that we wanted to gaze down the valley or that we might prefer not to have gasoline fumes mixed with our lunches. They reminded me of a gentleman I'd met in Wyoming, that evening with Mark and Mary Lou, who'd parked his 30-foot land yacht within 20 feet of my camping spot—when he'd had acres of empty space to choose from—and never noticed as I quietly carried my gear to a more distant site. These people aren't deliberately inconsiderate, often they're quite friendly, but they have an urban understanding of where to draw the line between intrusiveness and gregariousness, perhaps because they carry the city with them and never truly get away from it.

Even motorcyclists—who have much in common with bicyclists—may suffer from a similar problem. "I'd like to try bicycling," said a motorbiker I talked to a few days later, "but I could never go that slow." How could I tell him that even cycling is sometimes too fast, that cyclists too can become engrossed in speed and distance and forget what it was they left home to find? But the problem is magnified by the presence of an engine, and while there are always exceptions, the severity seems directly correlated to the size of the rig.

The camper parked beside us wasn't large by modern standards, and the people were friendly, but their goals were so different from ours we might as well have been from different worlds. They'd been to the Canadian Rockies—maybe as far as Alaska—but as the woman chatted while her husband worked, the only place she specifically mentioned was Edmonton, Alberta. "They have a mall up there," she said, "with eight hundred shops. It's almost unbelievable."

I had no answer to that. Shopping malls were just too far removed from my present reality. I changed the subject. "Where are you from?"

"Michigan."

That was something I could talk about; I'd lived there for eleven years. "What part?"

It turned out to be a small town in the center of the state. "Oh," I started to say, "my wife went to high school near there." But I bit it off. She'd think I was talking about Vera. So instead I told her I'd gone to Michigan State University and learned that her son had been there at the same time.

During this conversation Vera wandered off afoot. She'd been mumbling for several minutes about needing to find a "bush" — or more likely a ravine or ditch — and I concluded that desperation had set in.

Even in relatively civilized country, bathrooms are impossibly far apart by bicycle, and nonchalantly urinating by the roadside is simply part of the game. Since we'd both been on the road for some time we had abandoned conventional decorum. "I need a bush," had come to mean, "It's time to stop," even if no suitable shrubbery was in sight. Under those circumstances, the next line was likely to be, "Hold my bike and don't look back," possibly combined with, "Let me know if you see a car."

This time, however, was different. The woman in the RV represented a degree of civilization we'd almost forgotten about, and I found myself wishing Vera luck; we were in the midst of a treeless landscape where it would be almost impossible to get out of sight of the road, and gaps in the traffic were rare.

I continued talking with the woman while her husband's head remained buried in the engine. As we talked she kept stealing glances over my shoulder. She was too polite to say anything, but her repeated glances said more than words. *Where's she going?* must have been her first thought, followed quickly by, *She's not going to do what I think she is!* I kept asking questions, trying to distract her, but wasn't completely successful. Then her husband, who'd never said a word, closed the hood and started the engine. They were gone before Vera returned, but I could imagine the ensuing conversation. "You wouldn't believe it. . . ." she'd tell him, "That woman. . . ."

———————•◦•———————

After lunch we'd planned to rest, but more storms were moving across the valley and we both wanted to reach Kremmling. The first storm had already passed, and although there was another behind it we thought we could slip between them. After four days of this weather we were both beginning to feel confident of our abilities to dodge thunderstorms, though we also realized that eventually we would make a mistake—or simply meet a storm too big to dodge—and get drenched. But one thing was certain: If we stayed in one place too long we were sure to get wet.

So off we went, pedaling down the long hill into Kremmling, grateful that the storm had killed the wind and oohing and ahing at the play of lightning on the ridge 5 miles ahead, but realizing that both storms were still threats. Although the first had already passed by, it was moving slowly, and we were quickly catching up. The second storm was hanging to the ridgeline on our right, threatening to cut us off at any minute. At first the lightning was confined to the storm ahead, then we noted isolated bolts in the other, initially striking only the highest peaks but soon moving down the mountainside toward the valley. Together the storms were an awesome spectacle, blue-black clouds spitting fire at the peaks, throwing four or five bolts at a single location; jagged lines of actinic blue sometimes touching down with no apparent effect, sometimes erupting in orange fire as they seared an unfortunate tree.

I would have loved to stop and watch the storms, and even as I paused to survey the route below, I was impressed again by the raw power unleashed before me. And these were *small* thunderstorms.

But they were threatening to merge into something larger.

"It doesn't look good," I said when Vera caught up with me. "That last flash struck below us, somewhere near the road."

On my own I'd have stayed where I was, waiting for the storm to pass. I was in no hurry to venture into that exposed valley, with little but sagebrush for shelter.

But when it came to lightning, Vera was braver than I. "Let's go partway down," she suggested, and somewhat hesitantly I agreed.

We coasted down the hill, still hoping to slide between the storms before they merged. Within a couple of miles we realized that was impossible. Lightning was striking directly in front of us. It was time to hide.

I looked longingly at some ranch buildings to our right but couldn't figure out how to get to them. I was at the point of suggesting that we lie down in a ditch, when the road rounded a bend and we found ourselves in a deep cut. "This is it," I shouted. "Let's wait here." We were grabbing our rain gear as the first cold drops pelted us.

As quickly as it had arrived the storm passed, and within a few minutes the lightning receded to a safe distance. We'd gotten only slightly wet.

We remounted and rode on, but a mile later I stopped abruptly. "That white stuff on the hillside," I shouted, pointing, "it's hail!" Within another half mile we found half an inch of hail on the shoulder and big piles on the roadway itself, where the cars had shoved it aside. I stopped to pick up a handful. "Chick peas."

In another half mile we were again out of the hail, but the air was very cold. A mile later we were back in hail, deeper than ever, marble-size this time. "Boy, I'm glad we didn't get caught in this," I said. I had a new respect for mountain thunderstorms—and a new realization of what might happen if we failed to dodge them.

We quickly learned that hail isn't all that much fun to bike through, even *after* it has fallen. The traffic had made wide ruts, clearing a path for us, but passing cars sprayed us thoroughly, sending hailstones pinging off our spokes and saturating our legs with slush.

The second patch of hail lasted only a few hundred yards, and by then we were close to town. Anticipating a warm cafe, I started to sprint, until a glance in my rear-view mirror revealed a large RV bearing down on me from behind. I looked ahead and saw a truck coming toward me, uphill. There was no way to bail out—at 20 miles an hour I didn't dare hit the loose, wet dirt on the shoulder; I'd be certain to go sprawling.

The RV slowed but refused to wait. It started to pass, then squeezed closer to make room for the oncoming truck. By the time it finally got completely around there couldn't have been more than a few inches' clearance between it and my handlebars, while less than an inch of pavement separated me from the soft shoulder.

I was furious, but what I did next was deliberate and calculated. I learned long ago that cyclists must respond carefully to rude drivers; several times on day trips at home, drivers had come back to threaten me after I'd chastised them.

But this time I felt safe. I shook my clenched fist over my head. "Bastard!" I shouted and then sprinted after him. Town wasn't half a mile away, and if he stopped for gas or even a traffic light I'd have him. I wasn't sure what I'd do if I caught him, but I'd think of something.

A hundred yards down the road I suddenly remembered Vera. *What if he'd hit Vera?* I looked back and she was still there, so I sprinted on. I must have been going close to 30 miles an hour.

There were no stoplights, and the RV didn't stop for anything else. I gave up and braked to a halt at a cafe on the outskirts of town. I was still catching my breath when Vera pulled up, laughing.

"You should have seen what he did to your flag," she said. "It whipped around all over the place."

"Did he pass you as close as he did me?"

"No, but he was pretty close."

"I really wanted to catch him. If only he'd stopped. . . ."

She laughed again. "He saw you coming. Believe me, he saw you coming." She was laughing so hard, she nearly doubled over. "Pardon me, but it was so funny, you sprinting after him like that. He wasn't going to stop for *anything*."

I was somewhat mollified. At least he'd gotten the message. Then I laughed, too. "Ah, for Idaho or Oregon."

"Or Washington or Montana."

"Or even Wyoming!" But not California.

Still laughing, we propped our bikes under an awning in front of the cafe.

Thirty seconds later it began to hail.

———————•❖•———————

There were six other bicycles under the awning, so we weren't surprised to find the people we'd met earlier.

"Did you get hailed on?" I asked.

There were a half dozen vigorous assents. "Did you?"

Vera shook her head. "No, we waited for it to go by."

The others groaned, but I doubted they would have waited even if they'd known. I had the impression they'd rather be hailed on than take an unscheduled rest break. And a few minutes later they proved it by riding off in the rain, heading for Grand Lake 35 miles away.

But I was just as bad in my own way. For several minutes before they left I toyed with following them, drawn by the thought of Trail Ridge Road and its 12,000-foot summit.

I didn't know whether Vera knew what I was contemplating. "You don't owe me anything," she'd said when we'd first encountered the other riders, "and I know you're stronger than I am. Go ahead and ride with them if you want."

I'd turned down the suggestion at the time, and now I felt as though I needed an excuse to turn it down again. The weather pattern, I reminded myself, had been anything but conducive, and besides, once I crossed the summit I'd be leaving the mountains for good. But the fact remained that among U.S. mountain passes Trail Ridge Road was the "big one," and the lure of bagging it was immense.

Ultimately, the decision was simple. I didn't need an excuse to decide against being sucked into this group's form of white-line fever. If the norm for bicycle touring was too macho for me, I didn't have to accept it.

And if I still wanted an excuse, she was sitting beside me. Vera was one of the most congenial traveling companions I'd ever met. It was true that I owed her nothing, but the freedom afforded by that knowledge made her all the more valuable as a friend.

———————•••———————

When the rain abated we ran errands. The night before, Vera's father had given her a telescoping fishing rod, but she needed a reel, some bait, and a license. Meanwhile I'd finally decided that whatever route I took across the mountains, I'd head to Iowa in time for RAGBRAI. It had been a remarkably easy decision, a logical outgrowth of the process that had led me to stay with Vera instead of joining the faster group. While she was being shunted from one sporting goods store to another, I found a phone and let Jack know what I'd decided. RAGBRAI would serve marvelously for our Midwestern get-together, especially since this year's route began near his hometown.

The line was busy, so I went shopping for dinner.

I had told Vera that if she would supply the stove I'd cook. But I was starved for fruit and vegetables and went overboard on my shopping trip, buying green peppers, carrots, broccoli, fresh mushrooms, a potato, cherries, and a grapefruit, much of which I then had to ask her to carry.

We might have spent the night in Kremmling, where bicyclists were allowed to camp at the county fairgrounds, but Ruth and Steve—the cyclists we'd met near the Colorado border—were harassed by local kids when they camped here, so we decided to ride another 15 miles to a reservoir south of town. It was raining again, but we were beyond caring and there was blue sky just ahead. Soon we were riding in the sunlight, running before a strengthening tailwind; had we been so inclined we probably could have made it all the way to the next town.

Just before we reached our campground we passed a side road leading toward the dam that formed the reservoir. "PHONE" said a sign, with an arrow pointing to the right.

I sighed. "I'd better call Jack again. I doubt if I can from the campground. I wonder how far it is to that phone." I could see a town across the lake, and I had an unpleasant feeling that was where I was going. "I'll meet you at camp. With luck, I'll be only half an hour behind."

————— •●• —————

More than an hour later I bumped down the gravel road to the campground. Vera had selected a pleasant site on a low mound overlooking the lake. I propped my bike against a large sagebush — there were still no trees, even at 8,000 feet — and sat down heavily.

"How did it go?" she asked.

"That road was a killer. Up and down, up and down — steep little hills, $3\frac{1}{2}$ miles each way. I could have swum across faster!"

"Yeah, when I looked back and saw where you had to go. . . . Was he there?"

"The line was busy, so I waited and called again, but it was still busy. By the way, I brought back a gallon of water. I was at a lodge, and the woman who ran it said there wasn't any here."

"She was right. By the way, if you think your tent might leak you can share mine. I've got no problems with that."

I wasn't so sure. I knew my wife would have no objections to my traveling with Vera, and she trusted me. But I wasn't sure she'd approve of our sharing a tent unless it was absolutely necessary. I opted for the middle ground. "If it rains," I said, "I might take you up on that. Otherwise I'll pitch my own."

I didn't know how much sense that made to Vera — she had never been married — but regardless, one of the things I liked about her was that I knew she'd accept my preferences without taking offense. She shrugged. "Either way."

I suddenly realized how hungry I was. "For now, let's fix dinner. I'm bushed. That 7 miles wore me out!"

Before we could start we were joined by a tall blond man, about my age, with a surfer tan and the accompanying muscles.

"Hi," he said. "I'm Arvin, and I'm camped just down there." He indicated a camper near the bottom of our knoll. "If you two would like to use my stove for dinner, feel free. You can use anything else I've got, too."

That was an offer we couldn't refuse. So we gathered our vegetables and a pot and walked down the hill to Arvin's tent-trailer.

Arvin ran a sailboard concession at the lake, renting boards and giving lessons. In the winter he was a ski instructor. "I like rainy weeks like this," he said. "Then there's nothing to do but sleep and watch the lake."

Vera grinned. "It's a dirty job, but somebody has to do it!"

Arvin grinned back. "Right!"

The two of them continued to chat as I washed vegetables and peeled carrots. "I'd just eat 'em with the peels on," Arvin observed. "Here, would you like a cutting board?" But the board he proffered was stained and wet-looking, with a few gray flecks clinging to it that looked suspiciously like day-old meat.

"No thanks. I can do it fine this way."

"I think you're a bit of a fanatic about cleanliness," Vera whispered when Arvin was out of earshot.

I shrugged. "Not as much as Mark and Mary Lou." They'd kept everything as spotless as if it had been their kitchen at home. I thought of the catfish: Just as I hadn't seen the fish, Vera hadn't seen the cutting board.

Dinner was ready soon, and it was an immediate hit, a large pot of Ramen noodles choked with vegetables and covered with cheese. Arvin had said he'd already eaten, but he decided to sample some, then came back for seconds.

"You know," he said as we ate in the gathering twilight, "all those mountains across the lake are wilderness. It's called the Eagles Nest Wilderness. There's no roads over there—you can't go in except on foot."

Vera and I gazed across the dark waters toward the 13,000-foot peaks, their summits stark against the fading afterglow. Even here, at the edge of the wilderness, I could feel the familiar stirrings of primitive awe, a faint tug that called me to lose myself in the jumble of peaks, a feeling that there was something important there, just waiting for me to take the time to discover it.

I turned back to Arvin. "I didn't know there was much wilderness here in Colorado."

"Oh, yeah. There's a lot of it. Too much."

"Too much?" His change of tone had caught me off guard. Earlier, I'd thought I'd felt an echo of my own wistfulness.

"Yes, too much."

I could feel Vera stiffen beside me, but she was silent. "Why's that?" I asked.

"Because that's public land. It belongs to everybody, and everybody should have access to it. When they make it wilderness they don't allow most people to go in there. They should just run it like everything else. That's all it needs."

I didn't respond. It was a rational point of view, consistent with Arvin's career teaching downhill skiing and sailboarding. Antiwilderness sentiments, of course, don't necessarily follow from that, but such pastimes, oriented toward speed, skill, and excitement, are more similar to competitive sports than to the quieter, less mechanized activities associated with wilderness.

Vera turned to me as soon as we were out of Arvin's earshot. "You don't agree with him, do you?"

"Heavens, no. But why argue—I wouldn't persuade him. And he'd been so generous, it didn't seem right." I thought of Ben and his response to the cowboy in Idaho. Perhaps I'd learned something from him, that there were times to stand up for a principle, and times not to.

But one thing I did know was that it had gotten cold while we were huddled in the warmth of Arvin's campsite. It was so cold I could barely talk coherently, and as we walked, we joked about it, making shivering noises that only made us colder than ever. "You know," Vera said through chattering teeth, "your tent isn't pitched yet."

I groaned. At that moment, if she'd repeated her invitation to share hers I would have accepted, but she offered something better. "How can I help?" she asked. It was a simple offer, one I would have made myself if the circumstances had been reversed, and I wasn't too proud to accept.

———————•••———————

Our third day together was one of those days that makes or breaks a friendship.

It started simply enough, with neither of us stirring from our tents until at least an hour after sunup. Then Vera went fishing while I sat by the lake to work on my journal. Later, after a leisurely breakfast, we slipped over to Arvin's site to clean up the previous night's dishes. With all these delays it was midmorning by the time we broke camp, but for once I was in no hurry; we'd decided earlier that our goal for the night was a hostel in Breckenridge, barely 35 miles away. With any luck we could stop for the afternoon while Vera did some more fishing and I explored an off-road bike trail that climbed to the top of 10,600-foot Vail Pass.

It seemed a simple plan for an easy, relaxing day.

———————•••———————

At first it actually did go according to plan, as a tailwind blew us up the long, gradual hill to Silverthorne, the first of four resort towns clustered in a valley on the back side of the Front Range, only an hour's drive from Denver.

But something was wrong with my bike; the derailleur chattered as though it were perpetually out of gear. Nothing I could do would silence it, so when we passed a bike shop I stopped.

The problem proved to be a worn-out gear cluster (called a freewheel in cycling parlance). Fortunately the shop had a replacement, and I handed over my bike to have it installed.

Normally this shouldn't have taken longer than a few minutes. My hometown bike shop charged only $1.50 to remove a freewheel, clean it, and reinstall it. Putting on a new one should have been even simpler.

But this time the job took forever, as a continuous string of customers interrupted the mechanic. If I'd been alone I would have gone stir crazy. Instead, Vera and I took the opportunity to phone the hostel in Breckenridge. We learned that there was space available, but the accommodations were private rooms rather than the dormitories we were expecting. That was disappointing; dormitories are what usually make hostels such interesting places to meet people. It also meant we'd be assigned individual rooms and might not have anywhere to talk after dinner.

Since we were killing time anyway we played several rounds of "what would you prefer to do," eventually settling for a campground near Frisco, only 10 miles up the road. We could have managed all this in five minutes, but we stretched it to thirty, then spent another thirty fantasizing about what kind of ice cream we'd buy in Dillon, the next in the string of towns.

It seemed a good idea to have Vera's freewheel cleaned, too. She'd done a better job than I of keeping grit out of it, but it hadn't been professionally cleaned since she'd started. A good cleaning might keep her from running into the same problem that had stopped me.

By the time the mechanic was finished, at least an hour and a half had passed. "I'll give you a biker's special," he told me. "Seven dollars for the labor."

That wasn't really all that special for what should have been a ten- to fifteen-minute job—especially since I'd just paid a resort-town price for the freewheel. But it could have been worse.

Then he turned to Vera. "Four dollars."

I almost gagged. He'd done essentially the same work for each of us—if anything, he'd done more for Vera, and *she* hadn't bought an overpriced freewheel. Sexism, I thought, sometimes works to a woman's benefit.

————— ••• —————

A few miles later we were in Dillon, where I indulged myself in both a large ice-cream cone and a chocolate truffle. It was well after noon and I, for one, was famished. After the ice cream, Vera bought a roll of film at a drugstore and we were finally ready to tackle the remaining 9 miles to our campground.

"You know, we should probably buy dinner-makings while we're at it," I said. I had offered to cook spaghetti that evening, but we had none of the ingredients.

Vera gave me a long look, and we burst out laughing. Between the bike shop, the ice cream, and the film, we'd already spent three hours on a 1-mile stretch of road. Our relaxing afternoon was rapidly slipping away. Somehow we'd kept calm about it so far, laughing and joking rather than worrying, but enough was enough. "Let's blow this town," Vera said. "We'll get what we need in Frisco."

The route out of town led up a steep 300-foot hill to the shore of Dillon Reservoir, a beautiful man-made jewel lying in a basin surrounded by four of Colorado's most famous passes: Loveland, Vail, Independence, and Hoosier. Glad to be moving again, I surged up the hill, then turned to cross the dam, gritting my teeth as the change of direction turned the tailwind into a fierce crosswind. Vera was lagging badly.

"Ugh," she said when she'd caught up. "Too much sugar. That'll teach me to order a double-dip cone just because somebody else does! Why don't you go ahead and set up camp. I'll look for your tent when I get there."

I shrugged. "We've got lots of time. I'm not in a hurry." And that was true. It was the main thing I'd been learning in the last forty-eight hours. Riding with Vera had forced me to let her set the pace.

So we pedaled on, stopping once again for Vera and again 200 yards after that when the "perfect" picture rolled into view.

"Now I know you're not in a hurry," Vera laughed as I dug my camera out of my panniers. "But that *is* a good picture."

A moment later she muttered something far less enthusiastic.

I looked up. "Huh?"

"I can't find my film. I think I left it on the counter in the store." She searched her bags one more time. "I sure can't find it."

"Is it worth going back?"

We looked across the windswept dam and the hill descending into downtown Dillon. I thought about a 36-exposure roll of slide film at tourist-town prices.

I sighed. "I'll tell you what. You sit here with the gear and I'll strip down my bike and go get it." I began throwing sleeping bag, tent, and panniers on the road shoulder. "And when the sun comes out from behind that cloud," I handed Vera my camera, "take a picture across the lake. Without all that weight this shouldn't take long."

It didn't. I almost crashed twice in the first hundred yards, then became accustomed to the responsiveness of my unladen bicycle and sprinted into town, collecting the film and returning in less than twenty minutes. Vera was startled by how quickly I got back.

"It was great," I said. "Coming out of town I flew up that hill in less than two minutes. It was magnificent. I'd never have believed I could move like that, not up here at 9,000 feet!"

Vera grinned. "I *knew* you were going to race down there and back!"

I pondered that as we reloaded my bicycle. Was I that transparent? Not that I cared so long as the right people could read me. But I wasn't sure I'd known I was going to ride like that until after I'd gotten started.

Fifteen minutes later the wind had blown us to Frisco, a mile or two from our proposed campground.

We passed a supermarket and paused for a consultation, quickly deciding to worry about dinner later and find a campsite first. In exchange for the film Vera would come back to shop while I climbed Vail Pass. The path began in Frisco, and for a moment we considered separating while I climbed the pass and she set up camp. But the way the day had been going it seemed unwise. I might have trouble finding her that evening, and besides, it meant I'd have to lug my gear more than 1,500 feet to the top of the pass.

It proved to be the right decision. What showed on our maps as a single campground was actually three, two of which were enormous. And while there was a special area designated for bicycles, it was poorly marked and I doubted both of us would have found it independently. If we'd separated, we might never have seen each other again.

With that disaster averted we attempted to finalize our dinner plans.

"What should we get for the spaghetti sauce?"

"Oh, an onion, green pepper—or, you know, I saw a sign that said 'PIZZA' on the way into town. It's been on my mind ever since."

"Yum, I could go for pizza."

"Of course, spaghetti's fine. I don't mind spaghetti."

"Either's okay with me."

"Spaghetti's cheaper. But it'll be dark by the time we get to it."

"That's all right. I don't mind eating after sunset."

"But you know, pizza sounds really good."

It was a game we'd played before, the same one Vera had played with her mother—the old Alfonse/Gaston routine, with neither of us wanting to impose his or her will on the other, and thus never making a decision.

On an unconscious level we were trying to work by consensus, and we didn't know each other well enough to feel comfortable being assertive. It was a problem that would plague us repeatedly, and much later I realized it was largely the result of my small-town Midwestern upbringing, which had indoctrinated me in the virtue of hospitality while simultaneously drilling into me an aversion to accepting someone else's hospitality without first offering multiple protests.

The resulting discussions are sometimes comic, sometimes frustrating, beginning as one person makes an offer and ending some time later, when the other has decided whether the offer is genuine and whether it can be accepted without undue imposition. Reaching this conclusion is a negotiated process, with the parties presenting their positions through the strength of their offers and the vigor of their denials until each is fairly certain what the other really means.

That, at least, is what happens when both are playing the same game. What I hadn't yet figured out about Vera was that she didn't work that way, except with her mother. She is one of those rare people who usually mean exactly what they say and value directness above all else. "You keep deferring to me," she would later say. "That's not partnership. Tell me what you want and let me take care of myself."

But at the time these realizations lay in the future, and it took me a long time to hazard a true opinion. "Let's go for pizza," I said eventually. It was getting late; it was nearly five o'clock when we first reached Frisco. "You don't have time to shop for groceries if you're going fishing. Let's meet, say between 8:00 and 8:30?"

"Okay, but I don't want you to kill yourself thinking you have to be there at a specific time. That's the only trouble with the idea. I can write postcards while I wait, so don't worry about it, okay?"

"Fine. But my map says it's only 11 miles from Frisco to the pass. If I'm not back by 8:30, something went wrong, like a flat tire."

I should have known better: I'd just donned the straightjacket Vera had been trying to keep me out of.

I should also have known better than to trust maps.

———————————•●•———————————

I found the bike path easily, but the pass was a good deal farther away than I'd thought. As soon as I realized that, I questioned other people along the trail.

"How far is Vail Pass?" I asked a roller-skiing woman wearing a T-shirt from a college ski team.

"Seventy-seven miles round trip, I think."

"It *can't* be that far!"

"Well, you have to go up over the top then all the way down the other side."

"No, not the town of Vail. How far is the pass?"

Blank look.

I kept getting that answer from other people. None of them could distinguish the pass from the ski town on its far side.

Finally I found someone who understood—a pair of college-age women out for a walk.

"Fifteen miles from Frisco," they informed me. "You should have no trouble making it before dark."

But could I get back by 8:30?

———•———

I thought about that for a while, then made a decision. I hadn't used my watch since the day I'd left, but this time I would. I was going to be on time. It wasn't really that important whether I made the summit, and I'd committed myself to the return time, even if unnecessarily. I grinned. People back home would be flabbergasted. The Rick they knew didn't give up such goals so easily; on bike rides I had a reputation for returning late, having squeezed every possible mile out of the day. While I was making resolutions I also resolved not to kill myself on the ascent. I would enjoy the scenery and get as far as I got. Hopefully that would mean the top, but I wasn't going to be late, nor was I going to miss the scenery merely to bag the summit.

It was a spectacular climb. For the first 6 to 7 miles the path followed a creek along the bottom of a deep canyon. Above, the beehive-shaped ramparts of the highest cliffs towered so near it strained the neck to look up, while occasional shafts of sunlight threw entire cliff faces into golden relief. I paused now and then to crane my neck and let my thoughts drift toward those sculpted minarets 3,500 feet above me, standing in awe until eventually the mind regained the body and I could resume my passage without fear of forgetting such mundane matters as the next bend in the trail.

This was Colorado at its finest, my first glimpse of it since North Park. The rest of the state had been overcrowded, with too many views impeded by telephone wires, mining scars, or the zigzagging incisions of gravel roads, and too much traffic obscuring the scenery. Arvin was wrong. Colorado needs wilderness. It needs it now, before it's too late. In many places, it may already be too late.

It was odd that this path should inspire such thoughts, for it shared the canyon with Interstate 70, which lay less than 100 yards away on the other side of the creek. But somehow that wasn't a problem—I wasn't sure why, but perhaps it was merely a compliment to the people who'd engineered it that they had minimized the impact from the interstate while maximizing the scenery. The closeness of the cliffs and the knowledge that the mountains across the freeway were the same ones Arvin had pointed out the night before also helped. They belonged to the wilderness and were closed to motors and bicycles alike.

Above the canyon the valley widened and the bike path followed a circuitous route through the resort village at the base of Copper Mountain Ski Area. I had to stop for directions but eventually emerged on the other side and continued toward the pass, following a much smaller creek along the broad median of the interstate. I was running out of time but pedaled steadily and calmly, watching the stream dwindle to a small brook that I hoped meant the summit was near. Then, panting in air that was definitely thinner than I was used to, I crested a final, steep rise, crossed the parking lot of a freeway rest area, and rolled through the open summit of Vail Pass, at 10,666 feet the highest point I'd ever climbed by bicycle.

I coasted to the other side and descended 100 feet to the shore of a small lake, where I gazed at the jumble of mountains on the distant horizon and watched clouds scudding past nearby peaks. I took a few pictures—mostly just to show I'd been there—then turned back to Frisco and dinner.

The descent was slower than I'd expected; the upper part of the trail was so steep and winding I couldn't go very fast, and in the canyon the wind was against me. I still had a margin for error, however, and I reached Frisco with five minutes to spare. Determined to be punctual—though I knew a few minutes made no practical difference—I sprinted through town and arrived at the pizzeria one minute early, gasping for breath but delighted that I'd not only conquered the pass, but I'd been on time and I'd been willing to turn back if the summit had been too far.

Vera's bicycle was nowhere to be seen, so I paced around the parking lot until I caught my breath. I was about to go inside to reserve a table when I had a sudden thought: What if she'd caught a fish? Our whole plan was based on the assumption she would catch nothing. What if she was back in camp with all the makings for a fish dinner, while I was squandering the few remaining minutes of daylight here at the pizzeria? It wasn't an encouraging thought, but the solution was simple: I could pedal back to camp and check. It was only a couple of miles, and if I met her coming from the other direction, all I would have wasted was a little energy. I hopped on my bicycle and hurried through town, then out the other side to the turnoff for the campground. As I turned in, I nodded to four men in leather jackets and fierce beards who were sitting on motorcycles near the entrance. I was just as glad they didn't nod back.

Half a mile beyond the turnoff, the campground road split into two one-way segments that converged again within a few hundred yards. A half mile after that was the dirt path leading to the bicycle campground.

Even from the road I could see that Vera wasn't at our site. *Blast*, I thought, *I must have missed her on that one-way stretch.* I started to turn back but decided that as long as I was at camp, I might as well pick up my night riding gear—a reflective vest, a headlight that strapped onto my handlebars, and a taillight. One stretch of the main highway had no shoulder, and I didn't fancy being run over by the Friday evening traffic coming up from Denver and Colorado Springs.

I scurried back to the road and sprinted after Vera, mentally framing various versions of my story, trying to find the best way to word my apology. As I turned onto the highway I noted that the motorcyclists were drinking beer.

It had only taken ten minutes to get from the pizzeria to camp, but by now it was getting dark enough that fear of hitting an unseen pedestrian slowed me considerably. It was probably nine o'clock by the time I got back to the pizzeria, and again, Vera's bicycle was nowhere to be seen.

I nearly panicked. What could have gone wrong? Had I missed her again in the dark? Could she have gone back to camp searching for me?

There is a classic rule about such situations: When lost, stay in one place and wait to be found. I unpacked my pen and a stack of postcards and went inside to wait.

But it wasn't a good place for writing postcards. The general hubbub and smell of beer told me that, at least on Friday evenings, pizza wasn't the main order of business. Eight drunk college-age kids circled a table near the door, and one of them eyed me sullenly as I stepped inside. "Hey man," he slurred, staring at my reflective vest, "I can see you just fine."

I did my best to ignore him as I sidestepped one of his companions staggering back from the bathroom. This, I decided, wasn't my kind of place. And if I knew Vera, it wasn't hers either. If she'd been here earlier, she might well have left.

I flagged down a waitress. "Did a thirty-year-old woman on a bicycle stop here earlier?"

"Yeah. She didn't stay."

"How long ago?"

"Oh, just a few minutes."

I thanked her and left, cursing silently. If only I'd stayed put the first time. I went back outside to think. Where might Vera have gone? Another restaurant downtown? That seemed the most likely possibility. Since there were only two roads, it should be easy to find her bicycle.

For the second time I pedaled back into town, watching carefully to make sure she wasn't coming toward me on the other side of the highway.

Frisco's main street runs perpendicular to the highway, so I turned off and rode all the way through town, watching the storefronts for her bicycle. But it wasn't there. I stopped some pedestrians and asked if they'd seen another bicyclist, but no one could help. It was now 9:30, and I was hungry.

I thought about giving up and letting Vera fend for herself, but I was still afraid she was waiting for me somewhere, and the obvious place was back in camp. I couldn't leave her sitting there while I ate dinner, so once again I pedaled onto the main highway and passed the motorcyclists guarding the campground entrance.

When I reached the one-way fork in the road I stopped to think. There was only one road from camp to town, so Vera and I must have passed each other at least once. The only place where that could have happened was the one-way segment, where 50 yards of intervening trees blocked the view of the other lane. This time, I decided, I'd outsmart her and go against the flow of traffic, just to make sure it couldn't happen again.

To make doubly sure, I sprinted as hard as I could through the one-way section, wondering what I would say if I met a ranger coming toward me, then groped in the dark until I found the bicycle campground.

Vera still wasn't there.

I was almost ready to cry. I was hungry, I was so tired I was shaking, and Vera had vanished into thin air. The way my luck was going, she'd probably left only minutes before, and with logic similar to mine had also ridden against traffic on the one-way segment, allowing us to pass each other yet again. Either that or she'd fallen into a black hole, I wasn't sure which.

The worst part was that I expected this would be our last evening together before I turned off for Pueblo or Colorado Springs while she continued south for Santa Fe. The farewell celebration wasn't turning out as planned.

I was too hungry to stay around camp. I had to eat something. Vera would probably return to the pizzeria, learn that I'd been inquiring about her, and go eat somewhere else. I'd make one more attempt to find her, but this time I hedged my bets by leaving a note in her tent, telling her I was alive and well but had given up and was going to order a pizza. I didn't relish returning to the bar, but I didn't want to waste time trying to find somewhere else to eat.

I headed back to the main highway, again riding against traffic on the one-way section. This time I stopped every 50 yards to call her name so loudly that I imagined it could be heard by the motorcyclists at the campground entrance.

I pedaled by the motorcyclists again, wondering what they thought of this bicyclist who'd passed by four times in the last hour and wishing I had the nerve to ask if they'd seen Vera.

Then, just before I got back to the bar/pizzeria, I spotted a lone cyclist coming from the other direction.

I stopped. "Vera?"

"Rick!" I was afraid she'd be angry, but instead she was laughing. "That pizza joint just wasn't my kind of place, so I went to the other one!"

"What other one?"

"You mean you didn't see it? There's a Pizza Hut just on the other side of the Kentucky Fried Chicken." She turned to point. "I guess you *can't* see it from here. Not unless you know it's there. I found it when I did some shopping at the grocery store across the street, and I was sure you'd go there, too."

Vera's laugh was infectious. It had never crossed my mind that she would go anywhere but back toward camp. I told her about the hypothetical fish. "Have you eaten?"

Now she was laughing so hard I thought she might fall off her bicycle. "Yes. I'm sorry. I was hungry, and I didn't wait. But I *really* got caught up on my postcards. And I ate a whole pizza . . ." she was laughing harder than ever, "while you were riding back and forth in the dark! What are you going to do now?"

That was simple. "I'm going to Pizza Hut. Want to join me?"

She hesitated, then laughed again. "Sure, why not."

————— ◦•◦ —————

It was 11 before I'd downed a whole medium-size pizza and mounted up for the all-too-familiar trudge back to camp. Since I had my taillight and a reflective vest, I let Vera lead and gave her my headlight.

"You know," she said as we approached the same four motorcyclists and the pitch dark of the campground road, "this light is terrible. I can't see anything by it."

I chuckled, but Vera didn't find it funny. "Too much late-night journal writing," I said. "It needs new batteries." I fished in the pocket of my windbreaker. "I've got a regular flashlight, but its batteries aren't any better."

"What if we go past the campsite in the dark?"

I shrugged. We might well spend the next hour playing blind man's bluff in the campground, but now that I was warm, well fed, and out of the traffic for the last time, I couldn't work up the energy to worry. Besides, my bicycle could probably follow this path by habit.

A minute or two later we found the campground and crawled into our tents. I had barely zipped mine shut when I heard Vera's laugh from next door. "I found your message," she called. At least something had worked right.

I lay back, thinking about the evening and the comedy of errors that had put so much wear and tear on my nerves. Every step Vera and I had taken had been logical, but I wondered what the chances were that, if I'd gone through the same experience with my wife, we'd have wound up reacting in the verbal equivalent of "shoot first, ask questions later." Mentally I replayed the evening's events, trying to figure out what Vera and I had done in our three-day-old friendship that I could apply to a ten-year-old marriage.

One possible answer came to me over the breeze. In the distance I imagined I could hear Vera's muffled laughter.

———————•❖•———————

Neither of us rose as early the next morning as we'd intended, but even so we were on the move by 8 A.M., following an off-road bike path up the easy climb to Breckenridge. We paid resort prices for a breakfast smaller than the ones I used to get for less than half the price in Oregon, then stopped again at a bookstore, and yet again at a bike shop. Vera joked that after the previous day's episode she had no business visiting another bike shop, but I urged her to go ahead, waiting while she bought leg warmers and a handlebar-mounted rear-view mirror. We were planning to part company in 30 miles, and shortly after that I would drop all too quickly out of the mountains in a descent that would be exhilarating but would ultimately deposit me at the beginning of 700 miles of hot, windy prairie. I was in no hurry to leave either Vera or the Rockies.

The store was busy, and the service almost as slow as at the other bike shop, but eventually we finished and pedaled out of town toward Hoosier Pass, my fifth—Vera's ninth—crossing of the Continental Divide. The pass was 11,541 feet high, but the road was well graded, and it wasn't a difficult climb. I was surprised at how much I felt the elevation. I hadn't been below 7,400 feet since I'd left Wyoming, and I'd assumed I was altitude acclimated.

We reached the top in an hour and a half and basked in the sun, celebrating our arrival at the highest point on the Bikecentennial Trail. Vera had several more passes to climb, but for me this would be the last substantial grade before the Appalachians.

As we lounged at the summit another cyclist, a racer training out of Dillon, came up behind us, and two heavily loaded touring cyclists — the vanguard of an official Bikecentennial-sponsored group on a three-month crossing of the TransAmerica Trail — arrived from the other side. A few minutes later a car stopped, and the driver joined us; she had a cousin in the Bikecentennial group and was waiting to surprise him when he reached the summit.

The other Bikecentennial riders struggled up one by one, until eventually there were nearly ten of us gathered around the Continental Divide marker, holding an impromptu party to celebrate our arrival at the high point of our respective journeys. It was a special moment in many ways, and Vera and I lingered more than an hour, surrounded by 14,000-foot peaks, chatting with the other riders and sharing tips about routes, food, and lodging.

Throughout all of this I had fun watching the three-way interaction among Vera, me, and the racing cyclist who'd come up behind us. His name, if I heard correctly, was Allen, and he was clearly drawn to Vera. First he set about attempting to determine if we were a couple, asking questions that seemed calculated to give me an opportunity to clarify our relationship.

If he'd asked directly, I'd have answered equally directly, but since he didn't, I took an impish delight in not giving him what he wanted. Eventually he either decided we weren't a couple or concluded that the best way to find out was simply to plow ahead. He deftly separated us then turned his attention to her, cutting me out of the conversation.

As they talked, I thought about my relationship with Vera.

Unlike Allen, most people had simply assumed we were a couple. After all, a man and woman about the same age, traveling together — what else could we be? The illusion was furthered by the absence of my wedding ring; I'd left it in Sacramento because, on extended trips, it often became painful beneath my cycling gloves.

The illusion made me uncomfortable. Many people would think I shouldn't be traveling with a woman other than my wife, let alone an attractive single woman. When Vera and I were alone I didn't think about it; our companionship had taken on the easy familiarity of old friends who've been through much together and know what to expect of each other. But when strangers were around, I often felt the eyes of an older generation staring at me, disapproving. I became defensive, and often I found myself searching for ways to shatter the illusion by mentioning my wife.

In essence, I was saying, "You don't know this, but I'm married, and not to her. But it's okay, because I wouldn't tell you if it weren't." I wondered why I did it. I wasn't uncomfortable with our friendship; over the years, many of my best friends had been single women.

Ultimately, I knew other people's reactions weren't important. The unspoken—and often imaginary—censure I felt was a holdover from an era when I wouldn't have met a woman riding solo. Companionships such as Vera and I were developing come along only rarely, and I simply accepted her friendship as a gift.

————— •❦• —————

When we finally prepared to leave, Vera surveyed the winding 1,500-foot drop to the valley below. "I'll follow you," she said. "You've got more experience, and I'm never sure how fast is safe. I want to see how you handle it."

"Most people tell me I'm overcautious," I warned. "I really worry about wind shifts on the bends."

"Better overcautious than not careful enough." But within half a mile, the exhilaration of speed won over excess caution, and Vera, grinning wildly, slipped by me at 40 miles an hour. I followed slightly behind.

The descent was a joyride. The road was well graded, the wind blew strong and steady behind us, and for once the rain showers that had again formed over the higher peaks kept their distance.

Even after our route spilled into the broad, high-elevation meadow known as South Park, near the headwaters of the South Platte River, we continued to sail along at nearly 25 miles an hour, until—barely half an hour from the summit—we reached Fairplay, where Vera's route continued south to Santa Fe and mine would curve east toward the Great Plains of eastern Colorado and Kansas.

"This is where I'm going to stop for the night," Vera announced as we came into town. "The map shows a hostel, and that sounds nice. What are you going to do?"

I had no real plan. It was 40 miles to the next campground, but with the tailwind I could cover it easily in two hours and could push a lot farther before dark. On the other hand traveling with Vera had finally taught me to quit worrying about distances. Yesterday we'd covered only 30 miles; today we'd barely made that. But it wasn't as though I had a quota, and while eventually I'd have to put in some longer days if I was going to catch RAGBRAI, there was time enough for 100-milers when I was alone on the Plains.

It was another easy decision. "I'll join you. Maybe I'll fix that spaghetti dinner. I'd rather spend the evening with you than get a head start on tomorrow."

According to the map the hostel was in the South Park Community Church, which we located thanks to its spire, conspicuous among the other structures in town. It was a small church of trim, white frame and neatly tended lawn, a touch of New England transplanted to the treeless high country of central Colorado. The sanctuary, which could barely have held fifty people, was as tidy and unpretentious as the exterior, but no one was inside. We went back out, looking for the church office, but instead met a spry, eighty-year-old woman tending a flower bed.

"You must be looking for the hostel," she said. The tone of her voice and the sparkle in her eye told me she knew the secret of life and relished it to the full. Her name, she said, was Weltha. "It means 'Welcome.' I was the first girl after four boys, and my parents thought it was a welcome change." I later learned she'd just returned from her own six-week adventure in Scotland.

"Just check over there," she continued, gesturing to a house on the other side of the street. "I think the pastor's out, but his wife can show you where to stay."

A few minutes later we found ourselves wheeling our bikes into a third building, a single-story structure the size of a small ranch house that served as a combination community center and Sunday school. The pastor was indeed out of town, but he would be back that evening to collect the fee.

"Let's get dinner-makings," I suggested, eyeing the large gas stove in the kitchen. Since nothing in Fairplay was far from anything else, we set off on foot.

Dinner proved to be the spaghetti equivalent of the Ramen stew of two nights earlier, and as before, I was the chef. The availability of vegetables was again overwhelming, and we loaded ourselves down with cauliflower, broccoli, mushrooms, carrots, onions, and whatever else seemed even remotely appropriate.

"Let's get some beer or wine to top it off," Vera suggested. "Something special for our second, last dinner together."

I shook my head. "We probably shouldn't. We're staying in a church and they might object."

"You really think so?"

"I don't know. But this is a small town, and there's a pretty good chance."

I wasn't sure Vera was convinced, but she accepted in good grace, and we returned to the community center.

The pastor hadn't yet arrived. As I set up for dinner I wished I knew what the kitchen rules were. In some states, health codes regulate public kitchens extensively. Reluctant to take time-consuming precautions, I decided to pass up the extensive collection of pots and pans and use as much of our own equipment as possible.

Within fifteen minutes the sauce was simmering and the spaghetti water boiling. In a fit of rashness we threw the entire pound of spaghetti into the pot. It took a while to cook—we were at 10,000 feet—but eventually it was done, and we settled down on the front porch to an extremely filling meal.

After cleaning up I went downtown to call my wife, who'd just gotten home from a week-long conference.

"I've got news for you," she said early in our conversation. "I'm going to the University of Michigan for three weeks in August."

She went on to explain the research problem that had led to that decision and how the conference had prompted her to approach it aggressively, but I was too stunned to relate to what she was saying. As I'd told Vera a few days before, I'd half-expected some aspect of Jane's work to interfere with our vacation, but I'd never expected to lose the whole thing. All I had grasped was that she needed specialized equipment or assistance that she could access through connections at the university, where we'd both gone to graduate school.

It crossed my mind that I could abandon the bike trip in Colorado and fly back to spend time with her before she had to leave. But I knew she'd be busy and I'd soon be wishing I'd stayed on the road.

Jane must have been thinking along the same lines. Earlier I'd told her I wasn't sure I would have time to make it all the way to the East Coast and she responded by offering to forgo our vacation. She repeated the suggestion, pointing out that my alternatives were either to spend the three weeks alone in California or to join her while she worked in Michigan. Both sounded dull.

I said I'd think about it, but my head was already swimming with the implications. Only a few days before I'd been seeking a way to relax while still making it all the way across the country. Then I'd met Vera and obtained the first half of my wish, choosing the day-by-day pleasure of her company instead of the endurance race for the Atlantic. Suddenly I'd been given back the Atlantic—without the endurance race.

It was ironic that the opportunity came because my wife had chosen high-pressure goals—in her case, career goals—over a vacation. I didn't know enough to second-guess her decision, but it wouldn't be the first time a wished-for vacation had been consumed by research, and I was saddened by the thought that it wouldn't be the last.

Even so, walking back to the hostel I couldn't keep my heart from soaring with the realization that I now had time both to relax and to reach any point I chose on the East Coast. I would miss Jane, but I'd made my decision: I would spend the extra weeks on the road.

———————•○•———————

I got back just in time for the pastor's arrival.

"Glad to have you here," he greeted us. "The cost is three dollars apiece, and feel free to use anything you like." So much for my concern about state health codes. "But because this is run by the church, there are three rules we ask people to follow. One, no drugs."

We nodded. No problem there.

"Two. No alcohol. If you've already had some, don't worry about it. It's not that we're trying to regulate your personal behavior, but we use this building for other purposes and it's easier to tell the youth groups 'No' if we have a hard and fast rule against it."

"You were right, Rick," Vera interjected. She explained for the pastor's benefit. "We were going to get some wine for dinner, but Rick thought the church might object."

"Thank you," the pastor said. "Not many people would show so much respect. The third rule is a bit different. Because this is a church, we ask you to think for a moment about the people who built this place so you could be here, and—if you believe in God—to take a moment to thank him for the shelter of this structure. That's all. And of course, tomorrow is Sunday, and you're welcome to join us if you like, but there's no obligation."

"When's the service?" I asked. I'd already been thinking it would be nice to worship with these people.

"At 8:30 and 11:00. You need to have your gear out of here by 11:00, by the way, so we can hold Sunday school."

"Maybe I'll join you for the first service," I said.

———— •◦• ————

As dusk fell and the thin mountain air turned chill even inside the building, Vera and I settled down on the soft cushions of an oversize couch. We could have turned on the heat, but both of us were campers at heart, and so we wrapped ourselves in our sleeping bags and sat facing each other on opposite ends of the couch, leaning back against the armrests, our feet not quite meeting in the middle.

It was warm, comfortable, and companionable, and as we continued what we expected to be our last evening together we moved into a rambling conversation of the type more frequently shared around campfires — talk of life and purpose and aspirations, of Vera's long battle with cancer and what she'd learned from it.

I was amazed by how different were the lives that had brought us to this place. We'd both come of age in the tumult of the late sixties and early seventies but had reacted in very different ways. Perhaps because I'd lived in a small town, far removed from the hotbeds of political protest, I'd swung counter to the political pendulum of my generation. I'd viewed the Vietnam War as a regrettable necessity and would have served if my number had come up in the draft. It was only later, when many of my peers were shedding their idealism, that I became increasingly liberal.

Vera, on the other hand, grew up in New York City and had joined the antiwar movement. To her the only ethical alternatives had been either to protest or enlist; to sit on the sidelines hoping not to be called was never a consideration. She'd joined the drug culture in her early teens, and while she'd never dropped out — had instead graduated with good grades from Cornell — drugs and alcohol had figured prominently in her life until shortly before her cancer. The only thing our youths had in common was love of the outdoors, and it was unlikely that would have been enough to make us friends if we'd met only a few years before.

Six years earlier she was working at an animal shelter she helped found in Eugene, Oregon. She'd been depressed for some time, and one day she walked off the job. A few days later she found herself in Hawaii, living in an informal commune with an old friend, helping him grow marijuana but mostly fighting depression and trying to reassemble the pieces of her life.

Before succeeding she fell ill and was diagnosed with leukemia. "It was strange," she said as we sat on the couch. "When I was depressed, I'd wanted to get sick with something dramatic so everyone would have to take care of me. And then it happened."

Refusing admission to the local hospital, about which she'd heard a number of horror stories, she went home to Oregon for treatment instead. She phoned ahead to ask her sister, who lived in Portland, to meet her at the airport. She boarded the flight, barely catching it in time. "They told me later," she said matter-of-factly, "that I could easily have died on that flight. My platelet count was so low that if I'd started to hemorrhage I would have bled to death." In fact, she said, the doctor her sister contacted in Portland tried to stop her but was too late.

Nevertheless, she believed her wish to go to Oregon helped save her life, though she knew it would have been wiser to go to Honolulu for the initial treatments. "If I'd gone to one of the big cancer centers," she said, "I'd have been one of several leukemia patients. But I was the only one in that hospital in Portland, and I got extra attention."

Doctors gave her a twenty to twenty-five percent chance of long-term survival. "Even today," she said, "when I feel certain pains I get a flash of fear that it's a relapse, even if I know there's another explanation."

Vera exemplified what Friedrich Nietzsche must have meant when he wrote: "That which does not kill me makes me strong." She'd beaten the cancer, and rediscovered life. "I wanted to live," she said with far more intensity than when she'd spoken of the cancer itself, "each day—each week I had—and I took them as they came."

It was that desire to live that had shaped the person I'd come to respect so much. She'd stopped using drugs—today, she said, she'd like to work with "at risk" teenagers to help them see life more positively—and she'd developed the iron will and total self-confidence that were apparent from the first hour I'd known her.

On the fourth anniversary of her remission—a milestone made even more auspicious by having been off chemotherapy for half that time without a relapse—she hatched the plan for her bike ride. "I didn't ask my doctor," she said. "I just went in and told him what I was going to do; that way, he couldn't tell me it was crazy. Instead, he told me what warning signs to look for and what to do if I had problems."

At the time she didn't even own a bicycle, but a month later she and her housemate, Peggy, were on the road, doing 80 miles a day, even though she'd put in less than 100 miles of training. She told me again, "My doctor said I might never get my old stamina back, and I'm beginning to believe he's right. It doesn't seem to matter how long I've been on the road; after about 50 miles I start to get tired and really slow down."

I was more optimistic. "We did 80 miles that second day," I pointed out, "and what you did that first week on almost no training was amazing. Give it time."

She smiled. "Thanks."

"You know," she said a few minutes later, "I'm getting sleepy, but this couch is too soft. I guess I've been sleeping on the ground for too long." She headed off for the other room. "I'm going to sleep on the floor."

I probably could have slept comfortably on the couch, but I hated to lose the companionable feeling that had pervaded the silence as our conversation faded out. "I'll join you," I said, and tossed my sleeping bag on the worn carpet of the rec-hall floor, a few feet from hers. We weren't much farther apart than if we'd shared a tent that night with Arvin; I wondered vaguely why my sense of propriety accepted one but not the other.

In the morning I attended church for the first time since leaving Sacramento.

Vera didn't join me. She was Jewish by heritage but New Age—influenced by choice, viewing life as a smorgasbord of religious practices, all leading to the same goal. "What I don't like about many Christians," she'd told me the night before, "is their exclusiveness. They don't accept other religions as equally valid."

I'd heard that as a criticism of Christianity. "The reason," I'd said, "is that Christianity is different from religions that say the path to God is one of self-improvement. We say that's impossible, that first we must realize we can't perfect ourselves." I didn't know enough about comparative religion to know if that made Christianity unique. What I did know was that for me life involved a fundamental paradox: I had high ideals, but I knew that without help I'd always fall short.

When it came to recognizing our imperfections Vera and I weren't all that far apart, and the conversation had gone on from there with no resolution other than the realization that we each took our spiritualities very seriously. Despite our differences, it was something else we had in common. In the morning, Vera sat on the steps of the community center reading a book of meditations while I attended church.

The turn-out at the early service was small, but the sixteen people welcomed me despite my cycling tights and woolen jacket. Many—if not most—of the others were tourists or fishermen, and it was clear that the main reason this tiny church bothered to hold two services was for people like us. According to the bulletin, this congregation had been founded in 1872 by pioneer Presbyterian missionary Sheldon Jackson, who was later to acquire the nickname "Bishop of All Beyond" for his work as the foremost Protestant missionary to Alaska. The building itself had been in continuous use for 112 years, and the congregation's interest in meeting the needs of travelers indicated it had not forgotten its pioneer beginnings. Since I myself come from a Presbyterian background, I took pride in seeing this piece of my heritage so well preserved.

After the service I was invited to stay for cookies and coffee, which undoubtedly would have led to one or more invitations to lunch. I wanted to accept but couldn't. I'd told Vera that, if she waited until after the service, I'd ride with her across South Park and take my leave at the next junction after Fairplay, lengthening my route slightly but postponing the inevitable separation. So I said good-bye to the congregation, letting them fill my hands with cookies "for the road" for both Vera and myself.

I found her sitting on the steps of the community center, still reading. "Here," she said, handing me a handwritten sheet of paper. It was a passage from *The Prophet* by Kahlil Gibran, which she'd shared with me the night before in response to my concern that the trip might lose all meaning to the continuous pleasure of the moment.

Gibran's answer was both challenging and reassuring:

> *Pleasure is a freedom-song,*
> *But it is not freedom.*
> *It is the blossoming of your desires,*
> *But it is not their fruit.*
> *It is the depth calling unto a height,*
> *But it is not the deep nor the high.*
> *It is the caged taking wing,*
> *But it is not space encompassed.*
> *Ay, in very truth, pleasure is a freedom-song.*
> *And I fain would have you sing it with fullness of heart;*
> *yet I would not have you lose your hearts in the singing.*

Folding the quote into my address book for safekeeping, I felt a renewed sense of purpose. Yes, my odyssey could degenerate into nothing more than a self-indulgent escape in which the only goals were the search for the perfect tailwind or the ideal downgrade. The past few days had relaxed me, but I might yet wind up drifting aimlessly across the American landscape. Yet Gibran and Vera reassured me that there was nothing wrong with tailwinds or downgrades, and relaxing wasn't drifting; my

quest was to learn the lessons that might come from either pleasure or adversity.

———————•◉•———————

Five minutes later we were on the road, gradually descending and racing a tailwind to match the one that had blown us into town the night
before.

Four miles out of town, Vera suddenly pulled up beside me. "Your flag,"
she shouted over the roar of the wind, "you forgot your flag."

She was right. The orange triangle that, all trip long, had flapped behind me on its 8-foot pole was no longer there. I braked to a halt, thinking quickly. It had been on the bike the night before; I'd had to remove it
to get through the door of the community center. Presumably it was still
there, propped in a corner.

Vera remembered the slide film she'd left in Dillon. "I should offer to go
back and get it for you," she said. She turned to face the wind. "But I
won't."

It was decision time. I couldn't ask her to wait while I went back.
Against that wind, the roundtrip would take nearly an hour. I shrugged.
It wouldn't be right to part that way. "Let's go," I said, "It's not worth it."

———————•◉•———————

A dozen miles later we reached my turnoff. Again I stalled, suggesting
that I go with her up the short climb to the top of the next pass. Although
the summit was 9,300 feet above sea level, the climb from this side was
only 300 feet and within a few minutes we were there, sitting on the stone
bench that held the elevation marker, eating oranges and preparing to say
farewell.

Not for the first time that morning I was mentally rehearsing the distances I had to cover to meet RAGBRAI. Last night I'd finally contacted
Jack, and he'd suggested that instead of catching the ride at its start we
wait until the second day when it would pass near his hometown. Counting today, that meant I had eight days' time, and I figured that by the
shortest route it was at most 700 miles, with no major hills. I could see no
obstacle to covering the distance in a week—faster, if I picked up a good
tailwind.

That meant I still had a day to waste, and there was no reason I
couldn't accompany Vera as far as Salida, the next opportunity to turn
east. At the rate we were going we were likely to get there by midafter-

noon, and if the wind stayed behind me I might make another 40 miles beyond that by nightfall.

I told her my idea.

"Won't that mean you have to ride pretty hard the rest of the week?" she asked.

"About 100 miles a day if I get a good head start tonight." I'd held that pace on other trips on the Plains.

"Can you stay relaxed?"

It was a good question. I thought about it a moment, but 100 miles a day didn't seem unreasonable over level terrain. Even if I got headwinds, I could still cover a lot of mileage by starting at dawn, when it was calm. I nodded. "Yeah, I think so."

She gave me a long gaze. "I think so, too."

I grinned. It was our third postponed good-bye since Hoosier Pass. This one, however, would have to be real. The next east/west highway after Salida was another 75 miles away and would leave me so far south I'd wind up in Oklahoma instead of Iowa.

———————————•◦•———————————

Without further ado, we mounted our bicycles and began the 1,400-foot descent into the Arkansas River valley below.

At first it was unspectacular—a 400-foot drop into a dry meadow, flanked by low, wooded ridges. In the distance, above an intervening ridge, rose a single, snowy peak, a solitary reminder that better scenery lay ahead.

From the meadow we followed a stream bed around the end of the ridge, into a winding canyon strewn with grotesque boulders and isolated pines. The Sunday traffic intensified, and I saw less of the landscape than I would have liked as cars squeezed by on the narrow road, too impatient to wait for gaps in the oncoming traffic, even though we were often moving at 30 miles an hour.

When the road straightened, the view opened before us—a sweeping vista across a flat-bottomed valley toward a backdrop of snow-covered peaks rising nearly 7,000 feet above us, barely a dozen miles away.

We stopped at a scenic pullout to get away from the traffic and admire the view. A series of thunderstorms was forming behind the mountains, backlighting the peaks with all imaginable shades of gray. Heavy rain streaked from the clouds to our right, an ominous sign for the afternoon ahead; but even after a week of thunderstorm dodging it wasn't a view I would have traded lightly.

We weren't the only ones at the rest stop. While I unpacked my camera a Tennessee woman in her mid-twenties fell into conversation with Vera.

"Where did you come from?" she asked.

"Portland."

"You must be crazy!" She hesitated, realizing how strongly she'd said it. "Well. . . ."

"It's fun," Vera said.

The woman instantly reversed her opinion. "That sounds neat," she said with almost as much enthusiasm as she'd pronounced it crazy a moment before. She pointed to a rack on the back of her car. "But I've got my bike back there, and I'm dizzy already." She'd meant the comment as a reference to the altitude, but I chuckled, thinking it could be applied more broadly than she'd intended.

Meanwhile, a pair of older women were asking me non-stop questions. "Where's the river?" one of them asked. "I thought there was a river down there."

I pointed to a line of cottonwoods that marked its course. "It's the Arkansas," I said. "It's a big one."

"Oh, I see it. Yeah." Suddenly her pointing arm veered twenty degrees. "Is that the penitentiary? I hear there's a penitentiary around here."

I shrugged. "I don't know. I'm from California." *Why is it*, I wondered as they walked back to their cars, *that people always seem to think bicyclists know everything about the local geography?* Even at home that often happens: Drivers often flag me down to ask directions to places I've never heard of. Maybe they're unconsciously relating to the fact that, to a greater extent than driving, bicycling requires you to keep track of your surroundings lest you pedal 20 miles in the wrong direction. More likely, though, they simply assume you live nearby.

———————•●•———————

After they left, Vera and I looked at each other, then exploded with laughter. Still chuckling, we mounted our bicycles and coasted the remaining mile and a half into the valley, looking for a place to lunch.

We found a truck stop just on the other side of the river. Vera decided to phone the cousin she'd be visiting in Santa Fe. She'd only been gone a couple of minutes, however, when she came back in disgust. "My cousin wasn't in," she said. "I reached her roommate. 'When can I call back?' I asked. But her roommate refused to answer. 'She doesn't have a backbone schedule in her life,' was all she'd say." Vera's irritation turned to laughter. "What a phrase, 'a backbone schedule.' All I wanted was to know when to call."

I was laughing, too. "It sounds like something out of The Sixties." And while we, too, had no backbone schedules in our lives, even discussing it that way seemed alien to the free-structured existence each of us had been pursuing for nearly a month.

After lunch, we had what had become our typical conversation about the weather.

"It looks like rain," I said, "maybe we ought to wait it out."

Vera, true to her Oregon heritage, had no interest in waiting for rain. She tested the wind, which had been fair for Salida all morning. It was still out of the north. "I think we can make it."

I wasn't so sure, but in nearly five days we hadn't been caught yet. And with that tailwind it would take little more than an hour to reach Salida. "Let's do it."

Two miles out of town the odds finally caught us. The wind shifted 120 degrees, freshening to a gale that slowed us from 20 miles an hour to 8.

A few miles later the rain hit—cold drops followed by stinging hail that luckily was little more than overgrown sleet. But as fast as it came the rain was gone, and we'd barely changed into our rain gear before it was time to take it off, at least until the next squall.

As we neared Salida, it was again time for decision. My route veered east through town, while Vera's bypassed town and began a 2,000-foot climb to the top of yet another pass. She'd planned on camping in a na-tional-forest campground near the summit, while I'd intended to ride sev-eral more hours before stopping for the night. But it was already midafternoon, and the wind and repeated threat of rain combined to dampen my enthusiasm, especially since the traffic was still heavy.

"I'm thinking of staying here in Salida," I said, "Care to join me?"

Vera hesitated. "Sure." She hesitated again. "Why not." She laughed. "It'll only be our third last evening together!"

On the way into town we talked about camping. Other than the one in the national forest, the only campground on any of our maps was sev-eral miles in the wrong direction for her. But a town the size of Salida had to have other possibilities.

We explored a side road, hoping to find a secluded place for the evening, but there were too many beer cans and tire tracks for my taste, so we moved on. A mile later we passed a middle-aged man on a one-speed bicycle loaded down with aluminum cans and other scavenged items.

"I bet he knows a good place to camp," Vera said softly.

"Yeah, but I'm not sure I want to ask him. He's probably okay, but. . . ." I left it uncompleted. But Salida was a town of nearly five thousand, and to me that felt like a metropolis, with all the concomitant problems.

———— •• ————

It was 5 P.M. when we reached town, rolling through puddles left by a squall that had barely missed us. Though it was still early, Vera was famished.

We spotted a supermarket and hurried inside. The first thing either of us saw was a one-pound loaf of bakery bread.

Two minutes later we were outside again, ripping the package open and devouring big hunks. "What do you want to do for dinner?" I asked, helping myself to another chunk. The bread seemed the most wonderful thing I'd tasted in years.

"What do you want?" Vera returned.

"Well, we could go out to eat, or we could go back in the store and find something cheap. Which would you rather do?"

"Whatever you want."

And so we went around again, Alfonse and Gaston, until one of us — probably Vera — broke into laughter.

"Look," I said, "this really *is* our last evening together. Let's do something special. How about a Mexican restaurant?"

Five minutes later we were sitting at a booth, studying menus.

———— •• ————

As we waited for our meal, Vera began to squirm on her seat. Then she leaned across the table conspiratorially. "You know, Rick," she whispered, "I really ought to be doing this in the lady's room."

I tried to imagine what on Earth she'd been doing.

"I was taking off my leg warmers," she said, reading my expression, "when I noticed that the woman behind you was staring at me. I think I've been on the road too long!"

"Me too," I said. "I never noticed."

———— •• ————

Dinner was a smashing success, followed by not one but two orders of sopapillas, a Mexican dessert I hadn't seen properly prepared for years. "You know," Vera said, "I think riding with you has been hard on my waistline." She laughed. "I know it's been hard on my budget."

We pondered where to spend the night. The phone book showed a private campground west of town, but no rates were listed.

"I wonder if there's a city park?" Vera suggested.

The waitress gave us directions. "There's a hot spring in the park," she added. "You can go for a swim."

Vera was instantly enthusiastic. "I spent a whole day sitting in a hot spring the day before I met you. I could go for that again!"

———————————

Our directions took us easily to the park — a village block of shade trees and grassy lawn. The signs near the picnic tables said "NO CAMPING."

"Let's check out the hot spring," Vera suggested.

Wheeling our bikes to the park's centerpiece building, we found not the natural spring we had anticipated but a crowded municipal swimming pool, part of whose water was diverted from a spring miles away. The admission fee was several dollars, and for that price we weren't interested.

Vera turned to the desk clerk. "Can we camp here?"

The clerk took in our attire and the bicycles propped outside, then nodded. "Yes. Over there." He pointed to one side of the park. "The RVs camp there all the time."

"Thanks," we chorused.

Back in the picnic area I lay down on a table, relishing the breeze and the warm glow of the setting sun. The rain was apparently finished for the night.

"I don't want to unpack our sleeping bags until after sunset," I said. "There's no sense telegraphing our presence."

But as I lay there, I became increasingly uncomfortable. The "NO CAMPING" sign was prominent, and the only RV I could see was a pickup camper parked in an empty lot across the street. Somehow I didn't think permission from the swimming pool clerk would count for much if the police decided to chase us out at 2 A.M. Salida is an old mining and tourist town, somewhat gone to seed, and its atmosphere made me nervous — undeservedly so, no doubt, but nervous nonetheless. Lounging there, even without sleeping bags, we were telling the world we intended to camp, and I had no idea who might return in the small hours of the morning.

"Would you camp here on your own?" Vera asked.

"No."

"Neither would I. In fact, I'd be a lot more careful on my own. But having you here makes a difference. I feel safer."

I nodded but was less sure. I felt only marginally safer with a companion than I'd have felt on my own. I didn't like the place, if only because there were too many people going back and forth on the main road.

"Let's try that campground," I said.

Vera hesitated.

"I'll pay." She had no argument against that, so we mounted up once again.

"It's about twenty-five blocks out there," she said, remembering the address from the phone book.

"How far's that?"

"Well, there are twenty blocks to a mile. . . ."

"Those are city blocks. This is Salida. How many Salida blocks to a mile?"

Vera giggled. Everything today had seemed funny—the women at the rest area, the phone call to Vera's cousin, even the hail. "Salida blocks?" She was laughing in earnest now. "Salida blocks?"

———— •◦• ————

The campground was right where Vera had said it would be, straddling a creek that ran next to the highway.

"Six dollars," said the owner.

It seemed like a fortune. "Got a biker's special?"

"No, but you get to use the shower in the far motel room."

"We don't need a shower," I said, hoping Vera would agree. "Just a place for our sleeping bags."

"Six dollars."

I gave up and paid. *You're the one who wanted to stay here*, Vera's look said.

I grinned. *Well, it's a lot better than being rousted by the police.*

———— •◦• ————

The storms were definitely gone, so we didn't bother to pitch our tents, camping instead on the grass near the creek. Dusk was coming, but I pulled out my journal, trying, with Vera's help, to record all the things that had seemed so funny during the day.

Eventually I gave up, and we talked. But the calm of the evening was interrupted by the noise of a radio from an adjoining campsite. "That's why I don't like these places," Vera said. I agreed. Both the radio and the music it was playing were out of step with the life I'd been living, but even so, the campground was better—and probably quieter—than the city park.

I have never understood why people carry radios into the outdoors. Radios—or televisions or bright lights or any such appliances—erase the natural environment these people come to appreciate. I wonder if these technologically dependent campers return to their cities feeling at least vaguely unfulfilled.

It was more with irritation than thoughts like these that I eventually crawled out of my sleeping bag and padded over to the campsite next door. To my surprise, the camper obliged immediately, and I returned to our site for a sound night's sleep.

——————•●•——————

The next day, finally and unavoidably, was the day for good-byes.

We ate breakfast in a cafe and exchanged addresses. Then it was time.

I'm usually too formal—stuffy, some people might say—to hug friends, but this time was different. And with the hug, Vera gave me a few words I will never forget: "Thank you," she said, "for being you." Then, even as the wonder of that marvellous affirmation rose within me, she was gone, pedaling uphill without looking back. A moment later, I turned in the opposite direction for the long cruise along the Arkansas River to the Plains beyond.

——————•●•——————

The morning was cool and the air calm, with the wind still deciding which direction to blow. But it was difficult to fall back into the solo routine. I remembered previous partings—the tears with which I'd left my grandparents' farm after every childhood visit, the throat-constricting good-byes after high school and college—and the painful question of which friendships would continue and which would fade until even the memories were dusty with age.

It was hard to believe that Vera and I had met only five days before. Something about adventure travel deepens friendships, making them feel as though they've persisted for years. I'd had a similar experience the previous October on a bicycle trip organized by an Arizona club. A hundred and fifty cyclists had gathered from all over the country, and together we'd toiled over mountain after mountain as we fought rain, sleet, and headwinds, exulting in sweeping panoramas, thrilling descents, and warm, sunny days in the lowland desert. The trip lasted only eight days. But the experience had been so intense, and the companionship so strong—as we gathered each evening to swap stories and bathe the painful ones in the warm balm of shared laughter—that it had felt as though we'd been together always.

So it had been with Vera, and my life seemed strangely unfocused now that I was again on my own.

I was jolted out of my reverie about an hour out of Salida. The road had been smooth and—in pleasant contrast to the day before—little traveled. But some sections had no shoulder, and I was traveling on one of those when a van drew up from behind. It started to pass with ample room to spare, but as it pulled even it slowed, matched my pace, and gradually pushed me off the road into the loose gravel. As I skidded to a barely controlled stop, the driver gunned the engine and roared away.

Welcome back to the real world, I thought, as I calmed my nerves and prepared to start again. It wasn't the first traffic problem I'd had in Colorado, but it was the first that was clearly deliberate. Suddenly I was ready to get out of the tourist traffic of the mountains and into the slower-paced life of the Plains.

At the same time I was shocked into a more acute awareness that I really was about to leave the mountains. As the adrenaline receded I took renewed interest in my surroundings, watching the dark blue band of the river curving through a canyon barely wide enough to hold both it and the road. The wind was settling into a headwind, but at least it would slow my exit from the mountains, allowing me to savor the last few miles. As the day warmed, the river, always nearby, filled with bright yellow rafts and the happy excitement of river runners. I was faster than they, and it was fun to race them through the rapids, stop for photos, and scurry ahead again, looking for more rafts and more photos.

About 45 miles from Salida—still well before noon—I passed a turnoff for Royal Gorge, widely hailed as one of the scenic wonders of this section of Colorado. I had never been there, but I knew that the primary attraction was a suspension bridge 1,053 feet above the Arkansas River at a place where the gorge was so narrow it was nearly vertical. The main road to the gorge came in from the east, but there was a back road from my side; at the cost of a steep, 1,000-foot hill, I could bicycle across what has been called the highest suspension bridge in the world. It was an irresistible prospect.

At first the side trip exceeded expectations. The back road to the gorge climbed gradually, then steepened, and steepened again into the toughest hill I'd seen on the entire trip, with pitches approaching fifteen percent. But I was in good physical condition, well rested from my days with Vera, and I joyously accepted the hill's challenge, sweating profusely in the growing heat, reveling in the view that opened toward the mountains behind, and absorbing—seemingly through every pore—one last draught of the semi-arid beauty of grasslands scattered with evergreens, an open savannah that has always been my favorite of the West's many vegetation zones. Several movie directors, I later learned, had shared my appreciation for this region; somewhere nearby the movies *True Grit* and *Cat Ballou* had been filmed, as well as a collection of early silent films.

All too soon I was at the top.

For the duration of the climb I had the road virtually to myself. Like Teton Pass, it was simply too steep for most drivers. But as I reached the top I re-entered civilization. There seemed to be thousands of people, and the attraction appeared not to be the natural glory of the gorge, but the bridge itself, which could be viewed not only from the canyon rim, but from a gondola or from a cog railway descending into the gorge.

I couldn't get away from the people. It was the first major tourist attraction I'd visited since the Tetons; despite the heavy traffic the day before, I'd spent most of the last ten days in a world where crowds simply weren't a factor.

I lingered at the gorge for perhaps two hours, taking the gondola ride, which was included in the price of admission, trying to get a feel for the landscape. Apart from excessive development it was every bit as stunning as I'd expected: a dramatic, steep-sided gash through an open plateau, with the river—green, flecked with foam—impossibly far below. At the bottom of the gorge ran a railroad line, which at the narrowest point was cantilevered over the water on a hanging bridge that had been an engineering marvel when it was first constructed.

I was only partially successful in my quest to experience it without being overwhelmed by the crowds. Leaving the gorge, I looked back one final time at the mountains to the west, into which Vera had ridden that morning. Thunderstorms were forming above them. I wished her luck dodging the rain.

———————— •◦• ————————

I stopped again 15 miles later in Florence, gateway from the mountains to the Plains. In the previous few miles the afternoon heat had clamped down, and I'd suddenly felt drained of energy. A bank clock told me it was one hundred degrees, and that news refreshed me. I'd been afraid it was only in the eighties, that after two weeks when I'd seldom seen a temperature above seventy degrees I would react poorly to the hot days ahead. One hundred degrees is hot by any definition. If I could tolerate that, I could tolerate anything I was likely to encounter.

In Florence I met the first cyclist I'd seen since I left Vera that morning. Her name was Brenda, and she was traveling east to west.

Before I met her, if anyone had asked me what type of woman would pedal solo across the country, I would have thought of Vera's self-assurance or Peggy's reputed athleticism, but Brenda appeared to be cut from a different mold. Short, petite, she barely out-massed her loaded bicycle, and something about her—intentional or otherwise—seemed to cry out for a bigger, stronger companion. I grinned to myself. It demonstrated, as I'd always known, that among cyclists there are no stereotypes. Brenda had proven her competence by pedaling more than 2,000 miles. She'd started solo but had spent much of her time riding with the Bikecentennial group Vera and I had met atop Hoosier Pass. A few days earlier, she'd taken a side trip and was trying to catch up.

"How far ahead of me are they?" she asked.

I paused to calculate. From the pass they'd been going to Breckenridge, where they planned to spend two nights. That meant they'd left Breckenridge this morning, probably heading for Kremmling.

"How far to Breckenridge?" she asked.

I hesitated again. "I was there two days ago," I said, "but I took a roundabout route. The Bikecentennial Trail's shorter."

"Think I can get there tonight?"

I had no idea of the mileage, but I did know one thing. "You've got to go over Hoosier Pass. From here, that's a 5,500-foot hill."

"Oh," she said. "It is?"

I grinned to myself again. Like many cyclists, she was using Bikecentennial's maps. They're marvelous tools, but because they come in short segments it's easy to be taken by surprise when you flip from one to the next. Still, I was startled she hadn't checked to see what lay ahead on her first day in the mountains.

She changed the subject. "Where are *you* going?"

I told her about Iowa and RAGBRAI. But I had another state to traverse before I got there. "What's Kansas like?"

"Kansas," she said with feeling, "is a real test. Hot. Windy. Terrible-tasting water. But the people are the greatest. One day I was shopping at a general store when a woman came up to me and said, 'I bet it's been days since you've seen a shower. Would you like to use mine?' It was great."

"Did the people make it worth it?"

She didn't hesitate. "No."

Kansas was a real test.

In Florence I faced my next major route-finding decision. The Bikecentennial Trail angled southeast to Pueblo, then ran due east across Kansas. If I went that way I could continue to use Bikecentennial's maps, and I had the greatest chance of meeting other cyclists. Iowa looked a bit closer if I left the route and cut north to Colorado Springs—a route that would also keep me close to the mountains for a few more hours. So, even though the wind was fairer for Pueblo than Colorado Springs, I turned northeast and bade a final farewell to the TransAmerica Trail. My goal for the night was a campground a few miles shy of Colorado Springs.

Despite the headwind I expected no difficulty getting there. It was only about 28 miles, and I still had three hours of daylight.

It proved not to be so easy; none of my maps had revealed a 1,500-foot hill lying between me and my goal. Had I not found a campground at the summit, I would have been caught by dark long before I got to shelter. As it was, dusk was settling in as I pedaled the 2-mile gravel road to camp.

I created quite a stir as I rode in, and by the time I'd registered, I'd drawn a small crowd of campers. "Where are you from?" "Where are you going?" people asked, adding more of the usual questions about weather and traffic.

One of the most persistent questioners was a teenage girl, who was camping with her family while her father commuted to work in Colorado Springs. Boredom had apparently been a major factor in her summer, but that evening she alleviated it by cross-examining me vigorously. "But why?" she eventually asked, "Why are you doing it?"

I thought about telling her about relaxation and spiritual odysseys, but I was tired, so instead I gave her one of my stock answers. "You really get a feel for the country. And you meet the most interesting people."

"Am I an interesting person?" she fired back.

Touché, I thought, and added a mental note to delete *that* answer from my list.

The next morning I lingered in camp until rush hour would be long gone, then coasted into Colorado Springs to stock up on food, film, and other supplies. Shortly after noon it was time to turn my back on the mountains and begin the next stage of my journey.

CHAPTER 7

Kansas

Facing the Test

DAY 31 • Tuesday, July 15 • CUMULATIVE MILES: 2,263
Colorado Springs (vicinity) to Punkin Center

DAY 32 • Wednesday, July 16 • CUMULATIVE MILES: 2,408
Punkin Center, Colorado, to Winona, Kansas

DAY 33 • Thursday, July 17 • CUMULATIVE MILES: 2,517
Winona to Norton

DAY 34 • Friday, July 18 • CUMULATIVE MILES: 2,614
Norton to Mankato

DAY 35 • Saturday, July 19 • CUMULATIVE MILES: 2,702
Mankato to Marysville

DAY 36 • Sunday, July 20 • CUMULATIVE MILES: 2,773
Marysville, Kansas, to Verdon Lake St. Recreation
Area, Nebraska

DAY 37 • Monday, July 21 • CUMULATIVE MILES: 2,879
Verdon Lake SRA, Nebraska, to Elliott, Iowa

Kansas is legendary among cyclists—not only for its winds and summer heat, but also for the slow unfolding of its scenery. Most would agree with Brenda that it is a real test.

Headed east from Colorado Springs, I was confident that I would pass with ease. On previous bicycling trips I'd fallen in love with Nebraska and reveled in the prairies of northern Minnesota. Could Kansas be all that different? I resolved to approach it on its own terms, knowing I would eventually emerge at the Missouri River, one state richer for the experience.

There are two great myths about Kansas: first, that the wind always blows from the west, and second, that Kansas is flat. In the following six days the wind blew from many directions, but never more favorably than south-southwest. The only certainty was that it would blow and blow hard, beginning early in the afternoon and continuing unabated until well after sunset. Because of the wind, Ben had suggested that I cycle through Kansas after dark—and an approaching full moon made that feasible—but I doubted I could sleep through the 100-degree heat of the afternoons.

Nor is Kansas flat. For years I've wondered how the Great Plains got that reputation. True, they are not mountainous, but even at their flattest they undulate in long, slow waves, granting vistas every few miles across wide expanses of treeless fields, sweeping the mind away to unbounded horizons, to the line, sharp and distinct, where the sky's dome settles to the ground and, for a surprising distance to the east, puffs of cloud mark the afternoon thundershowers forming in the Rockies, invisible below the swell of the horizon.

For me, Kansas began the moment I left the last of Colorado Springs' urban sprawl and continued until I reached the Missouri River—culturally, eastern Colorado, Kansas, and Nebraska are dinstinctly similar. There is something about the western Plains, something that has sustained an unhurried pace of life and a tradition of hospitality refreshingly out of step with contemporary urban America. Perhaps it is the difficult climate—scorching heat in summer, blizzards in winter—or the relative absence of people. Whatever the reason, the residents of the Plains retain much of what makes America worthy of preservation. My journey into Kansas wasn't so much a test as a lesson in humility in the face of an extreme climate; a lesson in patience as the sage-covered rangeland gradually gave way to wheat fields, and wheat to corn; a lesson in endurance as the incessant wind tried first to expel me forcibly into Nebraska and then infuriatingly switched 180 degrees when I finally decided to indulge in that long-awaited run to the north.

But most of all Kansas is people. People who've seen many cyclists before but still have time to talk to one more. People who honk as they pass and give big, friendly waves—not merely the courteous two-finger salutes of Wyoming and Idaho, but open-handed waggles of the entire arm; a wave you might have given when as a child you spied your grandparents' car coming up the driveway; a wave that says welcome back to a long-lost buddy, and can bring tears to the eyes of a total stranger, letting him know he's welcome in America's heartland, where no one could possibly wish him ill.

I never had a bad incident on the Plains. Nobody passed too close, nobody honked rudely. And I met some wonderful people. On the first day, still close to Colorado Springs, I stopped for a milk shake at a sub shop— itself a remarkable find on the Great Plains—in tiny Ellicott, Colorado.

"What do you do at night?" one of the three women who ran the place asked me.

"It depends," I said, falling easily into a friendly-country answer. "If there aren't any campgrounds around, I can always ask a rancher or a farmer if I can pitch my tent on his lawn. Around here, I doubt anyone would say no."

"I'd let you stay," the woman replied.

"We get a lot of bikers through here," one of the others added. "We ought to start a guest book."

"I'd be happy to sign," I said, and someone handed me a scrap of paper, which I autographed for later inclusion in the book. Savoring my first taste of Great Plains hospitality, I promised to send a postcard from "somewhere interesting" back East.

———————————•◦•———————————

That evening I stopped for dinner at the two-building town of Punkin Center. With 40 miles to the next town, I contemplated riding on, even though I'd be riding by moonlight over the last few miles. "Where can I camp between here and Kit Carson?" I asked the waitress.

"There's not much there," she replied. "But you can camp here in the field behind the cafe. The RVs stop there all the time."

I thought about getting to RAGBRAI, realizing I'd only done 86 miles. Then I thought about my promise to Vera not to push too hard, and decided to stay. Even after the cafe closed, the staff let me stay at my table, scribbling in my journal until they went home at nine o'clock. As I left, the head waitress caught me at the door. "Here, have a cinnamon roll. On the house."

Kansas, I thought later as I drifted off to sleep, is going to be great.

———————————•◦•———————————

I woke in the morning to discover that, however friendly the people may be, no place is perfect. The turf I'd been sleeping on may have been acceptable for an RV, but scattered patches of brown, dead grass and a couple of empty chemical drums indicated that someone had been using it for filling—or possibly cleaning—spraying equipment. At least there were no brown spots in my immediate vicinity, so I hoped I'd avoided the worst of it.

I went back to the cafe for breakfast, where I was disappointed to find different waitresses on duty. I'd hoped to say another thank you for the evening's hospitality.

In the parking lot a truck driver struggled to remove a pair of wheel hubs from his rig. The wheels, he explained, had sheared off and bounded into the ditch. "I'm sure glad I wasn't passing anybody," he added. By the time he'd braked to a stop, he hadn't even been able to find one of the wheels. Now, as he waited for a friend to drive out from Colorado Springs, he was trying to remove what was left of the hubs, but the entire assembly spun freely whenever he tried to turn the tire iron. As we talked, he experimented with various ways to lock it in place. Finally succeeding, he grinned at me and nodded at my bicycle. "Driving a truck is like riding one of those things," he said. "You gradually figure out how everything works, so you can deal with almost anything on the road. Isn't that how it goes for you?"

I agreed and wished him luck as I headed out, feeling a sudden kinship for everyone on the road that morning—ranchers, farmers, truckers, RV drivers.

It was the best time of the day. The sun had been up only an hour, and the cool of dawn still lingered. I was taken by song and passed the next hour singing fragments of old folk tunes, immersing myself in the peace and beauty of this supposedly barren ranch country. Every now and then I would steal a glimpse of Pikes Peak receding into the distance behind— my last tie with the world of mountains, the only reminder that the Plains do not stretch infinitely in all directions.

————•◦•————

The wind was as close to a true tailwind as it would get. Starting out in the northwest, it died, then resumed from the south-southwest, never more than a crosswind as I traveled a long, shallow curve, first angling slightly south toward Cheyenne Wells, Colorado, and then slightly north into Kansas.

As the day wore on, the heat clamped down and my singing ceased. Around 11 o'clock I stopped in Cheyenne Wells, visited a small museum, and drew the usual crowd of curious residents.

"Are you traveling alone?" an old woman asked me.

"At the moment."

"Get a companion," she ordered.

I couldn't help grinning. After all, between Ben and Vera, I'd already had two of the best companions imaginable.

"Get a companion," she repeated, possibly misinterpreting my grin as a sign of disagreement. "Get a companion." And, as though to prove her point, she placed her arm firmly in her husband's grasp, and together they began their own octogenarian odyssey toward a house on the other side of the street.

———————•◦•———————

By early evening—probably around 7—I'd reached Winona, Kansas, having covered nearly 145 miles, the longest single-day trek I'd ever made with a full load of touring gear. With a good two hours of daylight I thought of going farther, but as I entered town my gaze was arrested by a city park doubling as a highway rest stop. It was the best camping spot I'd seen in two days, so I called it a day.

Kansas is famous for roadside parks, leftovers from the days before the interstates. Along U.S. 40—the route I'd been following—they're spaced at intervals of 20 to 30 miles, perfect for a cyclist wanting to hop from shade to shade, water pump to water pump. Crossing the state would be difficult without them, at least in the midafternoon heat. And each little town has its park, where a cyclist can dive out of the sun, prop his bike against a tree, and sprawl out on a picnic table, letting the breeze cool him and drinking quart after quart of water to slake a seemingly endless thirst.

The park in Winona was one of the best of the lot, with plenty of trees to provide shade and break the worst of the 40-mile-an-hour wind, and soft, thick grass. As at the campsite the night before, I was the only person there, but on the Plains I had no fear of camping alone, even in clear view of the highway. Once, not too many years ago, when U.S. 40 carried a heavy tourist traffic, I might have been more cautious, but the completion of I-70 has left it a quiet farm road with only local traffic, and precious little of that. It was unlikely anyone would disturb me.

I had dinner in the town's one cafe, chatting with the proprietor and customers. One of the things that most intrigues me about these small-town conversations are the questions people ask first. In Idaho and Wyoming the usual response to the news that I'd ridden all the way from California was, "Wow, you must have legs like pistons!" I must have heard that at least twice a day. (I'd always meant to ask Vera if she'd received similar comments, and if so, what people in Wyoming considered the ladylike equivalent of "legs like pistons.")

In Kansas, however, the inevitable first question was: "How many tires have you worn out on that thing?" It was a question that showed surprising familiarity with cycle touring. If people had asked how many flat tires

I'd had I wouldn't have been so surprised, but many people don't know that touring cyclists wear out tires at a prodigious rate—about one per 1,000 miles.

There was a handful of other common questions—"How many miles do you do per day?" "Do you ever get lonely?" "When did you leave?" Less common was, "Has anybody hassled you?" Earlier in the trip, that one had usually made me nervous, leaving me to wonder why the questioner was interested.

But Kansans never made me nervous, so I answered all their questions—even breaking my usual rule of being vague about where I planned to spend the night—and between answers wolfed down a hamburger and a mountain of French fries.

Afterward I wanted dessert, but the only things on the menu that appealed to me were gone. The proprietor tried to interest me in substitutes, but I was losing my appetite quickly. "I know," he said. "How'd you like some pudding?"

That sounded good, so he slipped into the house behind the cafe and soon reappeared with a bowl of chocolate pudding, probably from a can in his private cupboard. Of course there was no charge. This, after all, was Kansas.

———————•◉•———————

At dawn the wind was still howling out of the south-southwest. I'd intended to bicycle straight east, but with my first taste of the morning wind I abandoned that plan, letting the wind blow me north to the town of Colby instead.

From Colby I continued to angle northward, heading for southern Nebraska with the hope of covering as many as 150 miles. As long as I continued to angle in that direction the wind would remain partially behind me, doing more good than harm, helping me along as I again fell into the routine of scurrying from one shady spot to another. The temperature had been 104 degrees the day before; on this day it was only 102.

About 105 miles into the day, during the worst of the afternoon heat, the road turned due east, and for the first time the wind—now a crosswind—got a solid bite at me. Suddenly I was drained. As I tried to figure out why, I realized I hadn't been eating. In the continuing heat of the previous two days, the thought of food had become more and more nauseating, until I barely wanted anything unless it was cold, wet, and sweet. Unfortunately, the only thing that fit the bill in small-town Kansas was soda pop, and there is a limit to how much soda pop one can drink in an afternoon. It certainly isn't enough to fuel a succession of long days.

As I inched into Norton, the wind demonstrated that it was capable of more tricks than merely sapping my energy. Whenever I crossed a bridge or passed any other guardrail, an eddy awaited me, doing its best to flip me over. At head height it blasted unabated from the right, while below a strong suction pulled my wheels in the opposite direction. To fight the back-eddy I had to steer left, downwind, scrambling my already shaky equilibrium by riding directly contrary to what years of cycling had conditioned me to do.

When I finally reached town, the first thing I saw was a Dairy Queen. Cold, wet, sweet, no carbonation. At the moment I could think of no better definition of heaven. Only then did I notice a group of cyclists in the city park across the street. This was where I would spend the night.

A few minutes later, carrying a large chocolate shake and a big cup of water, I ambled over to the park.

The cyclists were enthusiastic in their greeting. They were a Christian Adventures group, bicycling across the country, a dozen or so college students and four or five leaders. Cycling, they said, was secondary to companionship and the opportunities to share their faith. They were an exuberant, cheerful bunch.

One of them noted my milk shake and grinned. "That's where everyone goes when they first get here!"

Another said, "Yeah, but has anyone invited you to supper yet?" And with that, they all urged me to join them for a taco-casserole dinner. Suddenly—perhaps because I was out of the wind, perhaps because the heat had abated slightly—I was famished, and I gratefully accepted.

During dinner we were joined by another cyclist. Yuji, a welder from Japan, had saved his money for eight years before setting out to tour the world on a bicycle of his own construction. Now nearly three-quarters of the way through a two-year solo expedition, he'd already spent ten months in Australia, five in New Zealand, and two in the U.S. He was heading for Chicago and would then fly to Europe and Africa, completing his journey seven months later in Nairobi.

The Christian adventurers greeted him like a long-lost friend. "Yuji! It's Yuji!" someone shouted. "Hey everyone, Yuji made it here!"

"He camped with us last night," one of the women told me. "He's carrying eighty pounds, counting his bike, and he's covered 101 miles today. Isn't that amazing!" The Christian adventurers had covered the same course, but a baggage truck had carried their gear.

I nodded. My loaded bike weighed the same as Yuji's—maybe more when all my water bottles were full. And while I'd fallen well short of what I'd hoped, I'd still ridden 109 miles. Yuji, however, had been riding due east, battling that crosswind for his entire 101 miles. That impressed me far more than the weight or the distance.

A couple of minutes later, four other cyclists rode down the highway. "Hey!" I yelled, waving like a madman and dashing into the road. "Hey! I know you!"

They looked at me blankly.

"In Colorado. Kremmling. There were six of you then, on your way to Grand Lake. It hailed. I was with a woman. Do you remember us?"

Recognition dawned. "Muddy Pass! Yeah!"

A voice called from the picnic shelter. "Want to join us for dinner? There's plenty left."

"It's good," I added. "Taco casserole."

But one of them was a vegetarian, so they were looking for other fare. They were camping in the park, though, so we agreed to talk later and perhaps ride together in the morning.

After dinner I hopped in a van with most of the Christian adventurers for a short ride to the city pool, where we showered and beat the remnants of the heat with a swim.

"One dollar each," said the middle-aged woman at the gate. "Oh, are you bikers? Then go on in. No charge for bikers tonight!"

Kansas was continuing to live up to its reputation.

———————— •◦• ————————

After swimming myself nearly to exhaustion—a surprisingly easy accomplishment—I went back to the equipment cage to talk to the woman who'd let us in.

"I'm a biker, too," she said. "Have you heard about the cross-Kansas ride we have every June?"

I nodded. It was RAGBRAI inspired, reputed to be beautifully organized. By coincidence, for most of the time I'd been in Kansas I'd been following this year's route. The ride had spread goodwill for cyclists all along the way, and I seldom made a rest stop without at least one person telling me about it or teasing me for being "only about a month late."

"Well," the woman continued, "it's a great ride. My husband and I have done it three years in a row."

They had also biked in many other places, and soon we were swapping stories. We shared mixed feelings about Colorado. Officially, it was a state that went to great lengths to encourage cyclists, publishing pictures of the governor and his wife riding bicycles and printing one of the finest cycling maps I'd ever seen. But too many Colorado drivers were in too much of a hurry.

"I remember a century ride my husband and I did," she said— referring to a club-sponsored 100-mile tour—"where one section of the route was full of ore trucks. The drivers got angry at us for blocking the road, talking on the CB about how 'Somebody ought to get one of them cyclists.' But the police must have been listening to the CB also, because suddenly there were police cars all over the place, cruising back and forth for the rest of the day."

It was a story that matched my own perception of central Colorado. Officially, cyclists were welcome, but some of the drivers, like the one in the van that had run me off the road, thought otherwise. It made me appreciate Kansas all the more.

———————— •◦• ————————

That night I was the only cyclist in our several groups who pitched a tent, and the only one who got a good night's sleep; the rest spent the night swatting ants. I'd learned that lesson the night before, sleeping under the stars. The bugs had come out in shifts: first the houseflies, then the no-see-ums (a kind of biting gnat), and finally, at dawn, the mosquitoes. It was the last time on this trip I'd sleep without a tent.

But that night in Norton I might not have noticed. Following my swim I was strangely tired; even the next morning I was groggy and had a stiff neck, feeling as though I'd slept the entire night so soundly that I'd never even rolled over.

I also had an upset stomach, possibly a result of too much taco casserole the evening before. So I skipped breakfast and started out with Yuji, the Christian adventurers, and Ken, one of the riders Vera and I had met at Muddy Pass. My original plan had been to continue riding northeast into Nebraska, but the others were heading east, and a wind shift during the night had left my original route directly into the wind.

I listened to the Christian adventurers talk excitedly about their scheduled stay in the homes of church members in the town where they would be stopping that evening. Although the adventurers had been eating far more varied meals than I had, food was their primary topic of conversation, and it was humorous to listen to them spin elaborate fantasies about what their hosts might serve for dinner.

I found the large group and the concomitant chatter distracting. It wasn't that they made me feel like an outsider, for the friendship that bound them was as warm and open on the road as it had been in camp. But until that morning, I'd spent my entire trip riding with no more than a single companion. To me, schooled as I'd been in the windswept expanses of Wyoming and the hospitable rangelands of eastern Colorado, the very friendship that knitted this group into a single, purposeful entity was also a barrier, muffling them and me, insulating us from Kansas itself.

Undoubtedly, that barrier had been part of their experience all the way across the country. And undoubtedly it gave back in group bonding much of what it stole from their contact with the land. To say I wanted nothing of such comradeship would be wrong. But I wanted both—the silence of endless open spaces and a close friend with whom to face them. That was the companionship I'd had with Ben and Vera.

Riding with the Christian adventurers, I was reminded that bicyclists feel safety in numbers. The larger the group the safer its members feel, and the more they dominate the road, directly competing with cars. So it was with this group. Although the highway had a full-width paved shoulder, the half dozen riders clustered with me preferred to ride on the smoother surface of the traffic lane, refusing to move over even when cars came up from behind. Ken and I, our senses tuned by miles of solo riding (Ken had ridden on his own all the way from California to western Colorado), would automatically move over when a car approached, but the Christian adventurers were oblivious, even when a car followed patiently as the driver waited for an opportunity to pass.

As this scenario replayed again and again, I grew angry. What kind of Christian example was it to hog the road all the way across the continent? Worse, what effect would this behavior have on the fabled hospitality of Kansas? I remembered the rock-throwing rancher in Wyoming and the deputy sheriff who'd admitted that many people in western Wyoming hated bicyclists because of just such behavior. It would be tragic if a small number of rude cyclists caused a similar transformation here, ruining the charm of Kansas for generations of cyclists to come. I tried to explain this to one of the adventurers, but he shrugged it off. To him, the road was wide, there were gaps in the oncoming traffic, and nobody was threatening to run him over. For the moment that was all that mattered.

It was merely another example of how large groups tend to isolate their members from what is going on around them. The adventurers were a delightful group, and I would long remember their invitation to dinner and the enthusiasm with which they'd greeted Yuji. Their problem on the road was simply that there were too many of them and they were too inexperienced to be aware of the difficulties. With mixed emotions, I took leave of them 31 miles outside Norton; as they angled south, I joined Ken's group and continued east.

The next $2\frac{1}{2}$ days were the most unpleasant of the entire trip. At first I assumed that the full impact of Brenda's "test" had finally hit me, that I was suffering from monotony, wind, and heat. But by the afternoon of the second day I knew something else was wrong, that my lack of energy and general malaise were actually symptoms of something more. I was sick. I didn't know what it was, but I'd been succumbing to it since I'd left Colorado.

I assumed it was a low-grade flu. The symptoms were certainly appropriate: feverish afternoons, evenings in which I had to camp close to a toilet, and entire days when I had no interest in food, feeling bloated whenever I tried to force myself to eat even a few bites.

Added to this was the fact that I found the local water supply almost totally unpalatable. Brenda had been right about that—after the cold, crisp drink of the mountains, the mineral-laden well water of the Plains was at best unappealing; after it had spent a few minutes warming up in a water bottle, it was barely potable. "I can't take many more days of this heat," I thought, but then the heat wave broke and I didn't feel any better.

The worst day came on the way to Marysville, my second night's stop after Norton, when a rough road initiated an overpowering need for a bathroom, a need that kept returning at a much greater frequency than the number of gas stations allowed. Pepto Bismol is wonderful stuff. I bought a bottle that evening, and by the next morning I no longer needed to run for the toilet. My fever broke during the night, and my enthusiasm for bicycling began to return.

Throughout all of this I continued to ride, covering 90 miles a day through a blurred chain of unmemorable towns spaced every 30 to 32 miles, each at the center of its county, each—in the heat, humidity, or headwinds that plagued me all the way from Norton—a seemingly impossible distance from the next. My reason for continuing was simple: Ken and his friends were going this way, and I preferred to struggle along with company than be sick alone. But even after nearly six weeks of cycling it wasn't easy.

Other than Ken, I never really got to know my new companions, partly because of my illness—which blurred not only the scenery but also my memory, so that afterward I couldn't even remember their names—

and partly because I'd been right when I elected to stay with Vera rather than join this group in Colorado.

Ken—himself something of an outsider—was the only one who slowed down enough to match my pace. We started each day riding together for a while, until I'd eventually wave him on so he could beat the worst of the wind to camp. The others disappeared in the distance each morning, and I'd seldom see them again until I set up camp in the afternoon.

Ken must have told me a lot about his trip, but I remember only one story. He'd started somewhere in California and headed straight across Nevada, carrying only his normal complement of water bottles. "I had a sign with me," he said, "that read, 'NEED WATER.' Whenever I ran out, I'd hang it out back. The first RV would always stop."

I never got to know the other riders well enough to find out if they were as macho as they'd seemed in Colorado. I was surprised I'd even caught up with them, though I had a vague memory of their telling me they'd stopped somewhere to visit friends for a couple of days. Now, they were doing 90 miles a day across Kansas—a reasonable pace, even in a headwind, especially since the alternatives, dictated by the regular spacing of the towns, came in 30-mile increments.

But they rode faster than I did; I'd have found them hard to keep up with even if I'd been healthy. They were also more schedule-oriented than I wanted to be, choosing each night's campground before beginning the day, then bulling ahead to reach it with only a few short rest breaks.

By the time I felt well enough to strike out on my own, it was too late to catch RAGBRAI on the day I'd planned, so I called Jack to make contingency plans. He suggested that if I could get to his home no more than one day late, another day's hard riding would allow us to cut a corner on RAGBRAI's zigzag route, letting us join it the following evening. If we didn't meet it then, it would be a long chase: The following day ran 88 miles, directly away from us.

In midafternoon on my third day after leaving the Christian Adventures group, I waved good-bye to Ken and his friends, turning north to begin the remaining 140 miles to Jack's home. I had a day and a half to get there; if the wind would cooperate, it would be easy. But, as had been the case ever since Norton, I had a headwind, and while I was feeling much better, I was still eating little during the heat of the day but soda pop and fruit juice.

It was after 6 P.M. when I slipped across the state line into the tiny town of Dawson, Nebraska. At that hour on a Sunday evening the only thing open was a tavern. I stepped inside hoping for food to take with me to my planned campsite in a nearby state park and was disappointed to find little but peanuts and potato chips, neither of which appealed to my still-queasy stomach.

As I was talking to the bartender and reconciling myself to a hungry evening, a half-drunk farmer broke into the conversation. "What's that shirt about?" he demanded.

I looked down at it, unsure what one I'd put on that morning. "Military Athletes Run Challenging Hunger," it proclaimed—the same shirt I'd been wearing when I met the mega-distance runner in Idaho. I explained how the twenty-four-hour relay had worked, noting that it was a fundraiser for hunger-related organizations. I saw no reason to add that my only connection with the military had been a friend whose team had suddenly needed an extra runner.

"Why give it away when the American farmer can't make a living?"

He hadn't become belligerent yet, but I was cautious. "Some people are starving," I explained, "because they don't have enough money to afford even the shipping charges on our surplus."

He thought about that for a long moment, then pulled two dollars out of his wallet. "Here, give this to those people, you hear me. Give it to them."

I grinned. God bless the American farmer. Even when he's half drunk.

———————•◦•———————

I reached Jack's house the next evening at about eight o'clock. He was off working on his parents' farm a few miles out in the country, but he'd left directions. I stripped the baggage from my bicycle and pedaled down a series of gravel roads into a rich pastoral landscape bathed in misty golden sunlight and the cool dampness of a Midwestern summer evening.

It had been a grueling day, more tiring than anything I'd done in the mountains. Although the wind had been calm for once, I'd encountered hills when I left Nebraska to cut across the extreme northwestern corner of Missouri. In the course of only 20 miles they wore me out.

No one who hasn't encountered them on a bicycle can truly understand what it is like to ride through the hills of northern Missouri and southern Iowa. Mile for mile it is at least as demanding as the Rockies, but with no summit to uplift your spirits; instead, at the top of each hill is only a view of more hills, as the road stretches ahead with geometric precision, climbing straight over everything in its path, bouncing over the same 50 to 100 feet of elevation as often as three times in a mile.

On an unloaded bicycle, riding though hills like these can become a game, as you use your momentum to treat them like an endless roller coaster, accelerating on the downgrades, then standing on the pedals to surge to the next summit in a few strong strokes. It's challenging, but fun.

With a loaded bicycle all of that changes. If you try to charge the up-grades, you stall out halfway up. Worse, the slopes change so rapidly there isn't time to shift gears—one moment you're going 30 miles an hour, the next, 3.

Ten miles of such terrain takes an hour, and 20 miles—even without a headwind—is a torturous workout. But as I moved north from Missouri into Iowa the hills gradually abated, allowing me to reach Jack's house well before sunset.

As I pedaled toward the farm through flat, river-bottom lands lush with well-watered corn and soybeans, it seemed strange that, after so many weeks of planning, I was finally about to meet my friend. I had little remaining doubt we could cover the 100 miles to catch RAGBRAI the next day, but I wondered what it would feel like to join such an enormous group. If the Christian adventurers had seemed large and boisterous, then RAGBRAI, with its rolling party of 7,500 cyclists, was going to be an en-tirely different world. I had ridden it three years before, and enjoyed it immensely. This time, I feared the contrast with the past few weeks might tarnish the earlier memory.

CHAPTER 8

RAGBRAI

"The Thing That Ate Iowa"

DAY 38 • Tuesday, July 22 • CUMULATIVE MILES: 2,984
Elliott to Perry

DAY 39 • Wednesday, July 23 • CUMULATIVE MILES: 3,082
Perry to Eldora

DAY 40 • Thursday, July 24 • CUMULATIVE MILES: 3,162
Eldora to Belle Plaine

DAY 41 • Friday, July 25 • CUMULATIVE MILES: 3,256
Belle Plaine to Washington

DAY 42 • Saturday, July 26 • CUMULATIVE MILES: 3,366
Washington, Iowa, to Cambridge, Illinois

DAYS 43 - 45 • Sunday, July 27 - Tuesday, July 29
Layover in Dixon

We woke early, wondering as we stumbled about in the pre-dawn light why we'd stayed up talking until well past midnight when we had nearly a week of evenings ahead of us. At the same time, I knew we'd do it again if we had the chance.

In many ways I have more in common with Jack than with anyone else I know. We'd met several years before, when we both lived in Minnesota, through an informal noon-hour running club. Over the course of three years we discovered that, in addition to running, we also shared interests in bicycling, cross-country skiing, and a variety of other endurance sports. Both of us were veteran marathon runners, and Jack had also run three ultramarathons, including one that covered more than 60 miles. This summer he claimed to be out of shape, but while I wasn't sure how fast he'd be able to go, I was certain of one thing: He could pedal all day.

As we packed, Jack made strong tea to jolt us into a greater semblance of wakefulness; at 6:45 A.M. we were loaded and ready to roll.

As we walked our bicycles to the road, it was all I could do to keep from laughing. Rather than using panniers, Jack had put everything into a large duffel bag balanced crosswise on his rack. While it would be convenient on RAGBRAI's baggage trucks, the bag had a tendency to slip to one side or the other, and not only was it top-heavy, it later proved to be unstable at speeds of more than 20 miles an hour.

RAGBRAI is an Iowa institution, one that put the state on the map for cyclists throughout the nation and has spawned dozens of imitators from California and Washington to Florida and Massachusetts. Then in its fourteenth year, it began unpretentiously when one columnist for *The Des Moines Register* challenged another to get back in touch with the real Iowa by bicycling across the state. The challenge was accepted, and the two columnists invited their readers to join in.

Much to their surprise, 200 people showed up. The next year the number exceeded 1,000, and within a few years participation was *limited* to 7,500. RAGBRAI was firmly established.

The RAGBRAI concept is simple. For a nominal fee, *The Register* provides maps, emergency services, traffic control, and baggage trucks—the year I'd been on it, there had been three full-size semis. Since the goal is to see the "real" Iowa, overnight stops are usually in small towns—so small, in fact, that the arrival of RAGBRAI's caravan of cyclists and support personnel often doubles or triples their populations. Motel rooms are almost impossible to come by, but county fairgrounds, high school lawns, and the front yards of willing residents quickly turn into mammoth tent cities that spring up overnight, then melt away with the dawn.

Iowans love RAGBRAI. The route changes each year, so nobody becomes jaded. Farmers quit work and sit on their lawns to watch the endless stream of cyclists flow down the quiet county roads that make Iowa perfect for such an event. At the overnight stops, community groups and churches compete to offer the most attractive dinners, while other groups turn each day's route into a succession of bake sales and lunch offerings.

It is more than money that motivates this fanfare, though there is enough money at stake to encourage small towns to compete a year in advance for the privilege of hosting the ride. But at heart the statewide interest in RAGBRAI seems to stem from a vicarious interest in being part of this spectacle of people in motion. On my previous RAGBRAI, it was this sense of process that had captured me most strongly. "I'm not going anywhere to get there," I wrote in my journal—

> I'm going merely for the sake of going—and the sake of doing it with other people. In many respects, it's a microcosm of so-called real life. Fifteen miles into a day, you might meet an interesting person. You chat for 5

miles, then, by conscious choice or an eddy in the pack, you separate, just as occurs in the rest of our mobile society. You are alone again. You put down new roots, talking to someone else. Again, you are separated. People who meet on the road seldom ride a dozen miles together.

So far that sounds depressing, but RAGBRAI represents a small universe. Even with 7,500 cyclists, you begin to meet repeats. After riding into camp one night, I was prowling though the pile of duffel bags (word of caution: don't bring a green duffel bag on RAGBRAI; there are thousands of them) when someone called my name. I glanced up to see a woman who'd occasionally been a running partner of mine back home.

As the evening wore on, I had similar encounters with two women who'd camped next to me one night, a guy I'd eaten dinner with the day before, and a group of college students I'd ridden with two days earlier. Before the evening was over, I'd had the pleasure of hearing my name called by nearly a dozen people.

This is RAGBRAI at its best. It is a free-form existence with friendships that ebb and flow and regroup in surprising patterns until eventually you develop a kinship with the entire group—even those you've never met—nearly as strong as your kinship with specific individuals. Not only is it a microcosm of society as a whole, it is a microcosm of the bicycle-touring experience. "Bicycle touring," I wrote in the same journal, "is a very simple lifestyle":

All you worry about is keeping the body and the machine running. Once you settle into the routine, it's relaxing and simple.

But RAGBRAI is even simpler. No route planning. No "Will I find a place to camp tonight?" No need to worry about food or water. No cars. It is as simple compared to normal touring as touring is compared to urban life.

It's an artificial lifestyle, to be true. I can't maintain it forever. But perhaps I can bring home some of the simplicity to the rest of my life. One of my friends at work once referred to his job as "life in the fast lane." He liked that. I didn't. Bicycling is life from the road shoulder.

———•———

Jack's decision to put his gear in a duffel bag rather than panniers meant he was committed to catching RAGBRAI before he wound up carrying his awkward load all the way across the state. That meant the second day in a row with a difficult goal. But I felt no pressure to succeed at all costs. Perhaps I'd finally learned to relax and could now attempt to chase down RAGBRAI without being consumed by the goal. When I got there, I hoped the tour would help reinforce the lessons in day-by-day living that had been my quest three years earlier, but which hadn't been sufficiently driven home by an outing of only one week.

The morning was cool and cloudy, and we made good time until an unfortunate route choice landed us on a backroad roller coaster. Eventually, after passing through a series of small towns with names like Griswold, Lewis, and Norway Center, we stopped at a convenience store in Anita. We were tired, but it was only 10:15 and we'd covered 35 miles. We were doing better than either of us had dared hope.

Riding along, we talked about farming. Jack's father had been unusually successful because he'd recognized that today's low prices in one commodity mean tomorrow's underproduction. That, Jack explained, meant prices would rise again in the future, and so it's a good idea to invest today—when prices are down—in equipment that might be needed later. According to Jack, his father had beaten several price swings that way, consistently coming out ahead when everyone else was scrambling.

After our rest we discovered a prominent "BRIDGE OUT" sign posted on the road to our next destination, Adair. A construction crew informed us that we could probably get through, and a nearby railroad track offered the reassurance of an adjacent bridge should we need it. We decided to brave the missing bridge rather than detour 7 miles.

It proved a good decision, carrying us into Adair within an hour after nothing worse than a 100-yard walk along a farm lane.

I was overwhelmed by the height of the corn along the lane. It had been a magnificent growing season, and the shortest stalks were a foot higher than my outstretched arm. Most were 10 to 12 feet high. I wanted to walk deep into the field, to lose myself in the endless array of corn stalks, admiring the tassels 6 feet above my head, folding myself into a green world of damp stillness and narrow horizons.

But I decided to save that experience for later. We still needed to ride hard to catch RAGBRAI.

———————•◦•———————

And catch it we did, meeting the course 7 miles before Guthrie Center, a town that had served as an overnight stop on my previous RAGBRAI.

When we first hit the course, RAGBRAI was long gone: It was mid-afternoon and we'd intersected its path only 18 miles into that day's 58-mile route. But the hand-painted signs—advertising the bake sales and lemonade stands—were still out, asking, "Are you getting hot, thirsty? One mile to lemonade, iced tea, shade!" Or, "Homemade sweet rolls—Panora Cafe, only 9 miles ahead." Or simply, "Go Diane!"

But we were the last riders. Diane had gone, and so had the food, the lemonade stands, the kids with hoses waiting to spray hot riders. Following in the wake of RAGBRAI was like entering a football stadium an hour after a big game. There was an undefined feeling that something momentous had happened. You could see it in the eyes of passing motorists, in the empty food stands, almost in the woods and cornfields themselves, just as a great victory or tragic defeat seems to linger in the bleachers after the game, as though the emotions and energies expended earlier have been absorbed by their surroundings and then gradually released in a gentle haunting, a subliminal reminder that *something* has happened.

But there is one major difference between RAGBRAI and a football game. RAGBRAI is clean. There were no great windrows of litter along the road, no candy wrappers to make the haunting tangible. Three years ago I'd wondered how long it took to clean up after RAGBRAI's hungry hordes. Now I knew: only a few hours, at least in places that weren't overnight stops.

Within a few miles we caught the tail of the monster—a handful of riders still lingering in Guthrie Center. But it wasn't yet the RAGBRAI I knew, for both the riders and the shopkeepers were quiet, subdued, no longer greeting us eagerly, but taking us for granted. Already the town was well into the post-ride cleanup.

Seven miles later, in Panora, we caught up with more riders. Now we had moved from the eddy into the main event itself. Only a couple hundred cyclists were left, but in true RAGBRAI style they'd taken over the town, propping bicycles against store fronts, napping in the park, eating and chatting and milling about on the sidewalk of Panora's one shopping block.

But while much of the RAGBRAI flavor could be found here, we quickly learned that this was still a different RAGBRAI than the one I'd experienced before, riding in the front half of the pack. These people weren't laggards. They were strong, experienced riders, some of them far stronger than I. But many were also heavy drinkers who had been riding from bar to bar all day. We had no interest in lingering with them.

We encountered one of RAGBRAI's numerous "sag wagons"—cars or vans used to assist riders whose bicycles or bodies have given out. We told the sag driver about our long chase to catch the ride, and our pleasure at doing so with six hours of daylight remaining.

"Would you like me to carry your bags?" he asked.

There was only one answer to that, and we gratefully unloaded. A week with someone else to carry my baggage had been one of the great appeals of RAGBRAI, beckoning me all the way across Kansas. And as we loaded our gear into the waiting station wagon I realized that now the chase was over: We were officially with RAGBRAI.

----•-----

The remaining 26 miles should have been easy, and at first they were. Unburdened, we rolled across the longest stretch of flat terrain I'd seen in several days. But perhaps because we'd started so early, or perhaps because I was still feeling a hangover from my illness, I gradually ran out of energy. Even with a long stop at a lemonade stand 10 miles from our destination, I was tired by the time we got to camp.

Getting a good night's sleep on RAGBRAI is an art, for the huge crowds and party atmosphere mean that many people are up and around—some of them noisily drunk—until the wee hours of the morning. On my previous RAGBRAI it had taken several sleepless evenings to discover that the trick was to avoid camping in the official camping areas—usually school yards or county fairgrounds—or at a minimum to carry my gear to the far corner of the campground. Mobility was the key to a quiet evening, since most riders, constrained by their heavy duffel bags, set up camp near the baggage trucks.

That first night I definitely wanted sleep, so I loaded my panniers back onto my bicycle while Jack picked up his duffel bag and we pedaled several hundred yards away from the trucks to the far edge of the large city park that served as the official campground.

Because we were late arrivals, most people had already pitched their tents, and we could pick our spot with reasonable confidence that we wouldn't later find ourselves surrounded by unexpected neighbors. To our surprise, we quickly found a large open space with 20 yards between us and the nearest tent. By RAGBRAI standards, that was the equivalent of deep wilderness.

During the afternoon my appetite had vanished as my strength had declined, but as the sun set and the temperature dropped, hunger returned. On RAGBRAI, one chooses dinners along denominational lines. Baptists, for example, are likely to serve fried chicken and are among the most likely to advertise at great distances from camp. That means they are also likely to be the first to run out of food. Methodists favor spaghetti, while Presbyterians and Lutherans are renowned for baked goods. All of the denominations and service groups have one thing in common: They generate immense food lines, and those serving the more popular entrees often have waits of up to an hour.

By arriving late, Jack and I had one major advantage: Most of the lines had already subsided. We were late enough, in fact, that we decided to forgo the churches and service clubs, opting for a pizzeria that had established an all-you-can-eat pizza and salad bar. Earlier, we probably couldn't have gotten close to the door; now, there were seats.

Half an hour after sunset we returned to our tents, and I stretched out contentedly in my sleeping bag.

I'd barely dozed off when I was awakened by a vastly amplified guitar chord. "What on Earth. . . ." I muttered, then unzipped my tent to look outside.

Two hundred yards away, with a large bank of speakers aimed directly at us, a rock band was warming up on an outdoor stage. I groaned. So that was why nobody else had camped here. Coming across that much room so close to the baggage trucks had seemed too good to be true, and it was. I thought briefly about moving my tent, but gave up and instead tried to will myself to sleep.

It was probably close to midnight when I finally succeeded.

———————— •◦• ————————

I was awakened at 5:00 A.M. by the clank of tent stakes at a nearby site, and by 5:15, even though the sun wouldn't rise for another forty-five minutes, the entire campground was astir.

Jack was among the early risers, and seemed unduly cheerful for such an early hour.

"How did you sleep?" I asked. "Wasn't that horrible?"

"No problem," he replied. "Those guys were good. I listened to them for a while, then rolled over and went right to sleep."

My view was just the opposite. "The problem was that they were good, and they kept playing stuff I knew, so I couldn't help listening. It would have been a problem even if they hadn't been so loud."

Jack shrugged. "Not for me. Give me good music and I can go right to sleep. It's bad music I can't stand."

We finished packing our bags and joined the procession loading the baggage van. Then we lined up for a pancake breakfast served by a local service club. Not long after six, we were on the road.

It was a pleasure seeing RAGBRAI from the middle of the procession rather than the end. The riders were fresh, strong, and exuberant, the morning was cool, and the miles rolled quickly by as the route slid north of Des Moines, heading for an overnight stop in the small town of Eldora.

For those who wanted it, this day was RAGBRAI's century day, and while the basic route was only 88 miles, a 12-mile extension had been provided to bring it to an even 100.

I was interested in something different, and midway through the day I parted company with Jack to take a side trip that in 10 to 12 miles allowed me to nip the corner of two counties, slightly off the route.

For years I'd been collecting counties as I bicycled. At home I had an outline map of the United States with the counties I'd visited by bicycle highlighted. By the end of this trip the total was going to be several hundred, and while most of my friends found it a strange hobby, I couldn't resist the prospect of bagging two extras on such a short side trip.

While I was off the route, the wind sprang up and the day grew hot; by the time I rejoined RAGBRAI an hour and a half later, I was again much more tired than I should have been. When I reached the point where the century route diverged, I elected to go the short way. After all, I thought, I'd already done several centuries on my own in the past few weeks.

The last 15 miles were gently rolling, but I found them as difficult as the last 15 miles of the day before. The afternoon heat again sapped my energy. I'd fallen far enough back in the pack that while there were still many other riders nearby, they were all much slower than I, even in my depleted state. Ironically, although I was surrounded by other cyclists, I was again riding alone.

Still, I was buoyed by repeated evidence of Iowans' love of RAGBRAI. A few miles out of town someone had set up a life-size mannequin of a farmer wearing a lumberjack shirt, blue jeans, and a baseball cap, holding a sign that read:

Welcome to Eldora

Oink in There

This is the Last Hill

Earlier, a farm lawn had been decorated with life-size dummies of an elderly couple in pioneer attire. I was tired enough to forgo celebrating when I reached town, but I appreciated the effort invested on our behalf.

As I rode into camp, members of a church group were passing out brochures offering quiet camping at a retreat center 5 miles away, with bus service for rider and bike. "No alcohol or drugs," read the flier, which also promised a "pasta smorgasbord" dinner. The prospect was alluring, but the last bus left in only a few minutes, and first I needed to locate Jack.

One of the amenities provided by RAGBRAI was a notice board to help people find each other. Even if Jack had done the full century I knew he'd have beaten me to camp, so I looked for his message. I found it right away. "Rick," it read, "I'm camped in the ravine to the southwest." He'd drawn an arrow to mark the direction.

I found a ravine right away, but five minutes of exploration failed to locate Jack. A quick check of the vicinity revealed few neighbors and no rock bands, so I gave up on both Jack and the church group and pitched my own camp on a bed of hay stubble I hoped would flatten out enough to provide a decent night's sleep.

Then I went in search of dinner.

———————•••———————

Hay stubble or not, that night I slept the sleep of the just—or the dead. Sometime before the first faint glow of dawn, though, the people next to me awoke and, talking all the while in normal conversational tones, began striking camp. After fifteen minutes of trying to ignore it, I could stand it no longer.

"Excuse me," I called across the 10 feet between our tents, "but loud talking at 4:30 in the morning is just as rude as loud talking at midnight."

The conversation halted, then resumed, with three of the four talking as loudly as ever, and the fourth soon rejoining them. *Well, he's awake now anyway,* I could almost hear them think. *So what difference does it make now?*

———————•••———————

All the weeks on the road had made me more than usually tolerant, and I was able to shrug it off. Later someone attributed my equanimity to a loneliness for human company. But that wasn't so, not since the day I'd met Vera. Perhaps it was because I'd had such good company for those five days with her, perhaps it was the marvelous people of Kansas and the fact I'd continued to meet other bikers on occasion, but except when I was at my sickest, I hadn't craved company since we'd parted.

I was relaxed. The days had fallen into a pattern, a rhythm that little could upset for long. I would rise early and strike camp efficiently, usually getting everything packed in fifteen minutes or less, but feeling no pressure to move quickly. Then I would hit the road, initially relishing the cool of the morning, singing as I pedaled—songs of freedom and quest, songs of open spaces of land and open spaces of the soul, songs for the prairies or songs of quiet, pastoral contentment. Eventually the heat would clamp down, as riding itself became serious business, punctuated chiefly by stops for food or cold drinks. The only real aggravations were the hills, which slowed my pace and brought on waves of perspiration, but they, after all, were part of the process.

RAGBRAI had surprisingly little effect on this lifestyle. I still rose early, packed my tent, relished the morning, turned contemplative, then sweltered through the afternoons. Among the surrounding riders I no longer sang, nor did I carry my gear. I still struggled up the hills, though faster than before, and each evening I would find a tent site, pitch camp, and continue my daily ritual of trying to maintain a journal.

The chief change was the addition of a new class of road hazard: maniac cyclists.

Too many people treat RAGBRAI like a race. And routes that cover long stretches of roller-coaster hills, are tailor-made for accidents. Traffic control reduces the risk of getting hit by a car, but riding with RAGBRAI is mile for mile much more dangerous than riding alone.

The reason is pace chains—groups of two to twenty or more cyclists riding in close succession, often two abreast, taking advantage of the windbreak provided by the riders ahead. When these groups, which can be traveling at 20 to 25 miles an hour on the level, encounter slower riders—or worse yet, slower pace chains—they often zoom by with shouts of, "On your left," or, "Track! Track!" regardless of traffic conditions or the skill of the slower riders. On RAGBRAI's first day each year, when it usually rolls through large hills, I'd been told that the ambulances seem to run all morning, treating injuries ranging from simple cuts and abrasions to broken bones and concussions.

———— •@• ————

Just as I was packing my tent, Jack appeared. "Ah, there you are," he said. "I was camped in that ravine over there." He pointed to the other side of the hay field.

"You mean there's two?" I asked.

"Yeah. When I saw this ravine this morning, I knew where you had to be. You about ready to leave?"

I nodded. "Five minutes."

Jack, I knew, was one of the early birds, and while officially the ride didn't start until 6:00 A.M., he had a tendency to get impatient by 6:05. "The best time to ride," he'd told me on other occasions, "is first thing in the morning, when it's cool and the wind is light."

On this morning he was more than right, and along with many others we broke the rules by getting on the road well before sunrise. Our route, which had stair-stepped northeast the day before, doubled back to the southeast, covering 76 miles to Belle Plaine. Given Iowa's basic topography—flat in the north and hilly in the south—that meant hills as we dropped south, and the prospect of afternoon headwinds on the southerly stretches.

With that in mind we decided to skip breakfast, planning on an early lunch 30 to 40 miles down the road.

We stopped a few miles early in Conrad, population 1,100, which hailed itself to all and sundry as the "Black Dirt Capital of Iowa." To prove the point, the city fathers had dumped a truckload of dark loam in the center of town. They'd also provided clowns for entertainment, and were serving breakfast for those of us who'd started early. Later arrivals would get lunch. The first 1,000 riders to pass through—which despite our early start hadn't included us—even got souvenir bags of that famous dirt.

From Conrad our route led south and east through a series of small towns each tempting us with delicacies ranging from homemade ice cream (fifty cents a cup) to watermelon (twenty-five cents a slice), from Iowa porkburgers to roast corn, reminding me that RAGBRAI is the only athletic event I know of where it is possible to burn off thousands of calories a day and still gain weight.

Despite the party atmosphere, RAGBRAI was abuzz that afternoon with the news of tragedy. One of our fellow cyclists had died. The story was muddled, but apparently he'd been sitting on the dock of a small farm pond in the ninety-five-degree heat, drinking a beer. He'd fallen off the dock and disappeared, with would-be rescuers unable to locate him in the murky water. It was unclear whether he'd died of a stroke and then fallen in the water, or whether the combination of hot summer sun and beer had caused him to pass out and drown, but either way it was a sobering intrusion of mortality into the dreamworld of RAGBRAI.

It wasn't the first time RAGBRAI had been marred by tragedy. The paper reported that there had been three other deaths over the years, and the rumor mill pronounced that one had been a heart attack, one a drowning, and the other had occurred when an out-of-control van plunged onto a sidewalk, hitting a rider as he was relaxing after dinner.

I wondered as I pedaled through that afternoon what the chances were, if you put 7,500 people of all ages together for a week, that one or more might die of natural causes. I figured the odds were actually fairly high, and RAGBRAI had probably beaten them in its fourteen-year history.

———————•◦•———————

Each year RAGBRAI serves up one good thunderstorm. It seems to be part of the program, like the corn, the porkburgers, and the enthusiastic reception offered at every town the ride touches.

This year the thunderstorm came in Belle Plaine.

Jack and I were camped beneath a spreading oak in a large city park, far enough from the baggage truck to find elbow room—a snoring neighbor probably wouldn't be close enough to keep us awake.

But a thunderstorm was a different matter, and, as is common in the Midwest, it struck in the late evening, prefaced by the flicker of lightning on the southwestern horizon, the rumble of distant thunder, and a sudden breeze springing up from dead calm.

It was the first rain I'd seen since Colorado—the first test of my new waterproofing—and my tent failed miserably. Water came in everywhere as the wind split the zipper on the doorway, robbing the tent of the tension that would have kept it upright and setting it to flapping violently.

Weathering a Midwestern thunderstorm in a tent is an all-too familiar experience. I once cycled 1,000 miles across Nebraska, Iowa, and Minnesota, drawing storms on ten days out of eleven. But with a broken tent zipper this one was even worse than the one that drenched me in Wyoming. It lasted only an hour but it seemed an eternity, as did the rest of the night in a sleeping bag that had sponged up most of the available moisture. I had another tent at home and made a mental note to ask my wife to ship it to me somewhere ahead.

———————•●•———————

The next day was RAGBRAI's last full one, most of it spent on roller-coaster hills like those in Missouri. It was hot and humid, and again, as the afternoon progressed, my stamina waned.

How could I bicycle 90-mile days through the mountains with fifty pounds of gear, but have so much trouble in Iowa unloaded? I couldn't understand it. Heat and humidity were obvious factors, but I'd been dealing with heat since eastern Colorado and should have gotten used to it.

Thanks to an early start and relatively few stops, I made it to camp early that afternoon in the town of Washington, stopping with Jack in the farthest corner of a crowded city park. As had been the case everywhere on RAGBRAI, the local swimming pool was open and popular. For once, I was early enough to enjoy it. After a brief rest I took a turn cooling off in a pool so crowded we must have resembled a rookery of sea lions.

I had been looking forward to visiting Washington. It was the largest overnight stop on the course, and I was curious about what this town of 6,500 would do for a last-night party.

It proved to be all that could be imagined. There were not one but three bands, shuttle service to the high school showers, and a wide selection of church and community groups vying to offer the best dinner.

If we'd only known, Jack and I also could have showered at any of a number of private homes. Washington brags that it is the "Cleanest City In Iowa," and to live up to its nickname (a cynic might say to keep us from tarnishing its image), the chamber of commerce had passed out placards reading "Biker Shower" to homeowners around town. The signs were to be taken down whenever a home ran out of hot water, and replaced after the water heater recharged. The goal was to go down in history as one of the few towns to provide hot showers for all of RAGBRAI's sweaty hordes.

Downtown, a carnival atmosphere reigned in the streets, which were so crowded that many were effectively shut down. While I'd been resting at the park there'd even been a basketball game in the town square, with the high school team, which had gone undefeated the year before, challenging a hastily assembled team of "RAGBRAI All-Stars" that included three present or former collegiate players. The local team had triumphed 50 to 47, much to the joy of the hometown crowd.

After sampling the street parties, Jack and I were back in camp by ten o'clock, with muffled music still coming at us from three directions.

"Oh no," groaned Jack. "I'll never be able to sleep through that."

I was just about to climb into my tent, but first I glanced in his direction. "Huh? What?"

"That," he said. "That *noise*."

I grinned. "That? No problem. I can't catch the lyrics. I'll be asleep in minutes."

"Not me. That's not good music. It's awful. I'll never get to sleep."

Minutes later I was asleep.

————— •◦• —————

For most people, RAGBRAI's last day mixes celebration, achievement, and the bittersweet realization that the ride is virtually over. Usually it's also an easy day, allowing even the weakest riders time to get home afterward, even after fighting the big hills near the Mississippi.

This year, the 53-mile distance was long for a final day, but the terrain was relatively flat, and there was only one stop worthy of note: the small town of Riverside, midway through the morning's ride.

Were it not for the ingenuity of its citizens, Riverside would be merely another dot on the Iowa map: eight hundred inhabitants, a food stop for RAGBRAI, little else.

But in one episode of the famous television series, "Star Trek," Captain Kirk reveals that he was born in Iowa. Riverside saw its opportunity, petitioning the network to be designated as the official future birthplace of Captain James T. Kirk. The producers agreed, and to ardent "Star Trek" fans everywhere, Riverside suddenly found itself on the map. The town responded by building a mock-up of the starship *Enterprise* in the city park, and when RAGBRAI rolled into town the *Enterprise* successfully competed with the usual food concessions for the riders' attention. But once you've stood beside the model and walked the streets where Captain Kirk will be born two or three centuries in the future, there is relatively little to do in Riverside even for "Star Trek" fans. Soon, Jack and I were back on the road, following the lead of Riverside's fictional hero, leaving it for bigger things.

Those bigger things were the Mississippi River and the town of Muscatine, population twenty-three thousand—by far the biggest city I'd seen since Colorado Springs—an old river town that had seen better days, snuggled on the flood plain at the base of the river bluffs.

Over the past few days Jack and I had generally started out together but parted company at the first major stop, when he'd be ready to return to the road sooner than I. Since today was our last day, we stayed together all the way to Muscatine.

Muscatine is locally famous for watermelons and cantaloupes, and I'd visited it many times en route from my hometown in northern Illinois to the Iowa farm—no longer in the family—where my grandparents had lived when I was a child.

Jack and I joined a throng of bicyclists at the waterfront, symbolically dipping the front wheels of their bicycles in the river, completing an odyssey that for many had begun with an equally symbolic dipping of rear wheels in the Missouri. RAGBRAI completed, we pedaled up a steep hill to the courthouse lawn, where Jack had arranged to meet his father for a ride back home.

It was the third major good-bye of the trip, this time to an old friend I might not see again for many years. But the lethargy that had been creeping over me every afternoon was on me again, robbing our parting of any deep emotion. The past five days had been relaxed, quiet, and uneventful, a tranquil interlude like a vacation within a vacation, with much of the atmosphere of an easy summer week at the beach. Perhaps that sense of unreality was a spin-off from the artificial environment of RAGBRAI, or perhaps it derived from the fact that, despite his penchant for early starts, Jack is one of the most truly relaxed people I've ever known. Either way the sense of peace and unreality lingered, and when his father arrived, I found it easy to shake hands and part, even though I gladly would have spent another week with him.

"I envy you," Jack said. "I wish I could come along."

"Me too."

Then, loaded down with panniers for the first time in four days, I pedaled a suddenly unwieldy bicycle toward the river, in search of the toll bridge that would lead to Illinois.

———————•●•———————

I couldn't have asked for a better place for RAGBRAI to end than Muscatine, for another of Bikecentennial's several trails began here and led to Bar Harbor, Maine, 1,400 miles away.

Ever since I'd learned I had ten weeks instead of seven I'd been trying to choose an ultimate destination. By the time I crossed the Mississippi I was fairly certain I would go to Maine. Virginia, the traditional end point for many transcontinental cyclists, was closer, but for a month I'd been hearing reports of record-breaking temperatures in the Southeast. Since I had time to go anywhere I chose, I decided to avoid the heat and adjust my pace to arrive in Maine at about the same time Jane finished her work in Michigan. If time permitted, perhaps I could detour north to visit her, or persuade her to meet me by car somewhere along the way.

Muscatine was a perfect end point for RAGBRAI for another reason as well. The small town of Dixon, Illinois, where I'd spent much of my youth and where my parents still lived, lay only 90 miles to the northeast, 55 miles off the Bikecentennial route. My plan was simple: to bike as far as possible that night, then arrange to have my father give me a ride home. I would have preferred not to ask a ride, but it would get me to town that night, Saturday, giving me the rest of the weekend with my parents. On Monday they could drive me back to the point where I'd left the route.

———————•●•———————

Western Illinois looks a lot like Iowa, with substantial hills near the Mississippi gradually subsiding into a typical Midwestern roller coaster as the river drops behind.

The Bikecentennial Trail kept away from the main highways, stair-stepping across the state on county roads which, like their counterparts in Iowa, always ran east/west or north/south, regardless of the terrain, following the geometric dictates of a survey pattern established long ago by the Northwest Ordinance.

Other than the combination of hills and the pigheaded obstinacy of road surveyors, there is one other great bugaboo to Midwestern cyclists, and that afternoon I encountered my first example of it since western Iowa: "ROAD CLOSED," proclaimed a sign, "BRIDGE OUT AHEAD." Another sign with an arrow indicated the direction of the detour.

I muttered to myself, then pulled out the map to take a look, locating the appropriate creek on the Bikecentennial map, and determining that the next river crossing would take me 8 miles out of my way—the better part of an hour in hilly terrain. The bridge that was out, however, was only a mile or two ahead. I wondered if I could get across despite the official closure.

It was an interesting choice: an 8-mile detour as a sure thing, versus 10 to 12 miles if I gambled and lost. Anyone who bicycles solo is at heart an optimist; I packed up my map and forged ahead to find out if the sign truly applied to me.

I won my gamble—barely. The bridge itself was impassible, but a construction crew had set up a treacherous plank footbridge nearby. Since I didn't want to risk falling into the creek with a heavy load, I shuttled my gear across in several trips—first my panniers, then my tent and sleeping bag, and finally the bicycle.

On the first trip I noticed a fence with a single strand of wire running close to the path leading from the road to the foot bridge, with white, ceramic cylinders separating the wire from the posts that held it off the ground. It was another of the bugaboos of the Midwest—one I'd never encountered by bicycle—an electric fence.

Growing up, I'd been jolted several times by electric fences—on one notable occasion while canoeing a river across which a farmer had illegally strung a wire. It wasn't an experience I cared to repeat, so every time I passed the wire I squeezed carefully by, making sure I didn't touch it with either my body or something metallic.

By the time I'd unloaded my bicycle, shuttled everything across, and reloaded, it had taken twenty minutes and as much energy as bicycling several miles.

I was beginning to run out of energy again, so I called my father the next time I saw a phone and arranged to meet on the courthouse lawn in Cambridge, 10 miles ahead, even though there was sufficient daylight to go considerably farther.

I arrived in town several minutes early, bought a bottle of soda, and sat wearily on the curb near the store. *Heat sapping my energy in the afternoon,* I thought. *No appetite until well after dark, and the only foods I want are cold, wet, and sweet.* It felt like Kansas all over again.

————— •● —————

I spent three days with my parents rather than the planned one, talk-ing and sleeping but not doing much eating. Monday morning my mother persuaded me to see a doctor. He listened to an account of my symptoms and a brief summary of my trip. "Colorado, huh," he said. "We'll have to do some tests, but I know what you've got. There's a para-site out there called giardia. Did you drink any untreated water?"

I shook my head. "No." But I was unpleasantly familiar with giardia from a previous bout. A single-celled organism, it lives in the small intes-tine and is excreted in the feces of infected people or animals. In the back-country it's become so widespread that many backpackers no longer consider it appropriate to drink *any* untreated water, no matter how re-mote the source. Since I'd had it before, I was surprised I hadn't recog-nized the symptoms. But I was having trouble figuring out how I might have been exposed.

The doctor was undeterred. "It's everywhere," he said. "Colorado's full of it. I can't believe you bicycled 1,000 miles with giardia. You must be in really good shape."

"Normally," he continued, "I'd want you to be tested before giving you the medication. But I'll start you on it right away so you won't have to stay in town so long. You should feel a lot better in a few days."

————— •●• —————

I drove back to my parents with a mixture of relief and puzzlement—relief at finally having a diagnosis, puzzlement at how I could have picked up the disease.

The incubation period for giardia ranges from only a few days to a month, and I mentally counted backward from the day I'd first been sick. A week put me on my second day with Vera; a month ran me nearly all the way back to Sacramento. I could have gotten it from contaminated food, but as the doctor had implied, the most likely source was untreated water. What bothered me was that I'd been careful to drink only from public sources such as city parks, highway rest stops, and restaurants.

People who'd given me water, however, might not have been as careful, so I reviewed my trip again, looking for the times I'd gotten water from someone else. I remembered sharing water bottles with Vera, and possibly Ben, but we'd always filled them at the same sources. Then I remembered the night Vera and I had camped at the lake near Kremmling. We'd ac-cepted water from Arvin, the sailboard concessionaire, and now I wondered where he'd gotten it. Some people seem immune to giardia. I've heard of hikers who regularly drink untreated water and claim never to get sick. If Arvin was one of them—and it fit his personality—he might well have pulled his water from a nearby creek. After all, it was a long way to town. There were other possibilities, of course, but if my doctor was right, Colorado was the most likely source, and now I had a possible route of exposure.

That night I called Vera's home in Portland. I knew she wouldn't be there yet—she'd planned to spend two weeks in Santa Fe—but she'd told me she was in the habit of calling home once a week.

I left a message with one of her housemates. "Tell her," I said, "that if she got ill a week or so after she left Colorado, it's giardia."

Suddenly the contact with Vera, however indirect, brought back a flood of memories, along with the knowledge that this was a step that greatly increased the chances we'd stay in touch. "Tell her I'm in Illinois," I added, "and that I'm heading for Maine." That would catch her attention. When we'd parted company, I'd been thinking mostly about the Southeast.

CHAPTER 9

Illinois

Prairie Interlude

DAY 46 • Wednesday, July 30 • CUMULATIVE MILES: 3,431
Cambridge to Henry

DAY 47 • Thursday, July 31 • CUMULATIVE MILES: 3,504
Henry to Odell

DAY 48 • Friday, August 1 • CUMULATIVE MILES: 3,636
Odell, Illinois, to Monon, Indiana

Returning to the Bikecentennial route, I found a headwind wait-ing. I had to stifle a grumble—since the day I'd met Vera, all the way back in Wyoming, I could count on the fingers of one hand the number of days with a favorable wind: $2\frac{1}{2}$ days with Vera, 200 miles in Kansas and eastern Colorado, and assorted fractional days in Iowa. It would have been easier to ride in the opposite direction. What had become of the jet stream, which supposedly produces a westerly airflow across the continent? I'd ex-pected a few days of foul winds, but recently the only issue had been whether the headwind would be angling from the north or the south. To-day, it appeared the choice would be south, at about 10 miles an hour.

A 10-mile-an-hour wind may not sound like much, but wind is a cy-clist's worst enemy. It is worse than hills, worse than heat. It saps your energy, holds your pace to a crawl, and frustrates you with the tantalizing thought, "if only it were blowing in the other direction." Even a minor wind is a major nuisance. Pedaling 15 miles an hour into a 10-mile-an-hour wind you'll perceive a relative wind velocity of 25 miles an hour. If you're carrying panniers—which have a wind resistance reminiscent of a small parachute—you'll have to be an extraordinary cyclist to maintain that speed for long. Reverse the wind, though, and you perceive only a 5-mile-an-hour breeze, and the pace will feel like a Sunday stroll. On level ter-rain, a mile into a 10-mile-an-hour wind feels twice as long as when the wind is behind you.

When the wind has a crosswise vector to it, as it did on this day, one can at least hope for an occasional windbreak. And as the roadside vegetation varied among corn, pasture, and soybeans, I was pleased by how effectively the corn blocked it.

Jack and I had made a similar observation on RAGBRAI.

"I think *The Register* should require all farms along the route to plant corn," I'd commented.

"Good, tall corn," Jack added. "Nothing puny."

"Definitely no soybeans."

"And absolutely no alfalfa. That stuff's useless."

"Maybe they should set up big fans. *The Register*'s got a lot of clout. And RAGBRAI's important."

"Yeah—a big bank of fans along the Missouri to blow us all the way across the state."

Today I added another to the list: Farmers should be prohibited from growing soybeans on the upwind side of the road and corn on the other. *That* was cruel.

————————•❖•————————

After battling the wind all day I was in a mood to gripe, and that evening I found myself listing the accumulated aggravations of a month and a half on the road.

Topping the list were mosquitoes. I remembered a camping trip a few years before when the mosquitoes had been so bad my buddy hadn't wanted to come out of the tent to eat dinner. As I fended off the worst crop of bugs I'd seen since the Rockies, I understood how he'd felt. All I wanted was to crawl into my tent, exterminate any mosquitoes that followed me, and stay there until it got too hot for them in the morning or my bladder threatened to burst, whichever came first.

Unfortunately, a second aggravation surfaced—the tent itself. I'd taken advantage of the Dixon layover to have Jane send me a replacement by overnight courier (even on a bike trip there are times when the amenities of the I-want-it-yesterday culture have their uses). My new tent was three pounds heavier than its predecessor, but it was roomy and had weathered many a storm. I had difficulty pitching it, because a pole connector had gotten pushed so far into one of the hollow poles that it wouldn't hold the next segment. I had a pair of needlenose pliers in my tool kit, but in the several minutes required to repair the tent the mosquitoes had a banquet.

I was also getting tired of having to pitch a tent every night only to roll it up again in the morning. I wanted the freedom and simplicity of sleeping under the stars as I'd done in the West, but as I moved farther into a land of dew and insects I knew I wasn't likely to have another chance.

The final aggravation was the city park in Henry, a town of 2,700 people, where I was camped. I'd expected quiet, especially on a week night, but as the evening wore on a string of teenagers cruised through the nearby business district, circling three sides of the park, then returning downtown in a loop that couldn't have been more than a few blocks long. Around and around they went, radios blaring, engines unmuffled, fragments of conversation peppered with obscenities drifting on the breeze. In a way it was funny, in a way, sad—I could have walked the entire cruising route in ten minutes—but I'd been counting on a good night's sleep, and the noise kept me awake well into the night.

It wasn't a place I'd have been comfortable camping alone, but entering town I'd caught up with a ten-member Bikecentennial group, and they were camped nearby. The teenagers might be noisy, but I didn't think they'd hassle a group this large.

———————•••———————

All in all it hadn't been a bad day. I'd felt my healthiest since Colorado; I'd met the Bikecentennial group just as I was wondering where to spend the night; and the wind hadn't been strong enough to stop me from enjoying the ride.

I'd covered 65 miles through gently rolling cornfields, looking out over the yellow-green sea of ripening tassels and watching tiny yellow butterflies chase each other across the road. I wondered how such gossamer creatures could fly upwind, and urged them to keep out of my way, applauding when they dodged me and mourning when occasionally their careless flights ended tragically in the deadly blur of my spokes.

But I was still tired of headwinds, and I wasn't alone.

"Have you had a plague of headwinds?" I asked the Bikecentennial group.

Everyone responded at once.

"Yeah!"

"I thought the wind blew from the west."

"We've had two days of tailwinds since Glacier. I've counted. Two days."

Maybe tomorrow, I thought, as a car revved its engine in the distance. *Maybe tomorrow.*

———————•••———————

And the next day the wind finally shifted.

At first, equipment problems stopped me from enjoying it to the fullest. This time, the problem wasn't my tent—it was my bicycle.

On a bike trip, a fine line separates smooth sailing and catastrophe.

Some things, like flats, you prepare for. But there is a limit, even with mi-nor repairs, to what you can fix on the road, just as there is a limit to how many tools and spare parts you can carry.

When it came to flats I thought I was well prepared. I'd left Sacramento with plenty of patches and two spare tubes, and so far, flat tires had been even less frequent than tailwinds. My luck had made me careless, and when I'd used one of my spare tubes I'd failed to replace it. Today, I paid for that blunder when I got two flats in rapid succession.

Normally that wouldn't have been serious—most flats are easy to patch. But this time the first one had come from a hole so tiny I couldn't locate it; eventually, I gave up and dug out my spare tube. But as I was putting the tire back on the rim, I slipped with a tire iron and poked an enormous, unpatchable hole in the new tube, leaving myself with a flat tire and no spare tube. I went back to hunting for the hole. Normally, patching a tire takes at most five to ten minutes, plus a few minutes more to take all the camping equipment off my bike, then put it back on again once the job is finished. It's a hassle, nothing more. This time I spent forty-five minutes hunting for the hole, inflating the tire and listening for the hiss of escaping air, spitting on suspicious-looking scrapes to look for bubbles, but finding nothing.

I couldn't count on help from the Bikecentennial group, because on impulse, half an hour into the day, I'd left the route to take a shortcut. It was there that I'd gotten the flat, and I didn't expect any other riders to venture off the mapped path. If I couldn't fix it, I would have to hitchhike back to Henry to buy a new tube.

It was clear that what I was doing wasn't working, so I sat back to con-sider the alternatives. A couple of hundred yards before I'd gotten the flat I remembered crossing a small creek. Leaving my bicycle where it lay, I scurried back to the bridge, slid down a steep abutment, and joined a group of cows seeking shade beneath the bridge. Under their suspicious gaze, I pumped air into the tube and submerged it in the stream, immedi-ately locating the telltale string of bubbles that marked the hole. A few minutes later I was back on the road.

I'd barely relaxed into the ride when I got a second flat.

This time it was a slow leak—indicating an even tinier hole than be-fore. Without a spare tube I was afraid to risk patching it, so I pumped it up every few miles and searched for a hardware store.

There wasn't one in the next town, however, or the one after that. Nor, I learned, after making a few phone calls, could I get a tube in the following town, Odell, which, with 1,100 people, was the biggest thing directly on the route for 100 miles. The Bikecentennial map showed a bike shop in Pontiac, 8 miles off the route. I saw no choice but to detour.

I found the shop without difficulty and stocked up on spare tubes, buying not just one to replace the one that leaked, but also two spares. Running out of tubes was a problem I didn't intend to let happen again.

By now it was five o'clock, and while I'd covered only 59 miles, it was time to consider my options for the evening.

I had two choices: to cut back to the Bikecentennial route at Odell, where the group was planning to camp, or strike out on my own, picking up the trail farther on. That meant I'd have to scrounge a place to stay, since the map showed no nearby campgrounds.

It seemed bizarre to stop so soon when I finally had a tailwind—especially because no tailwind since Wyoming had lasted more than a day—but I decided to opt for the sure campground. I was also interested in learning more about the people in the Bikecentennial group.

From the bike shop, Odell was an easy 12-mile hop up an old highway, the once-famous cross-country thoroughfare, Route 66.

In its heyday, Route 66 ran from Chicago to Los Angeles and was the path to the California dream for thousands of migrants during the Dust Bowl era of the 1930s. It spawned a famous TV show, although I'm too young to remember it well. Today, modern superhighways have replaced much of the old road, and I expected this segment to be little more than a service road for the nearby freeway.

It was rush hour, however, and that expectation proved wrong. Pontiac was a town of ten thousand, big enough to generate substantial local traffic, and the next few miles were an unpleasant reminder of the rigors of urban riding.

Even in the congestion I was amazed by how courteous the Illinois drivers had become in the decade since I'd last lived there. I'd felt I was taking my life in my hands anytime I ventured onto a highway. On this trip—other than the rush hour—I'd felt safe everywhere, and the sound of a car horn behind me no longer meant—as it once did—"Get out of the way, I'm coming through!" but, "Hi! How ya' doin'?" followed by a wave.

Reaching the outskirts of Odell, I met one of the Bikecentennial riders who'd already set up camp and was out for a late-afternoon spin. Her name was Beth, and of the group she was the one I knew the best.

"We're camped in the city park," she said, giving me directions.

But then she added a warning: "I should probably tell you that some members of our group don't like strangers. There was a guy who rode with us in North Dakota. Most of us liked him, but after a few days one of our members complained. We eventually decided he could ride with us, but not camp with us. Here, though, we're staying in a public park. You've got as much right to it as anybody."

———————————•◦•———————————

As I rode on into town my spirits dropped. One of the reasons I'd decided to camp there was to get better acquainted with these people, and it was disconcerting to learn I wasn't wanted.

I wondered how Bikecentennial would react if it knew. It wasn't as though the tours were posh, catered events that might view tag-along, solo riders as freeloaders. Each rider had paid $1,680—roughly $18.50 a day—to cover food, lodging, and group equipment such as stoves, pots, and pans. The leader's only pay was that he or she rode free. There were no support vans or sag wagons; except for the fact that the Bikecentennial riders were part of a group, we were on equal footing.

I looked for other things that might explain their cliquishness, but drew a blank. All I knew about this group was that their ages ranged from twenty-something to sixty-three, and none of them had known each other before they'd started.

Whatever the reason, these people had the right to choose their own company, and now that I was forewarned I would take my leave as soon as possible.

But whether they liked it or not, I was staying in Odell. After two flat tires and an unplanned detour I was in no mood to press on.

Making it clear that I wasn't trying to force my way into their group, I set up my tent well away from theirs, and I was careful to keep my distance as they cooked dinner—I didn't want them to think I was looking for an invitation. Some of them came over to talk, but I'd lost much of my enthusiasm for getting better acquainted, wondering instead who it was who didn't like strangers or thought I somehow represented a threat to his $1,680.

Eventually I headed downtown in search of food of my own.

———————————•◦•———————————

As soon as the other riders were out of sight, my thoughts shifted from the mysteries of group dynamics to an appreciation of Odell.

This tiny town is the quintessential Illinois farm town. More than any other I've encountered, it typifies small-town Illinois—so normal it's abnormal, so ordinary it's extraordinary. If you approach as I did, your first view of the town takes in a grain elevator and a water tower, a cluster of trees and a clump of houses, all neatly bunched together, with no stragglers intruding on the surrounding cornfields, giving the appearance of a neighborly place where people trust each other and find no need to isolate themselves by sprawling far out into the country. Some of the houses are weather-beaten, with peeling paint, but the town as a whole is tidy and clean, with nicely mowed lawns, paved streets, and a spacious, well-tended park, complete with picnic pavilion and swimming pool—the best camping spot I'd seen since Kansas.

But this is only a superficial impression. In downtown Odell, I found Illinois hospitality a match for that of Kansas. And, although I was following a mapped route, the trail was new enough that it felt as though I were passing through virgin terrain, not yet jaded by too many cyclists.

I stopped in a grocery store, where I immediately drew a crowd.

"Where are you from?"

"Where are you going?"

"Oh, wow!"

"How many gears on that thing?" (That was the standard question in Illinois—perhaps because they overestimate the mountains they don't have.)

"Yes, we get a few bikers through here—every month or so a big group stays out at the park."

And on and on. In a previous town a man had given me a fatherly clap on the shoulder after such a conversation. "Sorry to detain you," he'd said, "but I really enjoyed talking to you."

Then there were the children. In a town like this, each passing cyclist must represent a true diversion—a minor milepost in the hazy roll of summer afternoons.

"Excuse me, sir, but are you a biker?" When a ten-year-old greets you with words almost dripping with awe, then lapses into incoherent silence—obviously seething with questions but too shy to ask—you can believe you're special.

The hospitality wasn't unique to Odell. All day long people had been going out of their way to make me feel welcome. Many had volunteered elaborate directions to the next town—even when I already knew the route—while general-store owners often didn't seem to care whether I bought anything or not, satisfied just to have me stop in.

But the best—what ultimately made Odell memorable—came last.

I'd decided to eat dinner in a tavern the locals had told me made excellent sandwiches. Biting into a roast beef and jalapeño sandwich—a spicy combination I'd never have expected to find in rural Illinois—I was joined by a man and woman.

"Excuse me," said the woman, who introduced herself as Debbie, "but are you the cyclist?"

I admitted I was.

"Well, do you need a place to stay tonight? We saw your bike outside and saw you didn't have a tent, and if you're trying to get to a motel somewhere, you're never going to make it. So I told Pete—he's my husband here—that we had to come in and see if you needed a place to stay."

I was overwhelmed, both by the offer itself and to a lesser extent by the torrent of words. "I'd love to, but I've already set up camp at the park."

"Well, do you mind if we talk to you? I'd love to do what you're doing. I think it would be a great way to travel, though Pete isn't so interested. I mean, he's happy to ride around town with me, but he'd rather sprint short distances than go like you're going. So it's kind of hard to find someone to go with on a long trip."

Soon I was fielding a barrage of the usual questions, but this time from a fellow cyclist. "Is it lonely by yourself?" "Have you been harassed?" "How do you decide where to spend the night?"

Pete let us talk for some time, interrupting only to say, "Let him eat his sandwich! Go ahead, you eat your sandwich while she talks."

When she added, "Yeah, eat your sandwich, I'll talk," I didn't bother to suppress a grin. I myself can be a non-stop talker, but I knew I'd found my match.

"Is there anything we can do for you?" Pete asked, a few minutes later. "Do you need a shower?"

"Thanks, but I had one at the pool."

"How about another sandwich?"

I'd barely managed to finish the first.

"Well, can we get you something to take with you?"

"What do they have here?"

"Other than sandwiches? Beef jerky, peanuts, potato chips—bar food."

I groped for an inspiration. I wanted to accept *something*. "Maybe a bag of chips?"

His enthusiasm took over, and a moment later he returned with four bags of chips and one of fried pork skins. "An Illinois specialty," he said about the latter. While he'd been at it, he'd also paid for my sandwich.

"What else can we do for you? How about breakfast tomorrow? We live only a block and a half from the park."

That was something I could use. Debbie thought it was a great idea, too, so we agreed that I would ring the doorbell at dawn, then return to break camp so I could still get an early start.

"Your mother's going to love this," Pete told Debbie. He turned back to me. "She's eighty years old and lives with us, and she loves company, any time of the day."

I wasn't sure if he was serious or joking, but I knew the hospitality was real. "He loves to do things like that," the bartender said after they'd left. "My husband and I had pizza with him one evening and he wouldn't let us buy a thing."

I was glad I'd come to Odell.

———————•●•———————

Next morning, Debbie fed me a magnificent breakfast, telling me between homemade croissants, an omelet, strawberries, and two kinds of gourmet Fruit-of-the-Month Club cherries about her plans to start law school that fall at a nearby university. Her mother was just as Pete had said. I'd never have believed she was eighty, and as predicted, she was thrilled to have a guest, even at 6 A.M. Pete, whose job had started three hours earlier, was long gone.

Debbie was determined not to delay me. She told me the route to the next town was one she biked regularly and asked if she could join me. I was happy for the company.

Again, just as at breakfast, she did not delay me. Many cyclists are in a rush to get started in the morning, and she apparently assumed I was one of them. On the road she let me set a comfortable pace for about 15 miles, then, when we reached her turn-around point, she quickly said good-bye. Before she left, I made sure I had her address so I could add her and her husband to my growing postcard list.

———————•●•———————

By 10:30, thanks to a strengthening tailwind, I'd already covered 40 miles. After parting company with Debbie I'd met Beth and ridden with her for a while, then said a final good-bye when she stopped for a snack. It was the last I'd see of her or her group.

For the first time in weeks I was feeling strong again, as the giardia was fading to nothing more than an unpleasant memory. I was eager to cruise on before that tailwind, which was blowing a steady 15 miles an hour, but there was no need to hurry, and it was time for a break. When I spotted a Dairy Queen in the village of Ashkum I stopped for a milk shake.

I'd barely sat down when the manager, a woman about my own age, suddenly appeared beside me and threw a newspaper onto the table in front of me. "Are you one of these?" she demanded sternly, pointing to an article on the front page.

I looked down, wondering what I was being accused of doing. "400 Bi-cyclists to Descend on Ashkum" read the headline, or words to that effect. It went on to talk about something called BAMMI – "Bicycle Across the Magnificent Miles of Illinois" – a RAGBRAI-style tour leaving Chicago in three days, heading downstate. She was confused, thinking I was part of the ride and that somehow I'd gotten here early; her abrupt demeanor wasn't a challenge, but a mixture of confusion and barely contained excitement.

"No," I said, "I'm traveling by myself." For the next few minutes we talked about bicycling in Illinois and how much more pleasant it was now than when I'd grown up. "I think it has to do with the '84 Olympics," I said. "Everywhere I've gone since then, people seem to associate any cy-clist with the racers who won all those medals, and they treat us like he-roes."

———————•—•———————

Later I rode on across the magnificent miles of Illinois, running before an equally magnificent tailwind. As it worked out, for the next two weeks tailwinds were to be the order of the day, as nature paid me back for the punishment inflicted on the Plains.

Early in the afternoon I crossed into Indiana, where I stopped in the first town to mail pages of my journal home to my mother, who'd volun-teered to type them. As I addressed the envelope the clerk told me that passing cyclists often arranged to have mail sent to them through his post office, general delivery.

The clerk, who looked to be in his late-forties or fifties, was a thin, soft-spoken man whose manner was simultaneously bashful and talkative. Like the people of Odell, he seemed fascinated by the slow parade of pass-ing cyclists, and he told me about one in particular, an Iranian student who'd been traveling solo and stopped to ask about nearby campgrounds. The clerk had said he knew of none, then in a flash of inspiration, offered his lawn. The cyclist, obviously thrilled, accepted gratefully, so the clerk added, "You know, I live alone, in a big old house, and I've got lots of room. You can stay on the couch downstairs." But the biker would hear none of it – he was already afraid he was imposing – and insisted on set-ting up his tent on the lawn. "He was so grateful even for that," the clerk added, "that he promised to send a postcard." A note of disappointment crept into his voice. "But he never did. I suppose he lost the address, or just plain forgot."

"That's my greatest worry," I said. "Losing my address book. I must have fifteen people to send postcards to, and I'm afraid I'll lose their addresses."

"Where are you going to stay tonight?" he asked, changing the subject. I said I wasn't sure.

"Well," he said, "you can always stay on my couch. I live in a big house all by myself. . . ."

I grinned. "I'm afraid I can't. My bicycle's been acting up, and I need a bike shop before the weekend." For the last 30 miles my deraileur had been squeaking badly in certain gears, and the range of those that functioned properly had been getting smaller as the day progressed. A squeak I could live with, but something worse might happen. While today was only Friday, I didn't want to risk finding the shops closed on Saturday.

"According to the map," I added, "the nearest shop is in Rensselaer."

"Oh, it's only 16 miles over there. If you want to come back. . . ." his voice trailed off.

I thanked him but declined. With that wind blowing, the last thing I would do was turn against it and repeat a 16-mile stretch, no matter how appealing the offer. Then, since it was already two o'clock, I bade him adieu.

I hadn't gotten three blocks when I stopped again, this time to get a snack at a general store. Before I left, the two ladies who ran it produced their guest register, a spiral notebook used only for passing cyclists, and asked me to sign. I did so with a flourish. I'd only been in the state a dozen miles, but already I'd decided the people of Indiana were nearly as good to cyclists as the people of Kansas.

I started out of town but kept thinking about the postal clerk. He needed a postcard. I paused, then went back to ask for his address.

"You deserve one," I said. "Assuming I don't lose the address book, I'll send you one from somewhere back East."

He beamed, and without hesitation pulled out a roll of gummed address labels and glued one in my book. I knew as I walked out that I'd guessed right, and I prayed again that nothing would happen to that little book.

I headed toward the bike shop, arriving in Rensselaer at about four o'clock and stopping at a gas station for directions.

"Bike shop?" said the attendant. "I think it's closed."

Marvelous, I thought, *I'm down to only half my gears, and the shop is out of business.* According to the map, the next one was in Huntington, most of the way to Ohio.

Just to be sure, I asked directions to the old shop, figuring I might as well see for myself.

I got there—though Rensselaer, even with only 4,700 people, is an extremely difficult town to navigate—and found to my surprise that the shop still existed. I was greeted by a pleasant, slightly rotund individual in his mid-forties. "What can I do for you?" he asked.

I explained my problem, noting that it might be partly due to a worn chain. One way to test a chain for wear is to see how far you can deflect it from side to side. An inch is normal. I could push mine all the way into the spokes and out the other side of the back wheel.

"I can fix that for you real easily," he said, producing a new one. "Now, let's put your bike on the rack and have a look at the deraileur." He quickly disassembled it but scared me badly when he fumbled a small part onto the floor, lost it, and had to hunt up a replacement. The fear of doing exactly that was why I hadn't attempted to fix it myself. I could all too easily imagine losing one of its tiny pieces by the roadside, knowing it was vital and probably gone for good.

"Can't find anything wrong," he said. "Maybe it just needs cleaning. Let's clean it up and see what happens." He did so, and after he put the new chain on, the squeak was gone.

"How much do I owe you?" I asked.

"Let's say $5.30 for the chain, nothing for the labor. I haven't charged a coast-to-coast cyclist yet for labor, and I'm not going to start with you. Consider it an introduction to Hoosier hospitality."

I grinned back. "I've been seeing a lot of that. Cyclists talk all the time about Kansas, but Indiana's every bit as good."

———— •❦• ————

I tested the deraileur to make sure it hit the entire range of gears, paid, and rolled out.

Two miles out of town I had problems again, though this time the gears that wouldn't work were different. Apparently, fixing one problem had created another. I muttered a heart-felt "damn," dithered a bit, then turned back toward town. Maybe the store was still open.

It was closed for the day, so I headed on. I wasn't going to wait for morning. Besides, I wasn't sure he could help. What I probably needed was another new freewheel, and the wide-range gearing I'd want when I got to the Appalachians would be hard to find in small-town Indiana.

As they age, freewheels and chains wear to fit each other; if you replace one, you often need to replace the other. It's a lot like the Biblical parable of new wines and old wineskins—I'd been lucky not to need a chain when I'd replaced my freewheel previously, in Colorado, and now the chain I'd just bought was finding the worn spots on my freewheel.

I had fifteen of my eighteen gears, and while the loss of the others was unpleasant, it was definitely an improvement. If I could put in another 30 miles by nightfall, I could easily reach the bike shop in Huntington by midafternoon on the morrow. If Huntington didn't have what I needed, Fort Wayne was nearby, and its bike shops would probably be open even on Sunday.

So on I rolled before that marvelous tailwind, covering another 15 miles before I hit what cyclists call "the bonk." In ordinary English, I was out of energy, and hungry.

I took a brief rest—I couldn't take a long one since the sun would be setting in an hour—then studied the map for the nearest campground. I found one, 7 miles away, only a mile off the route. Better yet, there was a town en route where I could find dinner before scurrying to camp at dusk.

———————————•❖•———————————

I camped in a commercial campground named Thrasher Woods. I never asked what the name meant; "thrasher" could have referred to grain harvesting or a type of songbird, but since the campground was in the woods, I assumed it had to do with birds. By the time I got there, though, any birds had already returned to their nests, and the air was full of fireflies. It was the first time on the trip I'd seen them, and tired as I was after 132 miles, I paused to admire them.

Fireflies have to be the most inoffensive creatures in all of creation, as they blink their bioluminescent messages into the gathering dusk. Biologists say the purpose of their flashes is to help males and females find each other. But as I watched them I found it hard not to anthropomorphize, wondering if, like us, they felt the need to dispel the dark, to chase away the warm, soft night and peer beyond its veil, seeking the great mysteries of life and death.

But fireflies aren't the only insects in Thrasher Woods. Later, as I lay in my tent, I could distinguish at least two types of cicadas. One seemed to have taken possession of an entire nearby tree, with their massed chitterings rising in a near-palpable wall of sound that swelled and faded but never stilled. The second type were fewer in number but individually louder, their solitary "chir-rups" arising from isolated sources scattered in a variety of directions.

A single one of these insects would have driven me crazy, but en masse their music was beautiful and soothing, a two-part harmony surrounding and encasing me, shutting out distractions from the highway and neighboring campsites and quickly lulling me to sleep.

Unfortunately, there were still other insects loose in Thrasher Woods. Mosquitoes, to name one, and something far worse, a tiny creature, probably a breed of no-see-um, whose bite leaves a fearsome and unignorable itch—an itch that could wake me from a sound sleep, then persist for five to ten minutes before dropping to a bearable level. These insects have a fondness for feet, biting in such unpleasant places as the tips of little toes. I'd had a tent full of them in Henry after I'd finally made my peace with the mosquitoes and the cruisers, and it had been at least 2 A.M. before the last one got its fill and I could sleep uninterrupted. In Thrasher Woods I wished my new tent were smaller; size has advantages, but it also leaves more places for bugs to hide. I tried to hunt down the gnats, but there's a reason why they're called no-see-ums, and eventually I gave up.

CHAPTER 10

Alan

White-Line Fever

DAY 49 • Saturday, August 2 • CUMULATIVE MILES: 3,716
Monon to Huntington

DAY 50 • Sunday, August 3 • CUMULATIVE MILES: 3,847
Huntington, Indiana, to Bowling Green, Ohio

DAY 51 • Monday, August 4 • CUMULATIVE MILES: 3,944
Bowling Green to Oberlin

DAY 52 • Tuesday, August 5 • CUMULATIVE MILES: 4,027
Oberlin to Chardon

DAY 53 • Wednesday, August 6 • CUMULATIVE MILES:
4,109
Chardon, Ohio, to Glenwood Springs, Pennsylvania

DAY 54 • Thursday, August 7 • CUMULATIVE MILES: 4,191
Glenwood Springs, Pennsylvania, to Onoville, New
York

DAY 55 • Friday, August 8 • CUMULATIVE MILES: 4,264
Onoville to Portageville

I slept late, relishing the decadent luxury of not hitting the road
until at least three hours after sunrise. Otherwise I followed the same routine I'd followed since California, as the days turned to weeks and the
weeks stretched toward months.

It was simple and relaxed. Each day I cycled until I was ready to quit,
then set up camp and ate dinner. If I rode late into the evening—as I had
the night before—I stopped for dinner before reaching camp; otherwise I
ate about seven o'clock. In either case I'd retire at sunset, and now that
the nights were becoming longer as July turned into August, I read or
wrote until I became too groggy to concentrate.

In the mornings I usually awoke within a few minutes of dawn and
went about the leisurely process of breaking camp, never moving quickly,

never worrying whether it took fifteen minutes or an hour, never checking, in fact, to see how long it took.

Once on the road I would ride 40 miles or so before taking a major break—unless something took my fancy. The first break consisted of an early lunch or a late, second breakfast followed by an hour of reading or writing in my journal. Then I'd ride a substantial distance and take a shorter, midafternoon break and think about where I wanted to spend the night. It was a thoroughly relaxing lifestyle that made schedules an alien concept.

I had one hard-and-fast rule, one so thoroughly internalized I seldom thought of it: no watches and no clocks; time would be kept only by the sun.

All that changed when I started riding with Alan.

———————— •◦• ————————

I met him in the afternoon after leaving Thrasher Woods, as I cruised through the flat cornfields and winding river bottoms of north-central Indiana. Tall (6′4″), lanky, and effusively outgoing, he was a forty-three-year-old engineer from upstate New York who would write the theme for the eastern half of my journey just as Vera had set the tone in the west. For the next seven days he was an almost-constant companion.

I couldn't have picked two more dissimilar traveling companions. Although both Vera and Alan had something to prove to themselves and each possessed an iron-willed determination and quiet courage that either probably would have denied, all similarity ended there. Vera preferred to do as little planning as possible, letting her days develop according to the caprices of wind, weather, and her own energy level. Alan delighted in scheduling, and actually used alarm clocks and stop watches.

"There are only two things I insist on," he said during the first hour we were together, "a shower and a good breakfast."

Those two requirements led to others, for Alan was on a schedule. With his eldest daughter entering college the following year, it would be a long time before he could again afford the luxury of an expensive solo vacation. With his wife's encouragement, he'd decided this was the summer for the cross-country trip he'd dreamed of nearly two decades. By careful hoarding he managed to accumulate thirty-eight days vacation, enough to cover the 3,500-mile Bikecentennial Trail from Anacortes, Washington, to his home in upstate New York at an average pace of 92 miles a day, excluding inevitable side trips to campgrounds and restaurants. It was a schedule that left little time for relaxation, but while I might question his wisdom in not choosing a shorter route, his decision to emphasize the athletic endeavor itself didn't make him all that unusual.

———————•••———————

That first afternoon we rode into Huntington, Indiana, arriving a few minutes before the bike shop closed. Pedaling through town, a local cyclist spotted us and hurried over.

"Where are you going?" he asked.

"The bike shop, at the moment." I looked at the maze of twisting streets in this city of 16,000. "If we can find it."

"No problem. Follow me. It's only a mile."

He led us on a merry chase through a series of side streets down a hill into a downtown snuggled at the base of a bluff, hidden from the rest of town. Without help, we'd have been hard put to find it before the shop closed.

Our guide talked to Alan while I explained my problem to the salesman. Unfortunately, the chief mechanic had left town for an exhibition, taking with him most of the specialty parts, including oversize freewheels. It was discouraging, but my freewheel had been working better, and I thought I could live with it, at least until I reached the Appalachians. By then the new chain might wear to match the old gears, and the problem could cure itself.

Meanwhile, the other cyclist had been pumping Alan for tips on long-distance touring. "You see," he said, "I'm leaving tomorrow morning for a week, heading for Erie, Pennsylvania."

"That's the direction we're going!" Alan said. "Are you taking the Bikecentennial Trail?"

The other nodded excitedly. "Right."

By the time I'd finished talking to the salesman, the other cyclist had already headed home, and Alan informed me that he'd be joining us. "We'll meet him for breakfast at a restaurant near where we came into town at 6 A.M. That okay?"

It certainly was. I was ready for company again, especially a few days from now, when the route would plunge deep into the urban sprawl of Cleveland.

This meant we'd be spending the night in Huntington, even though there were still several hours of daylight left. Alan suggested a motel, and while I preferred not to spend the money, I could think of no better alternative.

———————•••———————

The next day was as close to perfect as summer in the Midwest can be. The 15-mile-per-hour tailwinds continued, and the day was cool with low humidity. Alan and I met our new companion right on the dot of 6:00. After a breakfast of pancakes and eggs—the first pancakes my stomach had tolerated since eastern Colorado—we were on the road, covering nearly 40 miles by midmorning.

We quickly got to know Bruce—a school teacher, probably a couple of years younger than me, 6'2", a basketball coach, and an obvious athlete. Like Alan, he was married and had three children, the youngest only two months old. He'd done some bicycle racing and had recently pedaled 100 miles in under five hours, far better than I'd ever been able to do.

And he shaved his head. At first I wondered if he did it to look tough—which he did—but later he explained that he had an immune disorder that caused his body to attack rapidly growing cells such as hair follicles. No one knew what caused it, but the problem had developed three years earlier, and within a year his hair was falling out in large, unsightly patches. Eventually he gave up and shaved off what was left, wearing a wig on formal occasions but not for cycling. "People ask all kinds of questions," he said. "Like whether I have cancer or even AIDS. It once bothered me but now I'm used to it. It's purely cosmetic."

———————•❦•———————

As the morning wore on I began to notice differences between Alan and myself, differences that were to set us at odds regularly during the next several days. Alan's goal was to complete the trip; the ride itself was secondary. Although we'd ridden across the same continent, we'd experienced entirely different worlds.

I found myself counting the number of times he used the word "boring." Montana had been boring. Illinois had been boring. Minnesota was boring. Today would have been boring without company. Bruce, who was himself quiet and a good listener, delighted in urging Alan into incessant monologues on the subject, but I reacted as though he were a supreme test sent by heaven to challenge how well I'd internalized the lessons I'd learned with Vera.

Open your eyes, I wanted to shout at him. *Open your heart, your soul, and see these states on their own terms.* Boredom comes from within and can be defeated from within. Many people *choose* to live in these places. There must be a reason!

I hadn't been bored since my second day on the road. Miserable, yes, but never bored. Perhaps that was the test of Kansas. Perhaps I'd passed without knowing it.

Well before noon we crossed into Ohio and met our most pleasant surprise of the day: The Ohio back roads were perfect for cycling. All were paved, most were smooth, and in the northern part of the state, where the glaciers had shaved the topography into a vast plain, they were truly as flat as Kansas was reputed to be. Even with rest stops we averaged nearly 14 miles an hour, logging 131 miles before stopping for the evening.

Bruce and I proved stronger than Alan, and we both ended the day with energy to spare. Alan had difficulty with the last 40 miles, especially when the route led crosswind for 15 miles. I tried to instruct him in crosswind drafting techniques—riding slightly behind the pace rider on the downwind side—but he had trouble keeping station and often positioned himself on the wrong side. He might simply have been tired, but I decided not to suggest drafting in a headwind, when he'd have to follow dangerously close behind. Unlike Vera, whose coordination I'd always trusted, Alan sometimes steered erratically and seemed unable to hold a straight line for extended periods.

Bruce and I worked well together. Our only problem was that whoever was on lead would never admit he could use a break. Whenever the two of us drafted, we quickly outran Alan and had to ease off until he caught up.

Originally I had planned to detour to Michigan to visit my wife, but when studying the map a few days earlier I realized it was farther out of the way than I'd thought. Getting there and back would take nearly a full day in each direction. Jane, on the other hand, was afraid that even with three weeks she wouldn't have time for all the work she wanted to do, and thought it unwise to take time off to come down to Ohio. Perhaps, she'd suggested, if she finished in time we could get together for a few days in Maine.

It was by then a familiar conflict—the fast-track career versus a decision to sample life from the road shoulder—but I found it hard not to feel a touch of resentment; my two-day round trip was her three-hour drive. She could meet me for an evening and be back at work by midmorning.

Still, I knew from my own career experiences that a few lost hours can seem infinite, and the past few weeks had relaxed me so thoroughly that the resentment quickly faded into disappointment.

Meanwhile, I had company, and meeting Jane meant that I didn't have to part with Bruce and Alan the day after I met them.

Our goal for the evening was a hostel in Bowling Green. We'd called ahead to see if we needed reservations and had learned that another biker was also staying there.

When we arrived we found her in residence, a wiry blond, probably in her mid-forties but possibly as much as a decade older or younger. As Alan and Bruce ordered a pizza, I talked with her as best I could between bouts of, "No anchovies," and, "How big is a large? Perhaps two mediums?" I asked if she wanted to join us but she'd already eaten, and maybe it was just as well, for throughout the evening Alan and Bruce showed no interest in including her in conversation.

She was riding by herself and had followed Bikecentennial's Trans-America Trail most of the way from Oregon through Kansas. Eventually she'd tired of the heat and, like me, decided to head for Maine. She'd angled across Missouri, Illinois, and Indiana, and was resting for the day. "I'm amazed at how beautiful Indiana is," she said. "I hadn't expected that." (I later passed that observation on to Alan, but he only snorted.) From Bowling Green she was riding to Sandusky, where she would take a ferry across Lake Erie then ride through Ontario to Niagara Falls.

Shortly before our pizza arrived she excused herself to make a phone call. In mid-bite, the things she'd told me suddenly triggered a three-week-old memory. Her physical appearance was right. The timing was right. I could barely contain myself until she got off the phone.

"Excuse me," I said, "but is your name Lynn?"

She looked at me quizzically. "Yes."

"I thought so. You rode with a woman named Vera for a week in Montana and Wyoming."

"Vera!" she exclaimed. "You know Vera?"

I explained how we'd met and some of what Vera had told me about the time she and Lynn had spent together.

"What did she say about me?" Lynn asked.

I was immediately grateful for Vera's policy of not speaking ill of people behind their backs. All I knew was that the two of them had parted company because Lynn had a habit, when they'd met strangers, of making unkind remarks about Vera—perhaps in jest, but not obviously so. That was all Vera had said and, curious though I'd been, I'd resisted the temptation to pry.

Lynn seemed afraid her birds had come home to roost, but thanks to Vera I could honestly say she'd told me little, other than that they'd ridden together. She'd also told me about a time when she and Lynn had wanted to sunbathe in Yellowstone, with one of them suggesting they change clothes "behind that log." The log turned out to be a buffalo. "Can you imagine," Vera had laughed, "if it had moved? I can just see myself running along with it, trying to finish putting on my swimsuit!"

I didn't think of that story at the time, though, so instead we swapped memories of Colorado. She told me she'd taken a wrong turn at Muddy Pass, winding up in Steamboat Springs, where she'd tried to get permission to camp on the lawn of a condominium. Permission had been refused, but she'd been offered a night's lodging in a posh recreation hall instead. The next day she'd hitchhiked back to the Continental Divide.

She also asked about Vera. Questions like: "Was she still doing 50 miles a day?" and expressing surprise that one day we'd covered 80.

I felt a note of condescension. *And a lot of it was uphill with a headwind,* I wanted to add. *And she told me she did 95 miles one day in Wyoming!* Instead I changed the subject, asking about the infamous hills of Missouri.

"Oh, they were terrible," Lynn said. "One day, as I was struggling up a hill, a girl came up behind me. 'Hi,' she said cheerily as she caught up. She wasn't going all that fast, but she was faster than me, and she had no pack. Pretty soon the van carrying her gear came along, and I threw my bags in, too. What a relief! I rode with them for two days."

It was the Christian Adventures group.

"Did they offer you dinner?"

She smiled. "They sure did. And I got to stay with them that night in a church."

"Was there a guy from Japan named Yuji?"

"Not then. But he came down to St. Louis to meet them on the second evening."

Sometimes it really is a small world. All evening I wanted to tell someone about it. Alan and Bruce listened, but they hadn't been there, hadn't ridden with Vera, hadn't talked an hour with Yuji, couldn't picture the cheerful faces of the Christian adventurers as they welcomed yet another road-weary guest. So the story fell flat, and I retired to my journal, staying up later than I should have but glad for it because, after all, that's what journals are for. I only wished there were a way to tell Vera, but from Santa Fe she was heading back toward Portland and would be on the road for another month.

———————————•●•———————————

During the next few days we rolled rapidly across Ohio. West of the Mississippi every state line had been an important milestone, but as I moved east such events became increasingly routine. Illinois had passed in three days; Indiana in two. And almost before I knew it, Ohio was disappearing behind us.

Geographically the state was a transition between the prairies and the Appalachians. In the eastern portion, our route had spent more than 200 miles on the smooth plain south of Lake Erie, one of the few truly flat areas in the northern U.S. But as we neared Cleveland—which we crossed surprisingly easily on a system of parkways—we began to encounter hills. By our last night in the state, in a small town a few miles beyond the city, we'd entered an Iowa-style roller coaster that would soon give way to the grueling, mile-long climbs and white-knuckle descents of northwestern Pennsylvania.

"I think we're gonna pay for this," Alan moaned whenever we started a descent, while Bruce and I hunched forward in anticipation, forgetting for the moment the near certainty that within a minute we would again be geared down, sweating rivers and thinking bleak thoughts about the Northwest Ordinance and its consequence: In Ohio, as in Iowa and Illinois, farm roads usually run in straight lines regardless of what lies in their way. I only hoped that it would be better in Pennsylvania, where no such constraint applies and the roads are free to wander where they might, following, I hoped, the paths of least resistance.

————————•❖•————————

Ohio was also a lesson in contrasts. The farm economy seemed more depressed than elsewhere on the Plains, and while many of the farmhouses were immaculate, often decorated with beautifully tended flower gardens, others were unpainted and dilapidated. On first glance many looked abandoned, but their windows still held curtains or potted plants, testimony that someone still hoped for better days.

In keeping with its depressed appearance, Ohio was the first state since Wyoming with places where I didn't feel welcome—like the tavern where we stopped for lunch the first day.

Taverns aren't generally the best places to eat. Even if the food is good it can be difficult for a cyclist to blend into the crowd—but at two o'clock on a Sunday afternoon I'd expected few difficulties. As I opened the door, two young couples looked up from a nearby table where they were playing cards. One of the men eyed our cycling shorts and the helmets dangling from our hands. "Looks like we've got a couple of bikers," he said. "You guys riding bicycles?" Something about the way he said it made it more a challenge than a question.

Before we could respond, another drinker, probably no older than me, but already forty to fifty pounds overweight with buttocks bulging over the top of a poorly cinched belt and face puckered from missing teeth, turned away from his beer and replied, "It's probably all they can handle."

"What a way to spend your Sunday afternoon," Bruce said as we left, "playing cards and drinking beer. There's got to be something better."

Alan was less charitable. "I think the highest IQ in there was about forty."

We all agreed that it wasn't the type of place we wanted to visit. There'd been something unwholesome in the atmosphere, a startling contrast to what I'd found in Illinois and Indiana only a few days before.

Unlike the patrons of the tavern, the migrant laborers working the fields were refreshingly friendly, often pausing to wave as we passed by. I was impressed by one farm in particular, somewhere east of Bowling Green, where a group of workers were picking cucumbers. In the background a stereo broadcasted Latino music; despite the noonday sun the harvesters were working with a will. I watched two men loading a truck. One stood on the ground, tossing buckets of cucumbers to his partner perched high above on the side of the open-topped truck. He deftly caught each bucket near the top of its arc, stopping it cleanly and letting the cucumbers sail on into the truck in an uninterrupted trajectory. In a dozen tosses neither man erred—the bucket stopped and the cucumbers continued as bucket followed bucket with hypnotic regularity, turning the simple task of loading a truck into an art with all the grace and beauty of a ballet.

I've always been out of my element in such places, feeling I was flaunting wealth and leisure. I had no such concerns about the farmers themselves—they'd chosen the farm life. Many were probably fighting desperately to retain it, and while cross-country bike trips were impossible for them, their life had its rewards: freedom and motion, sun and wind, hard labor and slow-paced living that had much in common with mine. But the migrant laborers and the increasing numbers of unemployed factory workers were different. They hadn't chosen their lifestyles. And I passed by riding an investment equal to several weeks' income and declaring that this summer, at least, I didn't need to work. "Why don't you get a real job?" someone shouted at me in Wyoming, and I wouldn't have been surprised to hear the same sentiments in Ohio.

———————— •❖• ————————

Despite the tavern, and despite the increasing urbanization as we approached Cleveland, Ohio wasn't without rural hospitality. A few hours after the cucumber field we spotted a hand-lettered sign tacked to a mail-box: "Bicyclists Welcome."

On my own I'd have stopped immediately, but riding as a group, we had a psychological inertia to overcome, and by the time we'd played the inevitable round of "Did you see that?" "Would you like to stop?" "Would *you*?" "Well, yeah, why not!"—we'd overshot by several hundred yards. But such an invitation couldn't be passed up, and after Bruce and I assured Alan we wouldn't stay long, we turned back, left our bikes on the spacious lawn, and, fending off the attentions of a friendly dog and cat, walked toward the house.

The animals must have learned their friendliness from their owners. Before we got to the door we were met by a mother and her seventh-grade son who offered us a pitcher of water, then brought lemonade without giving us an opportunity to protest that water would have been plenty. As we sat in the shade drinking, she invited us to camp on the lawn. Remembering the invitation I'd turned down in Indiana, I longed to accept, especially since this time it had come in the late afternoon, with a good chance for a home-cooked meal in the bargain. But Bruce had planned to sleep in motels each night and was carrying neither tent nor sleeping bag, while Alan had set his sights on Oberlin, still 25 miles away.

So I chatted and signed the guest register, adding another name to my postcard list and thinking again how terrible it would be to lose that little notebook with the names and addresses of so many people. As we talked I learned that our hosts were avid cyclists, that their son had just completed a ten-day, 400-mile trek around Ohio with a cycling "camp," and that the whole family planned on cycling through England the following summer. It wasn't the first time I'd received such hospitality from fellow cyclists, but these people were the most enthusiastic I'd met other than those who'd actually been on their bicycles when I encountered them.

Eventually we said our reluctant good-byes, cycling on to Oberlin where we arrived just at sunset to find that our only lodging option was a cramped, sixty-three-dollar motel room. Even at that price we could get only two beds, so we flipped coins to see who got to sleep alone. Alan won, and I shared a bed with Bruce.

———————•❧•———————

I struggled during the next few days with my feelings about Alan and the schedule that had been driving him for more than a month. At first I blamed myself for our incompatibility. Traveling with Alan had scrambled my daily routine—in much the same way that staying in motel after motel was affecting my finances—and I wondered if the basic problem was that riding alone had made me unwilling to compromise. But then I remembered how I'd continuously adjusted my goals with Vera, viewing the changing plans as a cheap price for the company. Why, I wondered, wasn't I flexing the same way for Alan?

As the petty aggravations of our odd-couple relationship began to penetrate to nerves so calmed by the previous weeks that they were slow to respond to irritation, I realized that I *was* flexing my schedule. But there'd been little compromise. More like capitulation.

There was the alarm clock. I didn't mind getting up early, but I wanted to do it naturally, awakened by sun and birds or the natural alarm of a full bladder. If my body didn't care to listen to these signals, then it could just sleep late.

The alarm clock also forced me to schedule how much sleep I wanted. Alan invariably set his clock for seven hours, and since he'd survived on that schedule for five weeks it must have been the right amount. I, on the other hand, had no idea how much sleep I needed—after all, I hadn't paid much attention to clocks.

On our second night, in the hostel in Bowling Green, I'd gotten Alan to agree to try it my way, without the alarm. But that morning my body chose to sleep in—possibly because I'd been up late writing in my journal, possibly because I wasn't used to sleeping indoors. Whatever the reason, we didn't get on the road until nearly 9:30.

"I think today was my latest start of the whole trip," Alan said when we were finally under way.

"It was late for me, too," I said. "But we crossed a time zone yesterday, so it's not quite as late as it seems. The sun didn't rise until 6:30."

But he was still uncomfortable, and I wasn't sure how well he understood that moving as slowly as one does on a bicycle makes the artificial divisions of time zones almost irrelevant. "Does this mean we'll lose an hour's sleep?" he'd asked the day before, as he set his watch ahead.

"Heavens, no. Only the numbers change. If you go by solar time it's better to think of yourself as losing five to ten minutes each day." But I don't think he understood, and at the deepest level still believed the sun rose at 5:45, just as it had in Indiana. Thus the insulating effect of clocks, which by dividing the day into preset divisions make it unnecessary to pay attention to the vagaries of latitude and longitude that give those divisions meaning.

Regardless of the reason, that morning in Bowling Green was the only one on which Alan allowed me to sleep without an alarm, for he'd gotten the impression that on my own I'd probably sleep until at least eight o'clock. And perhaps he was right. Riding together meant that the only times I had for reading, journal writing, or simply thinking about the day's events came after Bruce and Alan had gone to sleep, and the resulting string of six-hour nights was beginning to leave me groggy.

There were other changes as well. Before meeting Alan I'd tried to spend a few minutes each morning in prayer or devotional reading, and while it was a habit that had never gotten firmly established, it was impossible now, lost in the urgency to get on the road—or at least to the nearest cafe—before the sun peeked over the horizon.

Gone, too, were the free-form route choices, the I'll-decide-that-when-I-get-there attitude. Alan needed a specific goal each day, a target chosen the night before, with the route mapped before we began and altered only if necessary.

Then, shortly before we crossed the Ohio/Pennsylvania border, I had a revelation. It began with a flat tire.

"Good," Alan said, "I could use a break." He pushed a button on his watch. "Let's see how long it takes. I love to time these things."

I could almost feel my blood pressure rise. *Don't you dare*, I nearly exploded, *I've raced enough clocks in my life.*

But instead of shouting at him I started thinking. And somewhere between Alan's report of, "I hate to tell you, but that took thirty minutes!" and our arrival in the next town, I finally figured it out.

According to one medical theory, most people fall into two basic personality types, Type A and Type B. Type A's always find themselves racing time, frantically scheduling their days full of clocks and impossible deadlines, often seeking quantifiable accomplishments at the expense of personal growth. The B category, on the other hand, although it technically includes almost anyone who isn't an A, is epitomized by people like Ben and Jack—patient, creative, calm, adept at handling whatever pressures society throws at them.

To the medical community, the issue is whether Type A's are more prone to heart attacks than B's, but to me, the issue runs deeper. As I see it, the Type A syndrome is a psychological trap that can gradually deprive the victim's life of much that should give it meaning.

And that, I realized, was the crux of Alan's and my personality conflict—Alan was a Type A.

He didn't have the fully developed syndrome, which can manifest itself as a persistent, low-grade hostility toward anything that interferes with the schedule, but the manner in which he organized his day—in fact, the entire way he'd set up his vacation—was typical Type A behavior.

More important, Alan was an unrepentant Type A. He clearly viewed his scheduling abilities as a virtue, measuring everything in terms of tangible goals, then pushing as hard as he could to meet them so that at the end of each day he could collapse and rest. Unlike many Type A's, he managed to live within the schedule he set, but the succession of 95-mile days was obviously taking a toll on his stamina.

Watching him, I realized I was looking at myself as I could easily become. I, too, was a Type A—in many ways more dangerously so than Alan—for in my daily life I regularly set goals that required intense flurries of high-stress activity. My quest on this trip, I realized, could be viewed as a war with my own Type A behavior. That was why riding with Ben and Vera had been good for me. Ben, with his thoroughgoing Type B personality, had in many ways been a role model, while riding with Vera had forced me to change my goals in favor of compatibility.

But now, as we rode toward Pennsylvania, Alan was unknowingly trying to undo much of the good Ben and Vera had accomplished, sometimes even advising me to do things directly contrary to what I'd learned. "You know," he said one time, "You've got some honking to do if you're going to get to Maine on time."

"That's okay," I replied. "I'd rather not get there than push too hard. The best times I've had on this trip were the days I actually reduced my chances of seeing the Atlantic."

"Well, you've got to set a schedule now, don't you, if your wife is coming to Maine?"

"No! If we do get together, we'll meet wherever I wind up. If it's the coast, great. If not, so be it!"

"Just kidding, just kidding," he'd said, backing away from my sudden vehemence. But he hadn't been kidding, and I knew it.

After our first day together, Alan had mellowed in one way, becoming more restrained, somewhat less talkative than he'd been before, never again using the word "boring." Maybe I'd been too hard on him that day; his continuous talk may have been because he was starved for company. "I rode 2,800 miles before I met you," he said, "and after Glacier Park I never saw another cyclist going my way. Then, in two days, I met that Bikecentennial group, rode 40 to 50 miles with that girl, Beth, then caught you and met Bruce. I couldn't believe it."

———————•●•———————

We crossed the northwestern corner of Pennsylvania in a little under two days, bouncing along winding, narrow roads over hills steeper and longer than any we'd seen in Ohio, following a maze of twisty country roads that crossed and recrossed at odd angles, with the routes marked only by knee-high signs bearing confusingly similar, five-digit route numbers. Even with the Bikecentennial maps it was a wonder we didn't get thoroughly lost.

About two-thirds of the way to New York, we said farewell to Bruce in Corry, near his ultimate destination of Erie.

"I know how Bruce is feeling now," Alan said a few minutes after we pedaled out of sight. "I bet he's got that lost, all-alone feeling. Isn't that how you'd feel?"

I answered with a grunt, but Alan didn't notice. I hadn't gotten to know Bruce as well as I'd have liked, but somehow I doubted he felt lost and alone. He seemed perfectly competent to take care of himself—it had quickly become clear that he was the strongest rider of the three of us— and I'd been amazed that he didn't get angry when Alan gave him advice as though he were a neophyte. I was also intrigued by his ability to be equally at ease with both of us, and I wondered how he could adjust to two such different companions.

For me, Bruce was a much more compatible traveling companion than Alan—a veritable gold mine of agricultural trivia and local history. I regretted not taking the opportunity to plumb his quiet depths. Instead, beginning on our first day and continuing until we'd reached the hills of eastern Ohio, I was relieved when he kept Alan occupied while I occasionally dropped back or ran ahead for a dozen miles, unleashing a three-hour supply of pent-up songs, overflowing with joy for smooth roads, endless green fields, a tailwind, and the cool, haze-free skies that allowed us to see it all. Bored? Not me!

———————————

After parting company with Bruce, Alan and I rode together for another day and a half, first through Pennsylvania, then into southern New York.

The weather turned hot and muggy, with a bright, humid haze reducing visibility to only a couple of miles. As we climbed a long hill on the west side of the Allegheny Reservoir, near the New York border, a thundershower passed behind us, winding up just to our north as we approached a bend that would carry us in its direction.

"When we get to the top," I said, "we ought to check out which way that storm's going before we move on."

"What difference does that make?"

"Well, it's passing by, but I'd sure hate to ride into the back side of it when we turn the corner."

"You mean stop riding and wait for it?"

"Yeah."

"You've got to be kidding!"

I relented, and soon afterward we were immersed in a cold downpour that persisted for several miles. It was the first time I'd biked in rain since Colorado, and the only time, so far, when I'd ridden in more than a shower. When we reached a campground just beyond the New York border I was ready to quit for the day.

Alan had set his sights on a town another 8 miles up the road, and it wasn't until I flatly refused to pedal any farther that he abandoned his plan. I think he felt we'd been defeated, even though we were so close to his home that he no longer needed to hurry.

A hot dinner at a nearby cafe did much for his mood, though, and he perked up even more when he discovered that the campground had the cleanest showers he'd seen all trip.

———————•◉•———————

The next day, as we followed the shore of the reservoir deeper into New York, we rode through early-morning fog into gradually clearing weather. For the first time since Cleveland the road was wide, smooth, and flat, but later, as the route moved away from the Allegheny and again turned northeast, it returned to the parade of 500-foot hills that had been the dominant feature of the last two days. The hills are less frequent and the roads better graded than their counterparts in Pennsylvania, and I made good time, struggling uphill for 2 or 3 miles then swooping downward into the next valley, there to pass through a small town and repeat the cycle again, undulating from town to town except when convenient river valleys provided a few miles of relief.

Although it was hard work, I enjoyed the rapidly unfolding scenery and the startling green of this well-watered landscape of hills, woods, and fields.

Alan reacted differently.

"I feel sorry for you, Rick," he'd said the day before. "I'm riding on emotion now—I'm almost home. But I don't know what keeps you going through all these hills." I wondered whether he didn't believe my live-for-the-moment attitude was real, or if he simply didn't understand it. "I'd love to be able to take a trip the way you are," he told me on other occasions, "with lots of time to go wherever you want. But it's a luxury I don't have."

If he'd had the time, I wondered whether he really would have slowed down, or whether, like me, he'd have spent half the trip fighting the desire to draw the longest possible line on the map. The main reason I clashed so strongly with him, I knew, was that we had much in common: Alan was doing exactly what I'd been tempted to do a month before—what I easily could have wound up doing all the way to the Atlantic. I was determined not to let him draw me back into a schedule-driven mentality.

Had I not seen him so much as a symbol of what I was trying to change in myself, I would have seen more of his strengths and less of his quirks. He was warm, generous, and outgoing, a companion who would never desert a fellow cyclist in an hour of need, and as we prepared to separate, I became increasingly aware of how little I'd appreciated those virtues.

Nevertheless, after nearly a week of disagreements over pace and schedule I was ready to ride by myself. So although I awoke that morning at 5:30—a feat for which he complimented me enthusiastically, suggesting that maybe I was "beginning to see the light"—I gave him a head start, planning to meet him for breakfast in Little Valley, 24 miles and a major hill into the day.

When I got there, I could find neither Alan nor a cafe. I gave up and was about to settle for breakfast at a Seven-Eleven when he suddenly appeared from behind.

"When I got to town," he said, "one of the locals told me there wasn't a restaurant here. I didn't believe him, so I asked a girl in the Seven-Eleven. She told me there's one called the Bear Trap Restaurant on a side street—a real first-class greaser. The guy who ran it gave me all I could eat, then didn't want any money. I finally forced two dollars on him. You've got to check it out."

He gave me directions, and before I left we agreed to meet a few miles down the road.

The restaurant was everything Alan had said it would be—all the pancakes, home fries, and orange juice I could eat and an owner who wanted only nominal payment, at least from cyclists. It was proof that small-town hospitality hadn't ended in Ohio. I thought about Alan's attempt to force money on the owner, a trait he'd shown before, and earlier in the week I wondered how well he understood small-town people. He would tell me stories about their hospitality but generally finished with, "And I tried to pay him—after all, he'd spent nearly an hour of his time, and that would cost a lot back home." Invariably, the people in his stories wouldn't accept, and inevitably Alan persisted until his benefactor eventually broke down or seemed to get angry. That kind of hospitality is a gift—one that cannot be repaid except in your own hospitality to some other stranger—one that is better remembered with a postcard than a greenback.

I had a final taste of Alan's generosity when we reached the town of

Portageville, near the point were our routes would diverge. I'd been planning to push on for a few miles—I was looking forward to a morning without an alarm clock—while Alan was going to stay at an inn.

But as we neared town—one of the few times we were together that day—he had another suggestion. "Stay with me one more night," he urged. "I'll pay."

I thought a moment, then agreed. I'd have plenty of time to dodge alarm clocks as I zigzagged across New York, and riding separately most of the day had shown me I had yet to lose all of my carefully nurtured tranquility. Just as I'd passed the test of Kansas, I'd also survived the test of Alan.

There was a limit to how long I could have endured. "It's too bad I don't have another week to ride with you across New York," he'd said a few days before. I was glad he didn't, because I wouldn't have enjoyed telling him why I couldn't accept.

But for one more evening and one final alarm-clock morning, I could appreciate Alan as something other than a threat to my own Type A battle—enjoying his generosity and affability, and smiling at his quirks rather than gritting my teeth.

CHAPTER 11

New York

Finger Lakes, Auto Racing, and the Land of "No"

DAY 56 • Saturday, August 9 • CUMULATIVE MILES: 4,345
Portageville to Keuka Lake State Park

DAY 57 • Sunday, August 10 • CUMULATIVE MILES: 4,421
Keuka Lake State Park to Sampson State Park

DAY 58 • Monday, August 11 • CUMULATIVE MILES: 4,528
Sampson State Park to Selkirk Shores State Park

DAY 59 • Tuesday, August 12 • CUMULATIVE MILES: 4,628
Selkirk Shores State Park to Inlet (vicinity)

DAY 60 • Wednesday, August 13 • CUMULATIVE MILES:
4,675
Inlet to Lake Eaton Campground

DAY 61 • Thursday, August 14 • CUMULATIVE MILES:
4,751
Lake Eaton Campground to Crown Point State Park

The day I left Alan, the hot, muggy weather that had followed me since eastern Ohio finally broke. Until that morning my primary impression of New York and Pennsylvania had been the haze, which held visibility to only a few miles, shutting down the distant views and muting the colors of trees only a few hundred yards away. Morning and evening haze can be attractive, romanticizing barnyard scenes with streaks of mist, or suffusing the glory of the dying sun. But at midday—especially if the day is cloudy—it constricts the expansive vista that would otherwise reward each hill climbed, making that which is visible seem incomplete and insubstantial.

All that had changed. Alan had often praised the beauty of his home state, but that morning I saw it myself for the first time, as the haze was replaced by a crisp clarity of rolling, green panoramas, bounded on both sides by long, parallel ridges running north to south.

I was entering the realm of New York's fabled Finger Lakes—a young landscape only recently released by the last of the glaciers that plowed it into long furrows like so many claw marks in soft clay, forming the beds of the lakes that give it its name. But this isn't a landscape of soft clay. This is rock country, where the bones of the Earth lie close to the surface, forming rounded ridges that rise as much as 1,000 feet above steep, U-shaped valleys, on a 10-mile cycle that seems to repeat forever.

Near the south end of Keuka Lake, the first of the Finger Lakes I encountered, I detoured off the Bikecentennial Trail to the town of Bath in search of a bike shop. The freewheel problem I'd had in Indiana had cured itself, as I'd hoped, but then the derailleur began to act up. I was pleased to find a mechanic who was able to fix it—hopefully once and for all—simply by replacing a few bearings.

From the bike shop I headed north into wine country near Keuka Lake, stopping at the largest of the wineries—Taylor's New York Cellars—only a few minutes before its tasting room closed for the evening.

Entering the winery, I met three cyclists: a married couple from Cornell traveling with a visiting friend from Ireland.

"Don't go through Watkins Glen," the wife told me, apparently aware it was the next stop on the Bikecentennial Trail. "There's an auto race there this weekend, and the traffic will be even worse than usual."

I thanked her and asked where they were headed. "North. There's a little state park on the northern end of Keuka Lake," she said, pointing it out on my map. "That's where we're going."

I made a quick decision: The state park was only 20 miles away, and I was certainly not wedded to the Bikecentennial Trail. There were plenty of other good routes through the Finger Lakes. "Maybe I'll head that way, too," I said, turning back toward the winery in hopes that the tasting room hadn't closed.

Within a few minutes I was back on my bicycle, heading north. After riding with Alan for a week I hadn't thought I'd want company so soon, but they seemed a mellow couple, and I loved their friend's lilting Irish accent. I wondered if I could catch them before they got to camp.

Two miles later I passed another winery whose tasting room was still open. On the spur of the moment I pulled a U-turn into its parking lot. But bicycling and wine tasting are a poor combination, and I lost my balance on loose gravel, barely managing to hop free as my bike skidded out from under me. Nothing but my ego was damaged, but I was chilled by an unpleasant thought: Although the wines I'd sampled couldn't have amounted to more than a single glass, there was no doubt they'd been re-sponsible for my crash. What effect did wine-tasting have on drivers—es-pecially those who'd imbibed more than I had—on these winding roads? It was a question I didn't like to ponder.

Having stopped, I visited the winery anyway, but tasted only small samples and waited a few minutes before cycling. It was half an hour be-fore sunset when I reached the state park, high on a peninsula that split the northern end of the lake in two.

I quickly set up camp at a site adjacent to the cyclists. I already knew I'd made the right decision in coming to the park. I'd been disappointed in the lake, for the shore had been lined with cottages, and even though I'd followed it nearly 15 miles, I'd seldom had more than occasional glimpses of the water. But as I biked into camp along the flat top of the peninsula, I could watch the red ball of the sun sinking to the west, casting reflected highlights on the water hundreds of feet below, with no cottages or fences to block the view.

———————————— •◦• ————————————

The next morning I explored the peninsula with my new acquain-tances, first traveling the entire length of its spine, then dropping down to water level and following the lakeshore back north. They were going back to Cornell that evening, and on the spur of the moment I decided to ride with them most of the day, even though that meant detouring south through Watkins Glen, which I'd so carefully avoided the night before. On the map my route through the Finger Lakes was anything but direct, describing a large "N" as I ran north along the west side of Keuka Lake one day and on the next turned south between Keuka and Seneca lakes before doubling back north a final time along the far side of Seneca. Alan probably would have shaken his head in amazement. But I was enjoying this opportunity to return to a less structured existence, especially since I no longer had any worries about making it to the Atlantic. If all went well, I had plenty of time to follow the Bikecentennial Trail all the way to Bar Harbor. If need be, I could even finish in southern Maine.

We took our time on the way to Watkins Glen, stopping at a winery where I was more cautious than I'd been the day before, and not arriving in town until 3 P.M. My new friends still had 25 miles to go, so we ex-changed addresses and I waved them on their way, then turned to visit the famous state park at Watkins Glen.

For visitors uninterested in auto racing, the state park is the center-piece of the town. Its primary attraction is the Watkins Glen gorge, a narrow defile that follows a fault line slicing into a hillside southeast of town. The trail along the stream bed is an engineering marvel, with rock retaining walls, railings, and several bridges arching the river, while a sign at the entrance urges visitors to come back in the evening, when the walls are lighted for a sound-and-sight presentation billed as a walk through time.

My first reaction was negative. Watkins Glen is a tourist town of gift shops, restaurants, and heavy traffic, and the park entrance is only a few blocks from downtown. As I started up the trail it appeared that the park would be as heavily developed as the town, but deeper within the gorge, the magic of the stream bed began to take hold. With each step I left more people behind, and as the defile narrowed, with cliffs sometimes reaching 200 feet above my head, I entered a realm of racing whirlpools and rock basins sculpted into smooth, swirling patterns.

Remembering that the Finger Lakes region is a young landscape, I was in awe that the creek had probably cut the entire gorge in the short ten thousand years since the glaciers departed, in one place cutting so quickly as to leave a natural archway spanning the gorge. Everywhere water boiled from whirlpool to cauldron to waterfall, shouting an unanswerable challenge to rock already weakened by the ancient fault.

Had there been time I would have followed the creek all the way to the top of the gorge; instead, I turned back after half a mile. Rain threatened, and it was 28 miles to the first campground that wasn't too far off-route. Besides, the race would soon be ending, throwing heavy traffic onto the surrounding highways.

I didn't leave early enough. By the time I returned to the main highway the race was over, the traffic was intense, and far too much of it spilled north on the side road the Bikecentennial Trail followed along the eastern shore of the lake.

Following an afternoon of vicarious thrills, beer, and the invigorating whine of racing engines, the spectators apparently still felt the excitement when they got behind their own wheels, fancying themselves racers, revving their motors and demonstrating how much greater was the power of their cars than that of a puny bicycle. In the space of only a few miles I was honked, buzzed, and cursed at more times than in any comparable distance I'd ever pedaled.

The traffic died down eventually, and by the time a heavy rain descended on me two hours later, the overexuberant drivers had left me well behind.

The next day began gray, but by midmorning the clouds had broken into puffy clumps. The soaking rain of the evening before washed the air clean of haze, and more than any time since Kansas I felt I could see forever.

Pedaling away from the Finger Lakes, I entered a landscape that can be found in any of a number of northern states: New York, Michigan, Minnesota, Wisconsin. It is a land of flat valley bottoms separated by short, steep hills—of winding country roads and ragged fields gradually returning to nature, too recently scraped clean by the glaciers to have supported much in the way of agriculture.

Midway through the day I crossed what was once the main route of the Erie Canal. Had it not been identified on the Bikecentennial map, I would never have recognized it, except perhaps for the unusually straight course it cut as it skirted a nearby bog.

As I stood on a bridge I could have pedaled across in a few strokes, it was hard to believe that this was the canal that had done so much to open the frontier that is now the Midwest. Those barges must have been narrow, I thought, as I gazed at the stagnant water and tried to imagine this quiet area bustling with activity—muleskinners with bullwhips guiding their animals along the towpaths on either side of the canal, barge captains and their families living on the water. Today there isn't even an echo, just a straight line of stagnant water, its edges overgrown, the towpath lost, not a soul in sight, with the modern-day canal—which still carries some barge traffic—routed elsewhere.

I camped that night on the shore of Lake Ontario, pitching my tent in the teeth of a near gale that threatened to scatter my gear into the woods behind the shore. It was worth putting up with the wind in exchange for the invigorating crash of waves and the simple pleasure of unlimited visibility.

I had gone from the Finger Lakes to the Great Lakes in a single day; on the next I would go from the Great Lakes deep into the Adirondacks. Even though I'd left the Plains nearly a week before, it still amazed me that in the East one can travel through so many geographic provinces so quickly. And the changes would come even more quickly in Vermont, New Hampshire, and Maine. For the first time it occurred to me that I was nearing the end, that within a week I might have my first glimpse of the Atlantic, and that in ten or fifteen days I would be on my way back to California.

Meanwhile there were still the Adirondacks, the Green Mountains, the White Mountains, and the rugged coast of Maine to see — so much scenery in such a small region.

------------•◉•------------

My first taste of the Adirondacks was disappointing. I'd expected towering mountains, shimmering lakes, and the East's most spectacular wilderness housed in a park that, on the map, sprawls over almost a fifth of the state — nearly three times the size of Yellowstone. Instead I found unspectacular rounded ridges, heavy traffic, and towns. This wilderness, I realized — as I should have known simply by looking at a map — is heavily interwoven with private landholdings and dissected by highways that slice through from at least eight directions. On the map the wilderness areas looked like a clutch of eggs in a nest, and I'd barely noticed the road corridors separating them. By bicycle I was confined to the roads, and for most of that first day I saw only a continuous string of cars, or — when I finally managed to leave the main highway for a few miles of quiet side road — cabins and lake access points marked "PRIVATE," "NO TRESPASSING," "NO HUNTING," "NO CAMPING" — no public use. I seemed to have entered the land of "no."

It might have been different if I'd had a canoe rather than a bicycle. Many of the cars speeding by were carrying them; perhaps from the water this landscape displays the calm wilderness character I'd expected.

Riding along, I fought off a resurging desire to blindly rack up mileage. Perhaps I was reacting to the traffic — that endless stream of glassy-eyed motorists bent on reaching their vacation destinations as quickly as possible. But more likely it was a legacy from Alan.

Whatever the cause, it was a depressing throwback, made even more frustrating because it was unnecessary even from Alan's point of view. In the last two days I'd done the "honking" he'd urged, covering 207 miles. At that rate I'd be in Bar Harbor with several days to spare.

But I couldn't silence that Type A voice urging me to go-go-go-go-go, to build up extra mileage now in case I hit a delay later. It was a seductive trap — one I knew from my professional life — urging the sacrifice of everything that matters today in exchange for a future that, when it arrives, may simply demand more sacrifices. Maybe I hadn't survived the test of Alan as well as I'd thought.

I turned off the main road and the traffic slowed and thinned, and my own sense of haste receded, at least partially.

I couldn't see the 4-mile-long lake that I knew lay less than a mile away, but was rewarded by the sight of several deer. All were tame—later I learned that the people of a nearby town feed them in winter—and once I stopped to watch as a doe trailed by a pair of fawns stepped from the woods and walked across the road only a few feet in front of me. She hesitated when she reached the ditch on the far side, and the fawns rushed over and began to suckle greedily, almost violently. She stood and stared at me for a long moment, then stepped across her fawns and disappeared into the brush, heading toward the unseen lake.

Later I spied a doe with triplets and again stopped to watch. Soon a car parked nearby and disgorged a heavy-set woman, who walked toward the doe, throwing marshmallows as she approached. The doe refused the offerings, and the woman turned to me. "Why won't she eat them?" she asked. "That's what I feed them at the lake where we're camped."

———— •❂• ————

A half hour before sunset I reached Inlet, at the head of the largest of a string of lakes known as Fulton Chain Lakes. After picking up a map of the Adirondacks from a tourist center, I pulled into a city park, where I got my first good view of the lake from which this town derives its name.

For the first time I began to understand what draws so many people to this area. The sun was setting low across the water, turning the distant mountains—which seemed to have grown substantially larger since my last view of them—into hazy, blue silhouettes accented by a golden beam of sunlight reflected on the water and the dark outline of a dock jutting into the lake.

Pleasant as the scene was, this isn't wilderness. I was in the middle of a resort town, with the bustle of heavy traffic nearby and the endless "no" signs—"NO SWIMMING WHEN LIFEGUARD NOT ON DUTY," "NO PICNICKING." I had no intention of swimming, and stood beneath the latter sign eating a plum with the casual nonchalance of cyclists everywhere, who truly believe such signs can't possibly apply to them. Reluctantly acknowledging the inevitable approach of night and the remaining miles to the nearest campground, I remounted and turned my back on the setting sun.

———— •❂• ————

The next day I pedaled only 47 miles.

I'd like to say I did so as a deliberate declaration of war on the previous day's sense of urgency, but the unfortunate truth was that when I rode out of camp I intended to cover at least 80 to 90 miles.

As I penetrated deeper into the mountains, I discovered the real Adirondacks, and it was this that slowed me down, starting a process that in the next two days would finally nudge me back into the low-key lifestyle I'd been following when I met Alan.

As I moved beyond the tourist bustle of Inlet, civilization gradually dropped behind, the peaks grew taller, the cabins fewer, the traffic less frequent. Shortly after lunch, when my map said I was nearing the middle of the park, I abandoned my bicycle to hike to the summit of 3,700-foot-high Blue Mountain.

As I chained my bicycle to a post, I remembered the many warnings I'd heard from hiking and backpacking acquaintances about the steepness of Eastern trails. In the West, where I'd done most of my hiking, the scenery generally unfolds on a large scale, and while mountains may rise thousands of feet above the valleys, they often allow themselves enough elbow room to do so in noble style, unclouded by lesser peaks nearby, with gently sloping skirts that extend the climb over many miles. The western ramparts of the Sierra Nevada near Sacramento, for example, take 50 miles to reach their full height, and while various rivers have cut them into numerous rugged valleys, there is often room for trails to work their way uphill at leisurely rates.

In almost every Western mountain range the story is the same: The high summits are often inaccessible, so the trails wander through long valleys or over passes, with switchbacks easing the process where necessary. The few trails that actually go to a summit are often no steeper; they may climb 5,000 feet but take a dozen miles to do so, an easy gradient.

Not so in the East. Study a hiking map and you will begin to think that every peak has its trail, most of which runs straight for the top by the shortest possible route with no concern for the hiker.

So it was with Blue Mountain.

The peak rose above the highway in a single, hunch-shouldered swell, a raw granite dome covered with a few inches of soil woven together by tree roots, reminiscent of one of the great domes of Yosemite but cloaked almost entirely in a mantle of vegetation. There were no drainages to break the climb into easy stages, few switchbacks to ease the grade. At its lower end the trail was nothing but boulders and mud running in a swath across the forest floor. As it progressed it steepened, but still there were no switchbacks. Designed primarily to prevent erosion, not to aid the hiker, switchbacks aren't really necessary in the Adirondacks. The soil is so shallow that, when the rains come, they simply strip the upper parts of the trails bare without being able to cut deep gullies. On the trail up Blue Mountain the result is a winding slab of rock about the width of a sidewalk, lined with moss and broken into natural steps by fractured blocks of stone.

At the top I climbed a rickety fire tower to view the entire sweep of the Adirondacks, spread out in lumpy magnificence. The terrain reminded me of the Black Hills of South Dakota—an island mountain range rising from the surrounding lowlands in a vast dome, with rivers flowing outward in all directions. Although I was in the center of the park, I was only on the edge of the high mountains. To one side were the valleys and gradually steepening terrain I'd pedaled through for the previous twenty-four hours. In the opposite direction, 30 miles away, the highest peaks—more than 5,000 feet high—spread in an arc across the northeastern horizon. The valley floors are strewn with lakes, often strung out in long chains marking the paths of departed glaciers. In some places swamps mark the sites of deceased lakes.

It was a gentle wilderness, a land of sunlight glinting silver off the lakes, of mountains receding into the distance, ridgeline disappearing behind ridgeline, like a child's drawing of mountains, a landscape almost entirely clothed in vegetation—an endless forest stretching to every horizon, broken only by the shimmer of water, the bare granite of the high peaks, and occasional glimpses of the thread of the highway.

This was the Adirondacks I'd expected to find. I lingered long into the afternoon as the sunlight slanted closer to the horizon and shadows threw the hills into sharp relief. Then, with a mingling of satisfaction and the loss that always accompanies departure from someplace special, I left the summit and returned to the lowlands to pedal the remaining 12 miles to the nearest campground.

———————•—————————

The next day was a series of tranquil moments separated by intervals of contemplative cycling, as my route carried me away from the traffic and through the heart of the mountains, emerging eventually on the shore of Lake Champlain.

Twenty miles into the day I came upon a city park in the small town of Newcomb. The park itself was nothing unusual—only a small plot of grass atop a knoll. But it offered the best close-up view of the high Adirondacks I'd seen.

It was the first time since Colorado Springs that I'd truly felt I was in mountain country. Fifteen miles to the north Mt. Marcy towered 3,500 feet, and nearby, encircling the uppermost reaches of the Hudson, were several of the region's forty-one other 4,000-foot peaks, their steep sides—looking as though they'd been squared off by vanished glaciers—rising to flat summits, their flanks gleaming white enough to give the fleeting impression of snow where sunlight glinted off creek beds stripped to bare granite by time and water.

A middle-aged couple were taking photos. "You know," the woman said to her husband, "you can't get in there. Nobody goes there. There's no skiing and there's no roads, unless there's some four-wheel-drive tracks."

While her voice was calm, it seemed to harbor a touch of resentment, as if roadless land was wasted land. I couldn't keep silent. "This," I told her with a certainty I wasn't sure was justified, "is the heart of Adirondack hiking and backpacking country. That area's full of trails."

People do use it, and you could too, I thought.

And while I would have loved to bicycle closer, to the very flanks of Mount Marcy, there to leave even my bicycle behind as I again sat on a summit with my heart soaring over the emptiness below, I knew it was impractical. The only side road gets no closer than 7 miles from it, and dashing for the top on a marathon day-hike wasn't the way to relearn relaxation. I continued pedaling toward Lake Champlain.

———————•◦•———————

Only a few miles later, shortly after I'd crossed the Hudson River not far from its headwaters, I encountered another tranquil scene. But it wasn't the river that brought me to a halt; it was a small lake I found shortly afterward.

The scene held nothing unique: water, a dead tree, and a scattering of wildflowers—purple, gold, and white—growing on an embankment beside the road. But these elements blended together into the essence of the Adirondacks.

Close to shore the lake was shallow, choked with arrowweed and lily pads. Farther out lay a brushy island, and still farther, perhaps a mile, was the far shore and the ever-present forest. On its near edge were trees in a variety of shades—yellow-greens for deciduous, deep greens for pine—but as the forest mounted the hillside beyond, individual colors faded into a two-tone shag carpet, with the tall spikes of scattered pines protruding above the deciduous leaf cover. Farther away even the pines became indistinct, as the outlines of individual trees disappeared and the impression of "forest" became dominant, until eventually the colors blended in the distance. A few puffs of cloud completed the scene, a few wind ripples played across the lake, but for the most part, all was still.

I sat by the roadside, eating a snack and listening to the buzz of flies, the chirp of crickets, the occasional twitter of a bird, the light rustle of a breeze in the bushes. But mostly I simply listened to the stillness of a warm, calm day in the heart of the Adirondacks.

It is the stillness that gives the mountains their charm. It is a land of rounded contours, interrupted only by the peaks of the higher mountains. In places it is steep, but the forest cloak smooths everything into a panorama of gentle curves, broad valleys, and lakes and rivers that look like pictures on a jukebox. Perhaps because my usual domain is the jagged bare bones of the West, I felt no sense of spectacle; these mountains didn't tug at my heart in the manner of their Western cousins. Instead I felt peace and tranquility, the beckoning of an opportunity, at least during the warm months of summer, to escape the pressures of civilization in the eastern U.S.

The forest itself feeds that sense of escape. It allows this area to absorb many visitors—far more than could fit comfortably into the open terrain of the West. You can disappear into these mountains, hike down a trail, put two bends between you and the next party, and as long as nobody is too noisy, be on your own. You could do the same with a canoe, gliding down a quiet stream or into a tranquil lake, letting the trees muffle the noise of the roads and hide signs of other people. By my definition, this area is too heavily used to be true wilderness, but it is a close approximation—perhaps as close as the East has to offer.

Gazing across the lake, I could see an occasional splash of red from a tree prematurely proclaiming that fall wasn't far away; that this country isn't always tranquil; that summer here is a short, spectacular flourish, soon followed by winter.

If I were circling the U.S., as a few cyclists do, rather than merely crossing it, those colors would be a warning that autumn, with its cold rains and bitter winds, was on its way, and soon it would be time to head south, to follow the first touches of color down though Virginia, Tennessee, Georgia—leaving the north country to the silence and isolation of winter.

But those were experiences for someone else, or for another trip. My own journey was coming to an end. For several days people had been asking me if I would be bicycling back to California—here in New York, that was the prevailing question, like "How many gears do you have on that thing?" in Illinois, or "How many tires have you worn out?" in Kansas.

The answer was no. Would I do it if I could? Would I take the grand circle, turning south to the Gulf of Mexico, then crossing back to California to run up the Pacific Coast? It would mean a minimum of 5,000 more miles, but yes, I might.

A week earlier I'd probably have said the reverse: I was looking forward to the end of my journey. Perhaps that had helped fuel my renewed bout with haste. While I looked forward to reaching Maine—I would be happy either to meet Jane there or board a plane to return to her and home—I was no longer eager for the end.

After descending from Blue Mountain, I'd shared the evening with a cyclist from Michigan named Kevin. At first I thought I'd found a companion for the last leg, but it turned out that our paths intersected only that one evening. After the obligatory talk of routes and traffic, our conversation quickly turned to touring in general, with Kevin telling me he'd taken his trip to think about his job prospects after graduating from college.

"And what," he asked, "is your reason?"

It was the first chance I'd had since Colorado to articulate it to anyone but myself. I told him about my long battle between process and goal, between the question of whether I was cycling for the experience itself or for the accomplishment of completing the journey. I explained how my knee problems in California had forced me to take each day as it came, substituting the question, "Can I get to the next town?" for "When will I reach the Atlantic?" I told him about Ben and Vera and how the destination had become unimportant next to the simple pleasure of riding with them.

When I finished, I thought of the lessons in day-by-day living Vera had learned during her long recovery from leukemia, and I realized I was trying to apply a similar lesson to my own battle with the spiritual cancer of Type A behavior.

"It's all summed up in a line from an old song by Harry Chapin," I told him. "It says: 'It's got to be the going, not the getting there that's good.'"

Kevin seemed to be fighting the same war. "There are two parts of me," he said. "One wants to relax and take it easy. The other wants to log 90 miles a day. I haven't decided which one I'm going to follow."

I wished him luck in his decision, and as I sat by the lake near the headwaters of the Hudson River, I wished my own journey of self-discovery weren't ending so soon.

I left the main highway a couple of miles later in favor of a winding back road, a cyclist's dream with smooth pavement, a 2-foot shoulder, and virtually no traffic. It was hilly, but the grades were gentle and I had a tailwind. I didn't get many sweeping vistas like the one at Newcomb, but instead found close-up views of the mountains as the road sliced over their shoulders, bouncing back and forth between the 1,700- and 2,100-foot elevations. By western U.S. standards this isn't high country, but it felt that way—somehow I knew rock lay close below the ground. It is a sense I associate with altitude or latitude and granite bedrock, and I have felt it in many places, ranging from the Sierra Nevada to New Hampshire, from the Black Hills to the Boundary Waters of Minnesota.

I've never been sure how nature imparts this sense of elevation. Perhaps there are clues in the vegetation that ekes its existence from only a few inches of soil spread over a foundation of bedrock. But I feel it whether the woods are pine, hardwood, or a mixture, and I continue to feel it even if I close my eyes. Perhaps the clues lie in the smell of sun-warmed sap or of grasses curing by the roadside, perhaps in the gentle undulation of the road itself, in the sweep of unbroken trees to either side—impressions that stay vivid even after I close my eyes. But I think the answer is the smell, reminding me of the brittle dryness of the harvest season, arriving two months early.

Whenever I travel, I find myself collecting places to which I hope someday to return. And despite my initial disappointment, the Adirondacks firmly enthroned themselves on the list, second only to the rugged splendor of central Idaho. It was a lesson against hasty judgments, and a tribute to bicycle touring as a mode of travel which, by forcing me to take three days to see what I could have passed through in only a few hours by car, gave me time to recover from the error of my initial impression. It's a shame city life cannot be so forgiving.

A few miles later the road fell into the town of North Hudson. I would still be in the park until I reached Lake Champlain, but I was departing from the high country, and the final range of peaks—rising to only half the elevation of Mount Marcy and its companions—came as something of an anticlimax.

Lake Champlain itself was a different story.

The Bikecentennial Trail crosses the lake by ferry at Ticonderoga, but I decided to use a bridge at Crown Point, 16 miles farther north. The ferry ride was only a mile, but it would leave a gap in my route, making me feel as though I hadn't quite crossed the continent. It would have felt like cheating.

On one level I knew this was silly—a typical Type A obsession, much like my county-collecting in Iowa. But it seemed a harmless one, so I let it sway me. I didn't want to miss the famous fort at Ticonderoga, so after I'd bicycled the long way around, I rode the ferry back to visit it the next day.

Rational or not, going to Crown Point quickly paid dividends. The road was smooth and flat, following a narrow plain between the mountains and the lake. Just below the bluff of the Adirondack foothills—impressive once again as they soared 1,500 feet—I could look east across fields of corn and hay, with an occasional glint of blue water, to the Green Mountains of Vermont, nearly as tall as the Adirondacks and only 20 miles away.

It was perhaps an hour before sunset, and the slanting rays of the evening sun turned everything—corn, wheat, and pasture—to vivid green, lush against the blue outline of the Green Mountains to one side and the hazily backlit Adirondacks to the other.

Within a few miles I caught up with another cyclist going my way. He was an odd sight, heavily loaded with equipment, carrying most of it on his back in a pack he said weighed sixty pounds. Lashed to his handlebars was a huge tent, giving him the most awkwardly loaded bicycle I'd ever seen.

He said he worked as a bouncer for a bar in Burlington but had accepted a summer layoff while the college students were out of town. With his long, unkempt hair, shoddy equipment, and outrageously oversize pack, he looked the epitome of a new breed of hobo—the bicycle bum—although in his case, his hoboesque existence was as temporary as mine, and he was merely living on a more limited budget.

I remembered the only time I'd met a true bicycle bum—a person on an extended journey with no destination, living in one place for a while then moving on again, pedaling rather than riding the rails, but living a vagabond existence nonetheless. It was February, and I'd been driving across central Nevada—not a time or place where I'd have expected to meet a cyclist. His hair hadn't seen a comb in months; he had a long, scraggly beard, missing teeth, and ugly sores on his cheeks; his clothes the well-worn attire usually associated with street people. And while his lifestyle strayed far from society's norms, at least it was more interesting than collecting aluminum cans in a city park.

The closest I'd come to finding a bicycle bum on this trip had been back in California, the day before I'd crossed into Oregon. He was a young man, perhaps twenty-five, riding alone in the opposite direction on a bicycle piled high with inexpensive equipment—seemingly anything that might be useful, perhaps his entire store of worldly goods. But he appeared in good health, and beneath his odd assortment of gear was a new, expensive bicycle. He said he was from Boston, and had started cycling west in the middle of the previous winter. "I didn't want to do it the easy way," he'd said as I grimaced at the thought of all those miles, upwind and freezing. He'd made it to the West Coast, and when I met him he was headed south before ultimately returning to Boston by a more southerly route. I assumed he was planning on being on the road for about a year.

As with my present companion, this meant he wasn't a true hobo, even though he certainly looked the part. Like me, both of them were on journeys that eventually would reach a conclusion.

I thought again of the Harry Chapin song. Yes, I decided, life had to be lived in the "going," not the "getting there," but for me, whether it was physical or spiritual, there still had to be a "there"—however vaguely defined—toward which I was headed.

Impeded by his awkward load, my new acquaintance was going to his somewhere much more slowly than I. So when he spied an apple orchard and stopped to help himself, I said farewell. I thought I'd see him later, in camp, but I never did.

———————————•◦•———————————

Shortly before sunset I reached the historic fort at Crown Point, now a state park with a campground. A sign said the fort itself was closed, but since the gate was open I propped my bike out of sight where no one was likely to disturb it—or know I was visiting after hours—and went inside.

I had the place to myself as I strolled through the parade ground of the partially preserved structure, watching the final rays of sun bring forth an intense contrast of color as the neatly mowed grass glowed vivid green against the white stone of the barracks. I knew some of the fort's history, and as I walked I listened to the voices of ghosts from the past, seeing in my mind's eye the sailing ships running north and south along the lake, trying to imagine this fort in its heyday, when it mounted a battery of 105 guns and housed up to 4,000 soldiers in its $4\frac{1}{2}$-acre complex.

Lake Champlain is more than 100 miles long, a natural highway running from Canada deep into New York, but here at Crown Point it passes through a narrows only a quarter-mile wide. In pre-Revolutionary times, and again during the Revolution, it was a critical gateway to North America, a vital back door for expeditions from Canada to the Colonies, or the Colonies to Quebec. And Crown Point, like Ticonderoga to the south, was one of the keys to that back door, one of the principal guardians of the lake.

The fort lies on a low bluff on the north side of the peninsula that forms Crown Point narrows, giving its cannons a commanding sweep north up the lake. Standing on the embankment, I tried to imagine an enemy vessel approaching from the north, how close it would have to pass and how long it would be in sight as it ran straight toward the fort, directly into the teeth of those guns.

————————•◦•————————

The next morning I returned to the old fort, and again had the place to myself. It was an entirely different kind of day—a gray day that started with a light patter of rain then settled into a low, muggy overcast. I was in a pensive mood, and it was easy to again find the ghosts from the past.

I walked the perimeter of the fort, along a ditch carved a dozen feet into solid bedrock with a parapet beside it. Everything was silent and empty, quietly offering its story of a time long ago when wars were fought on a smaller scale and battle was a much more personal matter than modern technology has made it. What would it have been like to be a soldier in pre-Revolutionary times? I looked out over the fort's commanding position, both over the water and over the land. No wooden ship could have passed that battery—it would have been pounded to matchwood before it reached the closest point. No one would have made the attempt. Any effort to take this fort would have required an assault by land, and I tried to imagine charging across the open space around it to cross that ditch and scale the parapet, dashing into the face of muskets and cannons. The British did exactly that at nearby Fort Ticonderoga in an attempt to take it from the French. Fifteen thousand troops charged a garrison of approximately one-fifth their number, and when it was over, one in four of the British lay dead or wounded, with the fort still unconquered.

What would it take to hurl oneself into the face of concentrated fire? Why would anyone do it? I could understand why a general might order it, but how could he get his troops to obey? Could I have done such a thing? Would I? The reasons for the French and Indian Wars seemed so remote that I couldn't place myself in the position of the soldiers on either side, but I wondered if there were any cause today for which I would charge an armed fortress.

The older I get, the less I understand war. Oh, I can comprehend the political pressures that lead to it; I can understand the strategies of battle. I can even understand that I've reaped the benefits of the wars fought and won since this fort was built. But I can't understand the common soldier. More particularly, I can't understand that—even when history judges one side to be clearly in the right—both often fight with valor. Why? I asked the ghosts again, though none had fought and died here. The only time

Crown Point had been attacked it had changed hands bloodlessly, when one force withdrew in the face of overwhelming odds. But still, I asked, why?

The ghosts declined to answer.

Before leaving I stopped to admire the bridge that arched the lake into Vermont, a modern structure of steel and concrete rising practically from the ruins of Crown Point's earliest fortification, half a mile east of the British fort. It was an interesting juxtaposition of old and new—the historic shore battery that once guarded the backdoor approach to the Colonies, and the modern bridge, symbol of the highway system that has rendered Lake Champlain unimportant in the flow of American commerce. The back door to the continent, I thought, the onetime gateway to North America, is no longer guarded, not merely because there is no longer a threat, but because it's no longer a gate. The keys had been discarded, the guard posts decommissioned, the mountains conquered, the valleys plowed and farmed. What a change in only two centuries. I wondered what the men who fought for control of this lake during both the Revolution and the French and Indian Wars would have thought.

CHAPTER 12

New England

Ending or Beginning?

DAY 62 • Friday, August 15 • CUMULATIVE MILES: 4,803
Crown Point, New York, to Middlebury, Vermont

DAY 63 • Saturday, August 16 • CUMULATIVE MILES:
4,887
Middlebury, Vermont, to Lyme, New Hampshire

DAY 64 • Sunday, August 17 • CUMULATIVE MILES: 4,957
Lyme to Kancamagus Highway

DAY 65 • Monday, August 18 • CUMULATIVE MILES: 5,022
Kancamagus Highway, New Hampshire, to South
Paris, Maine

DAY 66 • Tuesday, August 19 • CUMULATIVE MILES: 5,107
South Paris to Damariscotta

DAY 67 • Wednesday, August 20 • CUMULATIVE MILES:
5,175
Damariscotta to Verona Island

DAY 68 • Thursday, August 21 • CUMULATIVE MILES: 5,268
Verona Island to Surry

DAY 69 • Friday, August 22 • CUMULATIVE MILES: 5,315
Surry to Bass Harbor

DAY 70 • Saturday, August 23 • CUMULATIVE MILES: 5,363
Acadia National Park

Dealing with adversity," Alan regularly had lectured Bruce.
"That's what it's all about—dealing with adversity."

And while I disagreed with the emphasis he put on the subject, Alan
was right. Dealing with adversity is a substantial part of the bicycling experience, especially if you're traveling alone. Minor problems loom dispro-

portionately, easily plunging you from joy into despair. Such was my first day in Vermont; of all the time I spent alone, this was the day on which I most wanted a companion.

After leaving the fort at Crown Point, I bicycled straight to the bridge and crossed into Vermont, feeling a pang as yet another state line reminded me I was on the last stage of my odyssey.

"No toll for bicycles," the attendant said cheerfully. "Just don't run over the traffic counter or you'll mess up the bookkeeping." It seemed a good omen, the perfect introduction to a state reputed to have some of the finest cycling in the nation. After an excellent breakfast of blueberry pancakes, I was in good spirits as I took off on a back road for the Ticonderoga ferry.

That was my first mistake. On the map the back road looked to shortcut the main road by 6 to 8 miles, and at first it seemed nothing more than a scenic byway along the lakeshore, with the Adirondacks hazy on the western skyline, and the Green Mountains lost in deeper haze to the east.

I was bucking a stiff headwind, however, and quickly realized it would take a while to reach Ticonderoga—but that was only a minor aggravation; the problem that spoiled my morning came 4 miles later. In itself, it too should have been minor, but it touched off a sequence of events that ultimately left me screaming to an uncaring apple orchard that all I wanted was to go home; I was fed up with cycling.

And what prompted this outburst? Nothing more than a flat tire.

Like the headwind, the flat itself was only a minor irritation, but as soon as I'd fixed it, the tire went flat again—before I'd even managed to reload my bicycle. Even this wouldn't have been a problem if both flats hadn't been blowouts that left large, unpatchable tears in the tubes, ruining in the space of only a few minutes both my original tube and a spare, leaving only the backup spare I'd bought in Illinois.

The only explanation was a defective tire—the tube had probably bulged out from under it, like an aneurysm through the walls of a weakened artery. Why the tire had waited until this point to reveal the defect was a mystery.

As I committed my last spare tube, I also put on my spare tire, praying the 3,500 miles it had spent lashed in a coil beneath my sleeping bag hadn't ruined it as well. Just to be on the safe side I pumped it up only partway, and when it held I sighed, loaded my gear on the bicycle, and rode off.

Half a mile later the road surface turned to gravel.

I should have turned back, but I was too stubborn to give up any of the precious headway I'd won into the strengthening breeze. Even though it was still several miles to the ferry landing, I rode on, slithering through loose gravel, up and down steep hills, riding my brakes hard and waiting for the inevitable tumble.

But I didn't fall. After 3 miles that felt like 30, I noticed that the bicycle was handling oddly. I looked down. My tire was flat again.

That's when I screamed to the nearby apple trees, kicking various pieces of my equipment (but being careful *which* pieces of equipment I kicked). Then I set to work, removing the panniers for the second time that morning, and, for the third time, removing the tire and hunting for the hole.

This time I couldn't find it. I pumped air into the tube and could hear it squirting out, but I couldn't locate the source. Three times I pumped it up, holding my ear close and running my hand along the tube, trying to feel the stream of air. Finally I found a pair of small punctures almost an inch apart—what cyclists call a "snake bite." A big chunk of gravel had probably pinched the tube against the rim.

Normally I don't try to patch holes like these; a single patch won't cover them easily, and it's difficult to place two patches so close together, but I was out of spares. I crossed my fingers and covered the hole with the biggest patch in my kit, hoping it would work well enough to allow me to limp along, with occasional stops to pump up my tire.

The pump handle went back and forth, but after the first 30 pounds or so the tire got no firmer. I stopped pumping, expecting it to deflate with a whoosh, but that didn't happen either. I pumped again and noticed the air wasn't going in the tube—instead, it squirted in all directions. My pump had broken.

Only so many things can go wrong before something snaps. Two ruined tubes, a headwind, gravel, a third, difficult-to-patch flat, and a broken pump was my limit. Since I'd already thrown my tantrum for the day, there was nothing left but philosophical resignation. The universe was perverse, Murphy's Law reigned supreme, and I was merely cataloging the details of this latest mishap.

I wish I could say I recognized the absurdity of the situation and laughed, but that didn't come until later. The best I could manage was a sigh and a quick look at the map. It was only 3 miles to the ferry terminal, and even with a loaded bike and a spongy tire I could walk it in about an hour. Another hour would get me to Ticonderoga, where I could find a gas station to pump up my tire. Buying a new pump would be more difficult; the nearest bike shop was in Middlebury, Vermont, 15 miles in the opposite direction.

I headed for Ticonderoga.

Frustrating as the morning had been, I quickly found out that if I'd needed help, it would have been easy to come by. While I was working on my first flat, a woman drove by, slowed, stopped, backed up, and asked if I needed assistance. "I'm okay," I told her, not knowing the extent of my problems.

A few minutes later, as I was struggling with the second flat, a tractor came from the opposite direction. "You need help?" asked the driver.

"I don't know," I replied. "I may have a problem I can't fix. Are you coming back this way?"

He nodded.

"Well if I'm still here then, I may need help."

He waved and headed off on his errand. Five minutes later he was back. "I didn't realize it would be that soon," I said. I was in the process of reloading my equipment, and I didn't know whether the new tire would do the job.

"Well, I'm working in a field a mile over that way," he said, pointing down a side road. "If you need help, come and get me."

I thanked him and he drove off.

By the time I'd gotten everything loaded, he and two friends were back in a pickup truck. "I can give you a ride to town if you like."

I grinned. "Thanks, but I'd just as soon do it by bike if I can." I knew I was being irrational, but I'd just pedaled to Crown Point to avoid a 1-mile ferry ride. Leaving a gap in my route while I rode a pickup truck would be an irritating "failure," but it was nice to know the option existed.

We talked for a while about bicycling and life in Vermont, then he turned his truck around and left. Only later did I realize that he and his friends had taken a break from their work to offer me a ride. I was over-whelmed. Vermonters had a reputation for friendliness, but this was one of the best examples of hospitality I'd encountered anywhere. Later, as I sat by the apple orchard with my broken pump, I wished I had accepted.

Surprisingly, the tire was firm enough to ride with only thirty pounds of pressure, and eventually I reached pavement and coasted down a hill to the ferry landing. Twenty minutes later I was on the boat, and a half mile after that I was pedaling up the bluff to Fort Ticonderoga. Back on pavement, I felt a renewed sense of confidence and decided to deal with the pump and tire after visiting the fort.

---·•·---

Unlike Crown Point, Fort Ticonderoga—one of few remaining intact Colonial-era forts—has been fully reconstructed. A ranger at Crown

Point wistfully told me that historical preservation regulations prevented a similar restoration there. "We can't do it," he said. "The British had a bad fire in 1773 and the fort blew up. We have to leave it the way it is." I preferred the unreconstructed fort at Crown Point to the reconstructed Ticonderoga; there are no ghosts at Ticonderoga—crowds of tourists scared them away.

Historically, though, Ticonderoga is far more the stuff of legend. It was built by the French in 1755 and attacked six times between then and 1777. On three occasions it was successfully defended; on three it changed hands. The bloodiest attack was the unsuccessful British effort during the French and Indian Wars (the British did manage to capture it the following year), but the most famous was the predawn assault by Ethan Allen and the Green Mountain Boys in 1775, at the start of the Revolution. With only eighty-three of his fiercely independent Vermonters, Allen stole into a fort that only a few years before had driven back thousands, placed his sword at the commanding officer's neck, and successfully demanded his surrender.

Allen and his men weren't after the fort itself; they wanted the cannons, and after their bloodless victory, the men hauled the artillery overland to Boston where it played a major role in driving the British from the city.

Startlingly, Ticonderoga isn't a state park. It was included in a land grant to Columbia College after the Revolutionary War, and in 1820, Columbia sold it as a private estate. It wasn't until 1909 that the family who bought it decided to open it to the public. It is an interesting commentary on our nation's onetime lack of interest in its past that as late as 1820 a key location such as this was allowed to fall into private hands, however enlightened those hands may have been.

Even without ghosts Ticonderoga was worth the visit, simply to see what the fort had looked like. I took a guided tour and learned about the surprising accuracy of the cannons that once guarded the lake. "A good gunnery crew," my guide said, pointing a seemingly impossible distance across the lake, "could hit that two-story house six times out of ten." After the tour I also listened to a fife-and-drum corps and watched a gun crew fire real shot from cannon and mortar.

Best of all, as I was leaving I encountered two cyclists, who loaned me a pump to top off the air in my tire. It had held pressure surprisingly well while I'd been gone, so I decided to risk going on to Middlebury rather than out of my way to Ticonderoga.

It was midafternoon and I'd been in the fort longer than I'd expected, so I didn't wait for the other cyclists—Vermonters out for a long weekend—but sprinted for the ferry, only to miss it by less than a minute. Watching it pull away, I remembered that exactly the same thing had happened when I'd come the other direction three hours before.

As I waited, the other cyclists joined me.

"Missing ferries by thirty seconds is a fine art," I told them with a laugh. "I've gotten good at it over the years." The trick, I explained, is to pay no attention to either the ferry schedule or the clock. On average, that should mean you only wait half the cycle, but I always seemed to wait longer. Whatever the statisticians might say, sometimes the laws of chance fail to even out—they merely chuckle behind your back.

The wait wouldn't have bothered me at all if I hadn't been concerned about the bike shop closing early. My jokes masked a growing sense of haste and frustration—I'd gotten myself into the position of having to race to the bike shop before it closed. By trying to fit in a thorough tour of the fort and still get to the shop, I'd fallen into another Type A trap. I would have to do a mini-Alan to get to Middlebury before five o'clock.

The wait for the ferry wasn't long, however, and soon we were cycling back into Vermont.

Although I had wished for companionship that morning, the mood had disappeared. The other cyclists were pleasant company, though, so I rode with them until they turned off a few miles later to spend the night with a friend. They invited me to join them, but I decided to press on to Middlebury. Maybe Type A drive had something to do with it, but it would be inconvenient to have to wait until whatever hour the bike shop opened in the morning.

Why, I wondered, did these invitations often come when I couldn't accept them? Then I realized it hadn't always been that way. I'd accepted Esam's invitation, shared a motel room with Vera and her parents, dined with the Christian adventurers in Kansas. Cycling simply generated more offers than I could accept, at least at the 500-mile-a-week pace I'd become comfortable with.

I reached town with time to spare, found the bike shop, and bought what I needed. Since it was getting late and I'd had a rough day, I decided to treat myself to a motel, a good dinner, and possibly even a movie—all the amenities of a college town of 5,600 inhabitants. Unfortunately it was Friday, and everything was booked. The nearest campground was 8 miles out of town and several miles out of my way, and there wasn't even time to eat a quiet dinner if I wanted to get there before dark.

With only the scantiest of dinners to console me for the rigors of the day, I scurried out of town, trying to beat dusk, and barely making it before I would have had to walk, thinking as I rode that this was anything but the perfect ending to the perfect day.

I was headed for Elephant Mountain Campground, and as I pedaled north along the base of the Green Mountains I tried to pick out the peak for which it was named.

Eventually I spied something I thought must have been it, a mountain whose flank, as it drops precipitously into the valley, looks like the rear end of an elephant. The peak beyond looks like the elephant's head, with the ridge beyond that looking like its trunk reaching forward to grab the tail of another elephant in front. It's a surprising likeness. At the campground registration desk I was equally surprised to learn that Elephant Mountain isn't the proper name of the mountain, but merely the one given it by the woman who ran the campground.

———————•◦•———————

I woke to a fresh realization that my trip was drawing to a close. Although the Bikecentennial route would reach its terminus 400 miles later in Bar Harbor, it would first touch the Atlantic north of Portland, Maine, a point I could probably reach in an easy four days.

The land between me and the coast was something of a mystery. I'd lived in Massachusetts for a time during my childhood and had visited parts of Vermont, New Hampshire, and Maine with my parents, quite possibly driving along some of the roads I was about to pedal. But other than the Old Man of the Mountains, my memories were vague, and all I knew for sure was that between me and the Atlantic lay two major mountain ranges—the Green Mountains of Vermont and the White Mountains of New Hampshire—both of which would entail substantial climbing.

The aura of mystery was heightened by the weather, which served up another morning of gray skies blurring to a dull white haze that hid the far horizon and softened the outlines of hillsides and trees less than a mile away. My tent and sleeping bag were clammy, and even my body felt as though it were dripping with condensation. I longed for the dry mornings of the Rockies and the Great Plains.

Mixed with the morning's gray sogginess came a feeling of trepidation, for rumors garnered from other cyclists and confirmed by the route description on the Bikecentennial map indicated that some of the worst climbs of my journey lay ahead, with grades reputed to reach fifteen to seventeen percent, nearly twice as steep as anything I'd encountered in the West.

For the first few miles the route flanked the base of the mountains, but it soon turned east and began to climb steeply. This was the first major hill on the way to Middlebury Gap—elevation 2,149—and I settled down to wait for the grade to become outrageous.

To my surprise it never did—or so I thought until it leveled off, and I looked back to see a sign that said I'd just climbed better than a mile of thirteen percent grade.

Expectations can have an amazing effect on athletic endeavor. Had that sign been at the bottom of the hill I'd have found the climb a grueling effort. But I'd managed it easily—a testimony to the phenomenal condition of a cross-country cyclist with a continent behind him.

As the road continued to climb more gently, a sign informed me that this is Robert Frost country, that Frost had returned here repeatedly, and a nature trail leads through the woods with posted excerpts from his poems juxtaposed with settings that might have inspired them.

The mosquitoes were out in force, driving me hurriedly through the exhibits. Later I decided that Robert Frost could be the poet laureate of the touring cyclist. Like him, we seek out the roads less traveled; our mode of transportation opens the heart to things that others miss—the life-changing process of experiencing America from the slow lane.

───────────•●•───────────

Leaving the exhibit, I reached the summit, crested the Green Mountains, and dropped into a narrow valley flanked by peaks that rose 2,500 feet above me.

As I descended into the valley the leaden skies broke into scattered puffs of white, the soggy haze abated, and for the first time I could really see the Vermont landscape. Everything was lush, green, and tidy—a cyclist's paradise.

Twenty-five miles later I left the valley, climbed another surprisingly easy hill—where an after-the-fact sign again informed me it had been a thirteen percent grade—swooped into the next drainage and across a covered bridge, and eventually, in the early evening, crossed the Connecticut River into New Hampshire. I had covered an entire state in slightly more than a day, and, if I wanted to, I could reach Maine in one more. The end was drawing ever nearer.

───────────•●•───────────

That night I slept in a commercial campground near the Connecticut River and woke to another morning of dew and soggy equipment. Instead of high clouds I encountered fog, and, as it gradually lifted to become a bank of low clouds, it muffled the surroundings, making me feel pleasantly isolated from the rest of the world.

At first my route followed a little-used back road along the Connecticut River, with the fog closing off everything that rose more than a couple
of hundred feet above. Occasionally the road climbed into the fog, and I
was surprised to discover that the sky became brighter the higher I went,
giving me hope that later I might punch through the fog as I headed into
the mountains. But then I would fall back down to river level and the
muffled peace of that early morning.

As on the day before, the weather robbed me of sweeping panoramas,
but I struggled to accept that which came my way and to find beauty in it.
I gazed across the valley at the folds of the nearest hills, already bleached
of color at a distance of only half a mile, with the fog settling over their
summits like a blanket of cotton, shutting the world into a narrow band
along the river. On the flood plain were cornfields, and behind them the
still waters of the river flowed peacefully, with nary a ripple to mark their
passage.

I passed a succession of farmsteads and villages of beautifully maintained frame houses, their white siding and brilliantly colored shutters as
neat and trim as if they'd been built yesterday, even though many bore
historical signs proclaiming they'd stood there two centuries or longer.
Something about the well-manicured lawns, the tidy houses, and the
clean roadsides not only made me realize how appropriate is the name
New England, but also bespoke a tradition of pride that this land has
been long settled but not abused, a recognition that it is possible for
people to live *with* nature and not against her.

Not everything was manicured. As I left the river and climbed into the
mountains, the mowed-grass farmyards became less common, often replaced by tall hay going to seed. Similarly, many barns no longer looked
like architecture lessons or picture postcards; they were functional,
weather-beaten, sometimes standing upright in apparent defiance of the
law of gravity.

What the mountains lack in amenities they make up for in scenery.

I was particularly impressed by the first of two passes over the White
Mountains. I left the last of the fog at the 1,000-foot mark, moving into a
land of still-hazy visibility beneath a sky of dense cumulus clouds. Emerging from the fog I glimpsed my first view of the mountains, silver-blue in
the distance, mottled green and yellow-green in the foreground, with
flecks of red and yellow suggesting autumn.

My route, a beautifully surfaced winding road, followed a stream up a heavily glaciated valley. Beside me granite slopes soared steeply on both sides, confining the road to the flat, 100-yard-wide valley floor, with occasional glimpses of 4,000-foot peaks to the south and east.

After a long hill marked as a twelve percent grade (I'd yet to see one of the dreaded fifteen percenters), I reached the source of the stream I'd been following. It was a small lake nestled at the base of the mountains, a perfect reflecting pond beneath hillsides that rose 2,000 feet above it. My map indicated that a hidden summit rose another 1,000 beyond that. Scattered boulders lay on the far side of the pond—smooth granite rocks as big as houses, mirrored in the still, dark waters along with the nearby trees and more distant slopes of the mountains above.

I was sitting near the edge of wilderness or near-wilderness, with the Appalachian Trail somewhere nearby. It was a stunning contrast to the tidy farmland only a few miles away, but as I sat by the lake the two landscapes seemed equally necessary—the gaily painted houses and manicured farmland of the valley and the wild places, where in the words of the Wilderness Act, "man is a visitor who does not remain."

You have seen the best that man can do, the granite cliffs and the distant, hazy summits seemed to whisper. *Now come see what God can do.* But that wasn't the end of the message. *You can't stay here*, they seemed to warn. *After you have come and seen, you must go back, take what you have learned, and apply it to your own works.*

It was a fitting message to hear in this, the last of many mountain scenes across the continent that had lured me to pause, forget schedules, and turn contemplative. Yes, we should tame the valleys—plant the crops and erect the painted fences—but we should also remember where the land, weather, and seeds came from, never forgetting that nature isn't merely a gardener, that we can't control everything, that some things cannot be improved.

———————————•◦•———————————

From the hilltop I dropped into a long, winding valley, superficially similar to the one I'd followed the day before. The terrain was wilder. Instead of farmsteads the valley floor was covered by timber, and the river roared and foamed as it plunged through rapids and whirlpools.

Riding a tailwind, I soared rapidly downhill into North Woodstock, principal staging area for auto visits to the Old Man of the Mountains and the 5,500-foot peaks a few miles to the north. As I competed for road space with weekend traffic and tourists hurrying about their errands, my biggest wish was to get out of town as quickly as possible. But first I had errands of my own. I bought a day's supply of food, then found a pay phone and tried to call Jane. I couldn't reach her — scheduling phone calls on a bike trip is always difficult — so I rolled out of town and began the climb to the 2,860-foot summit of Kancamagus Pass. From there it would be downhill most of the way to Maine.

Kancamagus isn't as steep as other climbs of the previous two days, but it's longer, stretching on for miles at a sustained nine percent grade. A thunderstorm appeared in the southwest, and I raced it to the summit, which made the pass seem much more difficult than anything I'd done since the Tetons.

Nevertheless I made good time, beating the storm with several minutes to spare. It seemed unwise to linger, and soon I was falling down the other side, beginning a 20-mile coast that would carry me halfway to the state line.

I stopped at a national-forest campground near the bottom, pleased that so far the thunderstorm appeared more show than substance. Unfortunately it also spelled the return of the heavy humidity that had plagued me since Crown Point. I could have gone a lot farther before sunset but stopped in hopes that the morning would be clear enough to give me one good, final view of the mountains before I left them for the 150-mile run to the sea.

———————•◉•———————

It didn't rain that night, and perhaps because of that I woke to yet another day of dismal skies and energy-sapping humidity.

I waited a couple of hours, but the weather showed no signs of improving, and eventually I moved on. A few miles later I pedaled across my sixteenth — and final — state border, into the rolling hills of southwestern Maine.

As my trip drew to a close, the day-by-day experience of bicycling felt increasingly unreal, as though a portion of me had detached itself from the trip and was already on the way home. Although the cloudy skies and humidity slowly drained my enthusiasm, a sense of detachment lingered even after the humidity dropped and the sun broke through. Off and on over the next few days I settled into periods of mental torpor punctuated by sharp, brief highlights, like rays of sun piercing gaps in the clouds.

The first of these illuminations came late that afternoon, but it had nothing to do with sunshine. It occurred when someone — perhaps a clerk in a convenience store, perhaps a waitress in a cafe — asked me how I planned to weather the approaching hurricane.

"Hurricane?" I asked. "Hurricane?" Hurricanes happened in Louisiana or Texas, not Maine. The images that came to mind were of palm fronds speared like impossible arrows through the walls of houses, or waves washing across low-lying barrier islands—not the lobsterboats and white pines of New England.

Suddenly the weather was foremost on my mind, and I asked everyone I met about it.

Yes, they said, there was a hurricane coming. That's why the weather was so bad—we were already on the edge of the storm. The hurricane itself was still somewhere offshore, expected to hit the coast that evening. We were far enough inland to avoid the killer winds, but we could expect torrential rain—perhaps as much as several inches.

I thought for a while about camping—in years to come, the tale of the night I spent tent camping in a hurricane would make a wonderful campfire story—but ultimately I opted for a motel, stopping early and spending the afternoon and evening reading a novel I'd carried all the way across the country. The expected downpour never arrived, and I felt vaguely cheated when there was only an inch of rain.

———— •◦• ————

The next day brought another ray of illumination, atop a hill 10 miles from my motel.

With the passing of the hurricane the humidity dropped, and by midmorning, although the skies were still leaden, visibility was nearly unlimited. I was standing next to an old farmstead, now crumbling to ruin. Overgrown fields flanked the house on one side; on the other was a decaying barn with a gaping hole in one wall where the doors and a couple of windows had fallen into the basement. Nearby was another overgrown pasture with two horses that ran to greet me when I stopped, while behind the barn was a sweeping view toward the hills to the west.

I could see why someone would want to live there; I felt as though I were on top of the world as I watched a squall run across a valley in the distance. Farther off, perhaps 30 miles, were the blue silhouettes of mountains, and behind them a band of pink sky lay on the horizon, indicating that the clouds might eventually clear. A few farmsteads dotted the nearby hilltops, their tin roofs reflecting the white sky, their vivid green pastures striking a sharp contrast to the forest that covered almost everything else.

The people who live on this land probably no longer farm it. More likely, they work in one of the nearby towns and commute here to enjoy the view, shiver in the wintry blasts and bask in the summer sun. The people of Maine are a hardy lot, and it would take a hardy person to live both summer and winter on this exposed hilltop.

I was in a changed mood—energetic and cheerful, ready to pedal on toward the waiting Atlantic.

—————————•◦•—————————

Several hours later I was startled out of my ebullient mood by the sound of a sharp pop in the distance, followed almost immediately by the ping of something bouncing off a nearby rock.

I knew without looking that someone was shooting at me with a BB gun, and I didn't dare look back lest I take a second shot in the eye. I hunched my shoulders to protect my neck, stood up on the pedals, and with a surge of adrenaline disappeared around the next bend, memorizing the address on the first mailbox I saw after I reached safety.

Three miles later, well after I'd begun to shake with adrenaline aftermath, I reached a junction with a small grocery store and stopped, first to phone the police and then to eat a succession of fudge brownies.

An officer was on the scene in minutes, listening as I described where the incident had occurred. "I was afraid to look back," I explained, "but there was only one house in the area, and it had to be coming from there. It was probably just some kid, and I'm sure it was nothing bigger than a pellet gun. . . ." I broke off, realizing I was apologizing for being shot at, as though a *real* cyclist ought to be able to shrug off little things like BBs. But the officer took the incident seriously.

"I'll go out there and see what I can find," he said. "Why don't you wait here, and I'll be back."

I nodded and went inside for another brownie.

Twenty minutes later the officer returned. "You were right," he said, "it was a BB gun. I found a little fella up there, probably about six years old. His grandma had set him up with a shooting range in the backyard, facing away from the road. But I guess he found you an irresistible target. So I told him that if I ever heard any more reports of his shooting at anybody, I was going to come out there and take away his gun. And from the look on his grandmother's face, I think he's getting a real tanning right about now. So unless you want to take other action, I think that's the best way to leave it."

I nodded, feeling my spirits lift as my view of the world turned from hidden oppressions and hostilities toward friendliness and trust.

"No," I said, "that sounds perfect. I just wanted to make sure he got stopped before he hurt somebody."

The officer grinned. "I don't think we have to worry about that. You should've seen his eyes get big when I told him I'd come back and take his gun away. He's going to remember that for a while."

After he left I ate one more brownie for good measure.

———————•◦•———————

I got my first view of salt water a couple of hours before sunset as I crossed a tidal creek near the small town of Damariscotta. I was still several miles from the ocean proper, but as I rolled into town I knew I'd finally reached the coast. Snug frame houses in bright colors proclaimed that at one time this had been a fishing village or a small port, though it is a tourist center now. The smell of salt marsh filled the air, rendered even more invigorating as the clouds finally broke. For the first time in days the sky was more blue than white.

I wanted to stay in the city park that night and sample the feel of this coastal town, but the free camping I'd grown accustomed to on the Plains is unheard of in the East. I had to spend the better part of ten dollars for a commercial campground a few miles out of town, where the nearby woods released hordes of mosquitoes that quickly drove me to grab a book and take shelter in the campground's general store.

———————•◦•———————

For the next two days I pedaled along the coast toward Acadia National Park. They were days of contrast—occasional vistas of blue water on my right, rocky mounds of granite on my left, and everywhere traffic, traffic, and more traffic, as seemingly the entire populations of Massachusetts, Connecticut, and New York streamed north and east.

Much of the way I had no choice but to bicycle along Route 1, and sections of it have no shoulder. On these stretches the traffic treated me as though I were invisible, passing disconcertingly close to my elbow, forcing me to pay continuous attention to my rear-view mirror, gradually fraying my nerves.

I took several opportunities to get away from the traffic, stopping once in a state park to climb a bluff for an overview of a bay dotted with islands, chatting with a Bikecentennial group three days out on a westbound journey, and pausing to explore an old fort and pedal up a little-traveled side road along the Penobscot River.

I stopped one night at a small commercial campground on the lower reaches of the Penobscot, indulging in the glorious opportunity to order a pizza from a nearby town and sit in the campground recreation hall, munching popcorn and watching videos, beginning the process of rein-jecting myself into mainstream civilization.

———————— •◦• ————————

East of the Penobscot the coastline is dissected by numerous fjordlike inlets that reach inland like fingers from as far as 15 miles out to sea. By the shortest route it is only 40 miles from the Penobscot to Bar Harbor, but I didn't get there for another forty-eight hours. I spent one day poking out to land's end on one promontory, and another exploring the back-roads of Acadia National Park, which surrounds all land routes to Bar Harbor.

In the meantime I thought about the impending conclusion of my jour-ney.

From one perspective, a return to civilization might be a good idea. One afternoon in Acadia I left my bicycle to follow a pathway of ladders and cables bolted to the rock—a route the National Park Service euphe-mistically called a trail—to the top of a 600-foot bluff. As I sat on the sum-mit, gazing across a panorama of waves and water, a pair of teenagers came up and sat on a rock 20 yards away.

I overheard one of them say, "You never know about guys like that. He looks okay, but you can't be sure he isn't carrying a switchblade."

It took a moment to realize he was talking about me. I couldn't decide whether I was stunned or amused—I'd built up some muscle on this trip and shed twelve pounds, but I'm only 5'6" and have never felt threatening to anyone.

Later I looked at myself in my rear-view mirror. The face staring back at me was familiar, but my body was tanned, lean, and hard. That I liked. But my hair probably hadn't seen a comb since I'd visited my parents—after all, it had spent most of that time in a bike helmet—and neither it nor my beard had been trimmed since California. I looked like someone who'd just time-warped out of Woodstock. Maybe I'd been on the road long enough.

I definitely wanted a day or two off—I'd been riding hard since Illinois, and I was road weary, gradually losing the incentive to break camp and get rolling in the morning. Part of it was the weather, which hadn't been conducive to early starts. A heavy dew blanketed everything each morn-ing, leaving my tent as wet as if it had rained. I doubted whether all of my gear had been dry at the same time since I'd left my parents' house three weeks before.

But these were minor irritations, nothing that wouldn't look better

after a day's rest—a day of not having to break camp, not having to struggle fifty pounds of gear over the outrageously steep hills that populate
much of the Maine coast.

Those hills had taken a toll of their own. That morning I'd awakened
with stiff muscles, stiffer than on any other morning of my ride. The culprit was a side trip I'd taken the day before to a picturesque village with a
Revolutionary War fort. It had been beautiful terrain, and for once the
day had been sunny, but the road traversed 9 miles of wicked roller-
coaster hills with grades that must have approached twenty percent. I'd
had to ride it twice—out and back—and it didn't take much of that, even
in a beautiful setting, to turn my legs to spaghetti and convince me that
another 10 miles would have been insurmountable.

Aside from needing a day off, I wasn't really looking forward to reaching the end. I did want to see my wife—especially since our plans to meet
here had proven impractical and she was already back in Sacramento—
but were it not for that, I easily could have turned around and pedaled
back to California, cutting inland in a big loop through northern Maine,
then south through New Hampshire and Massachusetts, through the
Catskills, the Poconos, and Pennsylvania Dutch country, down the Blue
Ridge Parkway or the Shenandoah Valley, circling the southern end of
the Appalachians and then heading west across Texas, New Mexico, and
Arizona, eventually returning home via the California coast.

And that was the bottom line. After nearly 5,400 miles the lure of adventure was still there. I was almost finished but easily could have decided
that I was only half finished, could happily have started another trip all
over again.

Why? In many ways, by the time I'd left Colorado I'd already accomplished the most important aspect of the trip: I'd relaxed to an extent I
never believed possible. The rest of the journey had largely been a test of
that accomplishment. Could I stay relaxed through the Kansas heat?
Through the bustle and commotion of RAGBRAI? Through my slow recovery from illness? With Alan, or the New England tourist traffic?

The answer had been a qualified yes. Riding with Alan had left a legacy of pressure I didn't completely lose until the magic of the Adirondacks
and that frustrating day at Fort Ticonderoga caused me to quit thinking
about schedules and distances, just as my knee problems had done back
in California. Later, as I pedaled up Route 1, the traffic had left me clawing
for space, wishing I could find someplace where for thirty consecutive
minutes there were no other people. Worse, it was largely tourist traffic,
and like tourists everywhere, too many were in a hurry, too rushed to
waste even a few seconds slowing down for a bicycle.

Even without the fear that someone might run me off the road, I found the very presence of so many hurried people cloying. It was as though I were surrounded by a horde of Alans – thousands of people on tight vacation schedules, thousands of cases of, "If I don't get here by noon, I won't be there by midafternoon, and I won't be somewhere else by tomorrow." I felt sad for the victims of a nationwide attitude that not only produces but actively encourages such madness.

I was profoundly grateful to those who hadn't succumbed – to the people, more numerous every year, who are willing to accept a bicycle as an equal on the roads. Often these people are locals, seldom in the dreadful hurry that characterizes tourists. Sometimes they're from out-of-state, bearing license plates from Ohio, Indiana, or New York, places that stand out for the respect with which they treat cyclists. And it's reassuring to see that some people, regardless of where they come from, remember that vacations are to be lived and enjoyed, not collected like trophies.

But why did I want to go on? Why did I still feel the call? Was it a desire to draw the widest possible circle on the map? If I was honest, I knew that was part of it. I wondered if it meant that after all these miles I still hadn't fully learned to relax. But that wasn't the case – I didn't want to set a new schedule for reconquering the continent; I was enjoying the journey itself so much I wasn't ready to return to a more ordinary life.

Most of all it was the old urge to explore, to find out what lies around the next bend, in the next county, the next state. Five thousand miles hadn't quenched that thirst. Neither would 10,000 or 15,000. And that was good. The urge itself was neither Type A nor Type B; what mattered was how I approached it. I resolved once again to resist the "do everything and live none of it" behavior I had scorned throughout my journey. I couldn't pedal back to California, but it was enough that I had crossed the country on a bicycle and lived life to its fullest.